TAX IMPACTS ON PHILANTHROPY

Tax Impacts on Philanthropy

Douglas Dillon

Gavin K. MacBain

Theodore A. Kurz

Edwin S. Cohen

Robert Anthoine

Edwin D. Etherington

Sydney Howe

John J. Keppler

E. Hugh Luckey

Ruth C. Chance

Homer C. Wadsworth

Howard Dressner

James L. Kunen

Boris I. Bittker

Paul R. McDaniel

Henry Aaron

Thomas B. Curtis

Symposium conducted by the

TAX INSTITUTE OF AMERICA

December 2-3, 1971, Washington, D. C.

Princeton

TAX INSTITUTE OF AMERICA

1972

A TAX INSTITUTE OF AMERICA PUBLICATION

The purpose of the annual symposium conducted by the Tax Institute of America [formerly Tax Institute Incorporated] is to focus attention on a major problem of taxation by affording an opportunity for discussion by informed paticipants representing different points of view. The publication of this volume carries with it, of course, no endorsement of the views—sometimes conflicting—of the various participants.

Library of Congress Catalog Card Number: 72-190506

International Standard Book Number: 0-912052-28-7

CONTENTS

v

SYMPOSIUM COMMITTEES

PROGRAM COMMITTEE

Chairman: LEONARD L. SILVERSTEIN, Attorney, Silverstein and Mullens

R. PALMER BAKER, JR., Attorney, Lord, Day & Lord

ARTHUR P. BECKER, University of Wisconsin-Milwaukee

KENNETH W. GEMMILL, Attorney, Dechert Price & Rhoads

B. KENNETH SANDEN, CPA, Price Waterhouse & Co.

STANLEY S. SURREY, Harvard Law School

COMMITTEE OF HOSTS

Chairman: ALLEN D. MANVEL, Consultant, Washington, D. C.

JOEL BARLOW, Attorney, Covington & Burling

W. KEITH ENGEL, CPA, Touche Ross & Co.

F. CLEVELAND HEDRICK, JR., Attorney, Hedrick and Lane

WILLIAM M. HORNE, JR., Attorney, Reed Smith Shaw & McClay

EDWIN L. KAHN, Attorney, Arent, Fox, Kintner, Plotkin & Kahn

THOMAS A. MARTIN, Director, Division of Taxation, American Petroleum Institute

JOHN MENDENHALL, CPA, Arthur Andersen & Co.

WILL S. MYERS, Senior Analyst, Advisory Commission on Intergovernmental Relations

SYMPOSIUM FUND COMMITTEE

Chairman: ARTHUR M. HAYES, General Tax Counsel, Standard Oil Company (N.J.)

DAVID FLOWER, JR., Director of Tax Affairs, Raytheon Company

CHARLES W. HALL, Attorney, Fulbright, Crooker, Freeman, Bates & Jaworski

GEORGE H. KITENDAUGH, Manager-Tax Accounting, General Electric Company

PHILIP WAGNER, Associate General Counsel, New York Telephone Company

FOREWORD

THIS IS a period in our history in which the strains upon all instrumentalities of our democracy have been unusually severe. The fiscal mechanisms of our government are bearing their share, if not more than their share, of these burdens.

The high drama on Capitol Hill which arose in connection with the Revenue Act of 1971 bears obvious witness both to the extraordinary efficiency of the taxing mechanism as a collector of federal revenues, and also to its volatility as a regulator and motivator of human conduct.

Of particular pertinence to this symposium is the role of the tax structure in relation to private philanthropy. In this framework, it seems altogether fitting that the Tax Institute of America should provide a responsible public forum for inquiry into the scope of the relationship between philanthropy and the tax laws.

As a perhaps unfortunate characteristic of the dynamics of the United States tax legislative process, there is often an insufficient substructure of thoughtful consideration of the framework of the tax laws, carried on in an atmosphere which is unfettered by the pressures of time and politics.

Therefore, this symposium is intended to provide a forum for development of this substructure, in the important field of the relationship between taxes and philanthropy.

LEONARD L. SILVERSTEIN
Attorney, Silverstein and Mullens,
and Chairman, Symposium Program
Committee

OPENING OF THE SYMPOSIUM

I AM HONORED and delighted to be in a position to welcome you to this symposium, dealing with the impact of taxes on philanthropy.

In a variation of an old story, I have heard it said that the job of a college or university president is really a very simple one. Success is assured if he can provide football for the alumni, sex for the student body, and a parking lot for the faculty.

The trouble with the story is that even this simple-minded academic program needs financial support and, if you think about it, suggests questions of the kind that are now perplexing American society in balancing social needs and economic costs.

It is remarkable that tax policy affecting philanthropy has been developed with so little reference to these controlling factors. Certainly a number of viewpoints will be expressed here today and tomorrow about the effects and wisdom of the Tax Reform Act of 1969 as it relates to charitable giving. I think it is also worth asking, however, whether the provisions of the act might not have been quite different in this regard had the Administration and the Congress been focusing at the same time, as they have been in this congressional session, on a national program for the conquest of cancer, aid to higher education, and reform of the nation's welfare system.

Our symposium is therefore a timely one indeed.

We are indebted to our speakers and panelists, to Chairman Leonard L. Silverstein and the members of the Symposium Program Committee, to Chairman Allen D. Manvel and the members of his Committee of Hosts, to Chairman Arthur M. Hayes and the members of his Symposium Fund Committee, and to our Executive Director, Mabel Walker, and her staff.

R. PALMER BAKER, JR.
Attorney, Lord, Day & Lord, and
President, Tax Institute of America

TAX IMPACTS ON PHILANTHROPY

PART ONE

THE ROLE OF PRIVATE PHILANTHROPY

INTRODUCTION OF DOUGLAS DILLON

"The stimulating topic to which this symposium is devoted illustrates the continuing need for an organization of this kind, dealing with issues of tax policy from informed and independent points of view. Our immediate point of reference is the Tax Reform Act of 1969. Our overriding point of reference, however, is American society itself. As to this, the contributions and knowledge of our speaker tonight are immense.

"There is nothing abstract about the phrase tax policy in his distinguished career. Mr. Dillon was vitally and imaginatively concerned with the tax treatment of international trade and investment as Under Secretary of State for Economic Affairs from 1959 to 1961. As Secretary of the Treasury from 1961 until 1965 he led and supported the development of a tax policy organization and tradition in that department having an élan and expertise that continue vigorously today.

"His credentials in private philanthropy are equally immense. Tomorrow morning he will preside in his capacity as Chairman of the Rockefeller Foundation at its annual meeting. Currently President of the Board of Overseers of Harvard University, Chairman of The Brookings Institution, and President of the Metropolitan Museum of Art—indicating but part of his activities—I am glad that he still has time for a personal life and leadership

1

again in the financial community as Chairman of the United States and Foreign Securities Corporation.

"I am glad, too, and proud for the Tax Institute of America that he is here this evening to speak to us on the role of private philanthropy in American society."

R. PALMER BAKER, JR.
Attorney, Lord, Day & Lord,
President, Tax Institute of America, and
Chairman, Thursday Dinner Session

* * * * *

INTRODUCTION OF GAVIN K. MACBAIN

"Our speaker personifies, as I think you will see, the corporate chief of a major multinational business. He views the duties of his post as encompassing the interests of the company but also its responsibility to the public in the broadest and most enlightened sense. While we shall all be extremely interested in hearing Gavin MacBain's discussion of the role of modern American business in today's society in relation to taxes, a word about Mr. MacBain's background will indicate to all of you his unusual qualifications to address the Tax Institute of America this afternoon.

"Gavin MacBain was born in New Jersey. He holds a degree from Columbia. His early training was financially oriented, joining Bristol-Myers Company, the organization of which he is now the Chairman, as Assistant Treasurer in 1944. From 1947 to 1961 he served as Treasurer of that company, and in January of 1965, Mr. MacBain, after four years as President and Board Chairman of Gristedes—so he's a gourmet besides—returned to Bristol-Myers to become its President. He was elected Chairman of the Board and Chief Executive Officer in January, 1967.

"Mr. MacBain also holds directorships in a number of companies, including the United States Trust Company, Kennecott Copper, Simplicity Patterns, and others. Of particular interest to this meeting, he is Past President of the Economic Club of New York and a former National Chairman of the United Community Campaigns of America during 1969. In this latter position, Mr. MacBain was responsible for raising the staggering sum of $840 million. He is also a founding and very active member of the Business Committee for the Arts.

"Gavin MacBain's service to his company, the business community, and the public thus provides him with an intensely practical—yet I believe you will see humane—perspective from which he can relate his views this afternoon.

"I think you will also find that he will inject a very stimulating note of realism into this discussion.

"It is a great pleasure to welcome Gavin MacBain to this symposium of the Tax Institute of America."

LEONARD L. SILVERSTEIN
Attorney, Silverstein and Mullens,
and Chairman of the Friday
Luncheon Session

CHAPTER I

THE ROLE OF PRIVATE PHILANTHROPY IN MODERN AMERICAN SOCIETY

DOUGLAS DILLON
Chairman, The Rockefeller Foundation;
Former Secretary of the Treasury

PRIVATE philanthropy in the United States appears to be alive and well. In terms of total dollars, it has been enjoying spectacular growth. Unfortunately, this dollar growth does not reflect a general increase in generosity, but rather an increase in population coupled with the effects of inflation.

With the increasing infusion of federal funds into many areas previously supported by private philanthropy, some, including myself, have been concerned about the future of the private sector. Taken as a whole, the provisions in the Tax Reform Act of 1969 seem to signify a decision by the Congress that it no longer feels that giving to private nonprofit institutions is as important as it has been for the last half-century. If this is so and if private giving fails to keep pace with the growth of our economy, the results will be significant indeed, and, to my way of thinking, most unfortunate.

But, first of all, what do we mean when we talk of private philanthropy in the United States? Last year, 1970, private philanthropy accounted for more than $18 billion in charitable giving— an all-time record. This sounds better than it really is. For example, individual giving went from $7 billion in 1960 to more than $14 billion in 1970—the dollar amount doubled, but according to the Internal Revenue Service, itemized contributions in 1960 amounted to 3.73 percent of adjusted gross income, as against 3.02 percent in 1968—a decline of almost 20 percent. Corporate giving grew from $482 million to $900 million a year during the same period—but the percentage of taxable profits given to charity increased by only 0.04 percent, to 1.15 percent. Foundation giving rose to $1.7 billion in 1970, up from $710 million in 1960. During the past year, however, grants by the 40 largest foundations actually declined by nearly $5 million. In any event, when we talk of private philanthropy in the United States we are talking of $18 billion in annual giving, a truly significant sum.

THE DIRECTION OF PHILANTHROPIC GIVING

Over the years, the direction of philanthropic giving has undergone surprisingly few changes. In the beginning we had tithing and other popular giving systems, directed mainly to religion, and religion still receives the highest percentage of private philanthropic funds, though its share is falling off. In 1960, religion received some 51 percent of all such funds, but in 1970 only about 44 percent was contributed for religious purposes. Education remained relatively consistent, at about 17 percent, but has not quite kept pace with inflation. Health contributions grew slightly faster than the rate of inflation and reached 16 percent of the total giving. "Other activities," which absorbed scarcely more than $0.5 billion in 1960, grew at an explosive rate, reflecting among other things the increasing popular interest in urban problems and in the needs of the arts and humanities. This category reached a total of $2.8 billion in 1970—more than a fivefold increase in terms of dollars.

In all of this the role of the individual is dominant. Individual givers are responsible for about 78 percent of the total given. Some 35 million taxpayers itemize philanthropic deductions on their tax forms. What is perhaps more important, the masses of people are not only contributing money, but time as well. Twenty-two large national charitable agencies reported in 1970 that they had benefited from the volunteer services of more than 43 million individuals.

THE GROWTH OF GOVERNMENT PHILANTHROPY

But private philanthropic funds, important as they are, are dwarfed by the sums flowing from government. In the years following the Depression, the federal government plunged heavily into education, into medical research, into recreation, and into many aspects of welfare originally pioneered by private philanthropy. The funds involved in this burst of activity now dwarf anything that private philanthropy could possibly muster. The total amount of money involved is difficult to trace—literally dozens of federal and state agencies are involved in large or small ways. Even if you omit those activities which are no longer considered phlanthropic, but simply national policy—such activities as social insurance, old age assistance, unemployment insurance, and workmen's compensation—the federal government alone still furnishes over $35 billion a year. As an example of the government's expansion, consider its contribution to health.

In 1935, government entities spent $543 million for health and medical care of all kinds. In 1969, these expenditures reached $22.6 billion—up fortyfold. State and local governments contributed about a third of this total. A measure of the relative importance of this growing public contribution, supplied by the National Information Bureau, indicates that federal, state, and local governments provided 87.5 percent of all funds for health purposes in 1965, and 91.8 percent in 1970.

THE IMPORTANT ROLE OF PRIVATE PHILANTHROPY

This raises an interesting question: Does all this federal activity make the large-scale philanthropists and their foundations, with their comparatively modest contribution to health—or, for that matter, the total giving for health from all private sources—any the less important? Are the millions of individuals actively engaged in health-oriented philanthropic activities simply, so to speak, spinning their wheels?

I think the answer is definitely no. The funds that come from private philanthropy are without question helpful. They are, for the most part, directed to local uses and are related to special local needs. It is important also that we do not get into the irreversible habit of looking to government for everything. The 35 million people who contribute either time or money, or both, give solid evidence of community concern in our country, and for that reason alone, private philanthropy deserves to be preserved.

But with all this, there is still the question as to what will become of philanthropy in the future. Pressures most certainly will accelerate the activity of government at all levels, but mainly along well-trodden paths. Nevertheless, popular private philanthropy is so deeply characteristic of Americans that it is unlikely to disappear or even to diminish markedly.

By popular private philanthropy I mean the relatively modest giving by the great bulk of the 35 million taxpayers who now itemize their charitable deductions as well as the giving, largely church oriented, of those whose individual contributions are too small to itemize and hence are included in the standard deduction. This giving tends to reflect the accepted tastes and desires of the times, and these are not apt to change rapidly or dramatically. Hence, while highly important in support of established philanthropic institutions of all kinds, we cannot expect much in the way of innovation from this type of giving.

A similar rigidity characterizes the operation of community funds. As anyone who has been associated with them knows, the pressures for a reshuffling of priorities mount every year, but relatively little change takes place—every contemplated change creates questions and conflicts. The safe path—leaning on precedent—usually wins out. Therefore we must not look to community funds to break important new ground or to innovate in a way which will affect the future.

Another area which is unlikely to provide innovation is corporate philanthropy. Corporations, in all probability, will become increasingly active as more and more of them recognize that the corporation is as much a social institution as it is an economic entity. But here again the sensitive relationship between an individual corporation and public opinion largely precludes the possibility of truly creative or innovative giving.

That leaves the foundations.

If foundations are to be measured only by their $1.5 to $2 billion annual contribution as compared to the $18 billion private total, or to the $35 to $50 billion government figure, they would seem to be relatively unimportant. But there is another side to it: consider the long and brilliant track record of the foundations, particularly the larger ones. The pioneering achievements of these organizations in medicine, agriculture, cultural development, and other areas have been monumental. There is no need to list them here.

INNOVATIONS BY FOUNDATIONS

The fact is that foundation innovations have set the pace for many activities which have long since ceased to be regarded as philanthropy at all. What is philanthropic today may be far from it tomorrow. When the Carnegie Foundation for Teaching set up its first retirement pension for teachers, this was philanthropy. But the pension systems now supplied by every college in the land are a cost of doing business, and in no way philanthropic. The millions raised by the Prosser Committee in the early thirties as *philanthropy* have been replaced by the welfare system as public policy. The provision of social security is now considered just as much a public obligation as is the furnishing of police and fire protection. The Green Revolution which will save tens if not hundreds of millions of our fellow human beings from the agonies of starvation is another foundation contribution to our society. Surely we should be doing everything in our power to encourage foundations to continue these types of activities.

On the fiftieth anniversary of the Rockefeller Foundation, the trustees indicated what they thought a foundation should aim for. They said:

The role of a private foundation [is] in meeting contemporary human need. A private foundation can take initiative; it can pioneer; and by mustering available knowledge and human competence, it can identify causes and experiment with solutions. It can move without the political complications created when governments are involved with other governments. It can encourage cooperative effort across national and political boundaries. It can bring a high order of individuality and diversity of viewpoint into the field of human betterment. It can provide a decentralization of social initiative and responsibility. And it can enlist the interest and support of vigorous, enterprising, and public-spirited benefactors.

In terms of today, what does this imply? To me, it seems to say that the foundation, as a constructive institution, is the only element in private philanthropy that can continually explore new and higher ground; that has the capacity to pioneer new efforts to solve current problems, or for that matter, problems of long standing. The foundation can, in short, point the way.

But what is happening to foundations?

ANTI-FOUNDATION ATTITUDES

There has been some feeling—recently reflected in congressional action—that funds normally going to foundations might better be channeled through taxation into the government till. This point of view has been fueled by some unfortunate instances of misuse—the use of foundations by certain individuals and corporations, relatively few in number, for the primary purpose of avoiding the payment of taxes or of promoting particular political or social points of view.

The anti-foundation feeling built up gradually and reached a climax in 1969 in the successful attack in Congress upon all foundations, good and bad alike. Unfortunately, the resulting reforms may well be doing less damage to the exploiters of philanthropy than to the ability of foundations to finance worthy projects.

This is surely regrettable, but it must be admitted that some of the responsibility for this result lies with the foundations themselves. After the revelations in the Patman reports[1] and after the 1965 Treasury report on foundations,[2] which outlined a number of possible ways of correcting the excesses that had become apparent, it seemed to me that the large foundations, none of which were involved in these excesses, should have taken a forthcoming attitude. They should have worked with the Congress and the executive branch to develop legislation that would have outlawed the relatively infrequent misuse of foundations while encouraging the great majority whose sole purpose was to serve the public welfare. But this point of view was not accepted. Feeling secure in the knowledge of their own good intentions, the major foundations generally took the position that no federal remedial legis-

---

[1] United States Congress, House Select Committee on Small Business, *Tax-Exempt Foundations and Charitable Trusts: Their Impact on Our Economy,* Chairman's Report, 87th Congress, Washington: Government Printing Office, 1962, 135 p.; United States Congress, House Select Committee on Small Business, Subcommittee No. 1, *Tax-Exempt Foundations and Charitable Trusts: Their Impact on Our Economy,* Chairman's Report—Second Installment, 88th Congress, 1963, 407 p.; Third Installment, 88th Congress, 1964, 330 p.; Fourth Installment, 89th Congress, 1966, 59 p.; Fifth Installment, 90th Congress, 1967, 1131 p.; Sixth Installment, 90th Congress, 1968, 491 p.; Seventh Installment, 91st Congress, 1969, 165 p.

[2] United States Congress, House Committee on Ways and Means, *Treasury Department Report on Private Foundations,* Committee Print, 89th Congress, 1st Session, Washington: Government Printing Office, 1965, 110 p.

lation was needed and that everything could and should be handled by stronger enforcement of existing state laws—laws that had obviously failed to do the job. The result was that while federal legislation was delayed for a few years, its final form was much harsher on all foundations, including those with unblemished records, than would have been the case otherwise. Instead of legislation directed at closing loopholes in the laws regarding foundations, there was broader legislation, much of it directed against the foundation as an institution. Today our task is to consider whether this legislation in its present form is truly in the longer run national interest, and if not what to do about it.

First, let us look again at the role that foundations can and should play in our modern American society. Theirs is a unique opportunity and responsibility. Properly used, their $1.75 billion in annual expenditure can go a very long way in exploring new and difficult problems and in supporting worthwhile undertakings that are not in a position to obtain adequate public or private funding. This can be most helpful to government at all levels, allowing their much larger funds to flow where the ground has already been broken by foundation innovation.

THE NEED FOR RESEARCH AND DEVELOPMENT IN PHILANTHROPY

Philanthropy in modern society needs continuing research and development in the same way as all technologies need it—and the foundations alone are in a position to provide this research. Private foundations could become—and I think should become—the nerve center for all philanthropy. They have this potential if they can function efficiently and objectively and without harrassment.

The Congress has both the right and the duty to make sure that the tax-free assets of foundations are spent solely for charitable ends and with no advantages direct or indirect to their creators or managers. But with that assurance foundations should be allowed to function freely without unnecessary legal impediments. One member of a congressional finance committee was quoted recently as saying that "under the new tax law, foundations are not likely to be any braver than their tax counsel." This is certainly not conducive to much-needed experimentation and innovation.

With reasonable freedom, foundations could explore the deeper causes of social and economic problems and seek out possible long-term solutions. They need not limit their efforts to finding immediate remedies for acute symptoms which, to a large extent, is the role of government, but can look farther ahead. When a new and obviously successful avenue of approach is opened up by foundations, sufficient pressures will be generated sooner or later to stimulate substantial individual giving or governmental appropriations. Note, for example, the federal cancer program, which is simply an expansion of private efforts in an attempt to achieve a result within a time limit that would be clearly impossible for private capabilities.

The horizon for foundation efforts is virtually limitless—in funding promising ventures, in opening up new approaches, and in supporting worthy causes that have not yet caught the public fancy in a way that can guarantee the needed public or private support. Looking backward it is clear that without the contributions of foundations over the past 60 years, our world today would be a far poorer place in which to live. In short, the major role of foundations, a role that in our free democratic system can be filled in no other way, is to serve as the cutting edge of progress in our voyage toward a better life for all.

APPEAL FOR NEW LOOK AT ROLE OF FOUNDATIONS

With these considerations in mind—the immense possibilities for good on the one hand, and on the other, the unfortunate tendency to blame all foundations for the misdeeds of a few—I would like to appeal for a new and wide-ranging look at the role that foundations can play in our society and at the regulations that are required to avoid misuse. Foundations should not be used to dodge taxes, or to meddle in political matters. But surely, in preventing these abuses, it is not necessary to shackle foundation operations in a maze of complex regulations, or to prevent major givers from creating new foundations dedicated to the public welfare, or from supporting existing ones.

On the contrary, I feel certain that only by encouraging and helping foundations to do the kind of work they can do best, can private philanthropy make its optimum contribution to American society.

CHAPTER II

THE PHILOSOPHY OF CORPORATE PHILANTHROPY

Gavin K. MacBain
Chairman, Bristol-Myers Company

AMERICANS are a generous people, constantly forming private philanthropic organizations to alleviate suffering at home and abroad, to advance religion and culture, and to improve a wide variety of conditions that affect special groups and the general welfare. This generosity is reinforced by a widespread belief that such private initiatives strengthen our traditions of self-reliance and freedom. But they accomplish even more. In the words of a 1965 report by the Treasury Department on private foundations:

> . . . Beyond providing for areas into which government cannot or should not advance (such as religion), private philanthropic organizations can be uniquely qualified to initiate thought and action, experiment with new and untried ventures, dissent from prevailing attitudes, and act quickly and flexibly. . . .
> . . . In doing so, they enrich the pluralism of our social order. . . .[1]

Failure of Taxpayers to Respond to New Incentives

Our tax laws obviously reflect these beliefs and practices. The Tax Reform Act of 1969 increased the amount individuals can deduct for charity. Yet, disappointingly, individuals still continue to give at the past rate—slightly more than 3 percent of their adjusted gross income.

There are a number of possible explanations for this failure to take advantage of these new incentives: First, the recession. Sec-

---

[1] United States Congress, House Committee on Ways and Means, *Treasury Department Report on Private Foundations*, Committee Print, 89th Congress, 1st Session, Washington: Government Printing Office, 1965, p. 5.

ond, the progressive weakening of religion in our lives, once the primary motivation for compassion and charity. Third, a growing conviction, especially among many of the younger generation, that only government can and should be the effective instrument for social improvement. And, finally, the inhibitory effect of taxes on the accumulation of great private fortunes which in earlier decades were a major source of philanthropy in a number of important fields.

Philanthropic Causes Looking for Corporate Support

Not unexpectedly, philanthropic causes are turning increasingly to the business corporations for support. At the same time, the corporations are being subjected to intense scrutiny by the consumer and by other influential public-interest groups. Few of these deny that the corporation is a uniquely effective instrument for coordinating men, material, and markets for the production of goods and services. But they do question how the corporation and its economic and financial rationale and performance relate to the value system of our culture. They claim that while economic growth measured by an increase of private-consumption economic goods is an important social objective, that growth is sometimes achieved at high social costs, though unintended.

Who, for example, is to bear what share of responsibility for air pollution which is in part the social cost of producing cars within the price range of millions of Americans, even though such an achievement is generally regarded as a social benefit? The output of a steel mill is a positive value, but if it pollutes a lake, who bears the cost of cleaning up the lake for swimming?

In brief, the corporation is inescapably involved in questions of public policy, many of them extraordinarily complex. In the process of helping to solve them the corporation will inevitably discover that its survival and growth will depend on its willingness to conceive of itself as more than simply an economic instrument.

Change in Corporate Attitudes

Many corporations now acknowledge that their interests are almost co-extensive with all the factors in the environment, natural and human, which affect the ability of their enterprise to flourish.

And they are beginning to accept the obligations which they would not too long ago have rejected as irrelevant to their concern with productivity and profitability. Last January, John Davenport, writing in *Fortune* magazine, reported Alden Clausen, president and chief executive officer of the Bank of America, as saying that business "has to concern itself with nonbusiness problems today if it wants to be around tomorrow . . . in the long pull, nobody can expect to make profits—or have any meaningful use for profits—if the whole fabric of society is being ripped to shreds."[2]

Corporations are now active in helping to eliminate urban blight, to employ more members of minority groups, to improve job satisfaction, to control air and water pollution, to cooperate in urban planning, to ease loan standards in depressed areas, to train school dropouts, and to be more helpful to consumers.

Corporate philanthropy has expanded from contributions to health and welfare projects in plant communities to religious and ethnic groups, civic causes, education, art, and general culture, on both local and national levels. Corporate support of higher education, once restricted to projects narrowly related to business interests, now encompasses the humanities. This reflects a growing acknowledgment on the part of business that men at the helm of a modern corporation must have broad cultivation and knowledge to cope with the general cultural, political, and social environment within which the corporation has to function and grow.

What I am describing is an emerging trend, not a flood tide. But the trend has the backing of the heads of many of the largest corporations. Their attitudes, frequently expressed in public, are bound to influence the rest of the business sector well before the decade is out. Corporations form the second largest single reservoir of unrealized income potential for American philanthropic institutions and organizations. At present, they give slightly more than 1 percent of the 5 percent allowable, or a total of nearly $1 billion. I am convinced they will give more as they begin to apply to their philanthropies the same rationalized methods they apply to their other activities.

---

[2] John Davenport, "Bank of America Is Not for Burning," *Fortune*, January, 1971, p. 152.

EMERGENCE OF CORPORATE SUPPORT FOR ARTS

Perhaps the most dramatic indication of the change in corporate attitudes is the emergence in the past five years of a movement for corporate support of the arts—the whole range of the arts, visual and performing, including individual artists and such institutions as ballet companies, symphonies, museums, and arts centers. In a sense, this movement, still in its infancy, is the most crucial example of the new corporate philosophy, because it would appear the least likely to engage corporate interest. Yet corporate support of the arts increased 24 percent between 1968 and 1970, and over 160 percent since 1965 when the movement first received its impetus with the publication of the Rockefeller Panel Report, *The Performing Arts: Problems and Prospects.*[3]

The report expressed alarm at the grim financial condition of the arts in this country and proposed "an organization patterned on the Council for Financial Aid to Education to stimulate corporate support of and involvement in the arts."

The following year, David Rockefeller took up the proposal, outlined in broad terms what its objectives and program should be, and urged businessmen to express their response to it. The proposal received enthusiastic expressions of support from business leaders across the country and on October 15, 1967, the formation of the Business Committee for the Arts was announced by its first chairman, Douglas Dillon.

Corporate support of the arts affords an interesting case study of the way in which corporate obligations are linked to its short-term and long-range interests. Why should a corporation support the arts? David Rockefeller eloquently expressed the general philosophy when he said:

Too often the tendency is to regard the arts as something pleasant but peripheral. I feel the time has come when we must accord them a primary position as essential to the nation's well-being.

In our increasingly mechanized and computerized world, the arts afford a measure of consolation and reassurance to our individuality, a measure of beauty and human emotion that can reach and move most men. They are indispensable to the achievement of our great underlying concern for the in-

---

[3] Rockefeller Brothers Fund, *The Performing Arts: Problems and Prospects,* New York: McGraw-Hill Book Company, Inc., 1965.

dividual, for the fullest development of the potential hidden in every human being.[4]

I believe the case for the arts can also be put in terms more specifically related to corporate interests. First, there is the obvious public relations benefit from support of a cause of actual and potential interest to large numbers of people. Now that government is becoming the overwhelmingly dominant factor in such traditional fields of corporate philanthropy as education, health, and welfare, corporations will discover that the arts, together with efforts to repair the social and economic structure of our cities, provide unparalleled opportunities to render important service with great returns in visibility and good will.

Second, corporations are up to their eyebrows in the arts whether they realize it or not. Product design, packaging, point of sale and media advertising, public relations, design of company vehicles, headquarters and plant architecture and interior design —all of these require conscious concern with art and design. Unfortunately, it rarely occurs to businessmen that the use of art to move products in the market place would be impossible if there were no art museums, composers, orchestras, painters, film-makers, writers, playwrights, and choreographers who are dedicated exclusively to their art. The television and radio spot commercials, design and copy of ads, and annual reports all sooner or later reflect the work of such artists. Businessmen in Europe have known this for centuries and they have been dedicated patrons of the arts.

The South Kensington Museum in London, established in 1852, had as its primary goal raising the quality of British manufactures. The museum's departments were organized according to materials, and its appeal was directed to artisans who might come there and find inspiration and guidance. It was hoped that by improving the level of the native artisan's taste, design, and workmanship, the eventual result would be reflected in increased retailers' profits. And this happily proved to be the case.

The arts are essential to business in other specific ways. Companies find that the existence of art and culture in their head-

---

[4] David Rockefeller, "Culture and the Corporation," Address at 50th Anniversary Conference, National Industrial Conference Board, New York, September 20, 1966.

quarters and plant communities is an important factor in their efforts to attract and retain highly trained and educated managerial and professional personnel. A survey conducted at the Wharton School of Finance and Commerce showed that graduate students listed art, music, entertainment, and the presence of intellectual stimulation high on the list of requirements that had to be met by the communities in which they chose to locate with their families. An increasing number of companies are beginning to describe their company's involvement in the arts when they recruit on campus.

Retail merchants find that the existence of theatres, opera, music, and museums in and around the city's shopping center contributes significantly to the volume of business.

Finally, but not least important, some business leaders are beginning to study contemporary movements in the arts as important barometers of the social condition. Tensions in society are often first reflected in works of art and, perhaps, one day our business leaders will learn to study the arts as a prelude to planning for their company's future.

A few years ago Dr. Frank Stanton, Columbia Broadcasting System president, pointed out that the emergence of the corporate patron is essentially a democratizing movement. He said:

> It is better, for example, for several officers or directors to be involved in the acquisition of a great picture, even if most of them think they may be against it, than one man accountable only to himself. It spreads the word, and it interests more people, directly or indirectly, in the picture. The broader base that business brings to support of the arts is perhaps also more of a predictable and less whimsical one than the individual patron, because the commitment that the corporation of today makes in the arts is not apt to be made lightly, while the patron of yesterday could as easily be indulging some temporary personal oddity as a lasting thirst for the sublime.[5]

The mechanics of corporate patronage, the ordering of priorities, the development of criteria and expertise, and questions such as who in the corporation should determine the allocation of funds—all these are undergoing intensive study, often in close cooperation with the Business Committee for the Arts.

---

[5] Frank Stanton, "The Importance of Arts to Business," Address at Arts Councils of America and Americas Symphonic Orchestra League Joint National Conference, Washington, D.C., June 18, 1965.

Corporations are already discovering that they can contribute a good deal more than money to help enrich our cultural life. A company can also make valuable contributions by making available equipment which it owns, manufactures, or uses; by providing office or exhibit space, professional assistance in accounting, promotion, financial planning, and "audience development." Also by participating in united art fund drives, by commissioning original art works or sponsoring art projects, by encouraging executives to serve on the boards of arts organizations and art councils, by full or partial subsidy of employee attendance at performances, by using the work of local artists in public areas of the company's office and plants, and, not least, by persuading other companies that are still unaware of the plight of the arts to do something about it.

What Role Should Tax Laws Play?

In line with what I believe you will now agree is a demonstrable need for more, not less, corporate involvement in affairs of culture and social welfare, we should ask ourselves what role our tax laws should play. I speak, of course, as a corporate manager, not a tax expert. From that perspective, I suggest that the tax laws recognize that those corporations which respond to public needs in fact incur costs which are comparable in business terms to any other "ordinary and necessary" company expense. For this reason, the statutory limitation governing corporate charitable contributions —set at 5 percent—has no proper relevancy to comparable limitations applied to individuals. Similarly, the inhibitory rules which apply to those company foundations which are intended to serve corporate philanthropic purposes could well be favorably modified. And, in a form which will not induce tax avoidance, corporate contributions of property should be encouraged. More generally, I urge that our tax laws be framed and administered to play a more positive role in stimulating corporate philanthropic activity.

If the movement sustains its momentum—and we of the Business Committee intend to see that it does—then one day we might have the kind of society that once existed in Florence at the height of the Renaissance. As John Addington Symonds has put it:

From the Pope upon St. Peter's chair to the clerks in a Florentine counting-house, every Italian was a judge of art. During that period of prodigious activity the entire nation seemed to be endowed with an instinct for the beautiful and with the capacity for producing it in every conceivable form.[6]

---

[6] Quoted in S. Harrison Thompson, *Europe in Renaissance and Reformation,* New York: Harcourt, Brace & World, 1963.

PART TWO

THE TREASURY VIEWPOINT ON IMPACT OF 1969 LEGISLATION ON PHILANTHROPY

INTRODUCTION OF THEODORE A. KURZ

"We are certainly very fortunate in the quality of the speakers we have on the program. I am sure everyone who was here this morning agrees that we have an outstanding program, and the rest of it is going to be equally challenging.

"We are all disappointed that Eddie Cohen could not be with us at lunch today, and I guess he is about as disappointed as anyone. His schedule was open when this luncheon was first planned, but the monetary conference in Rome was rescheduled for this week, and as I believe all of you know, he has been a member of the United States team for that conference. He is on his way back —I believe his plane left the Azores a few hours ago. He is anxious to give you his views, and he will be here tomorrow. So you will have an opportunity to hear Secretary Cohen and to question him.

"But he has also very kindly agreed to have Ted Kurz come here today. I think Ted has been instructed not to encroach on what the Secretary is going to tell us tomorrow, but he is probably going to give us some very interesting observations on the Treasury's views and experience with the 1969 legislation on philanthropy.

"Ted has been on Secretary Cohen's staff for about a year and a half now. He was formerly with Debevoise, Plimpton, Lyons & Gates in New York. He is a graduate of Princeton University and the Yale Law School. I am sure you will be very interested in what he has to say, and he has also agreed to answer any questions you might have after he finishes."

ARTHUR M. HAYES
General Tax Counsel, Standard Oil Company (N.J.), and Chairman, Thursday Luncheon Session

*   *   *   *   *

INTRODUCTION OF EDWIN S. COHEN

"Our speaker presents me with a great opportunity and pleasure of introduction. He is known to all of you, of course, so we shall not burden you with his educational background and other details, except to say that I can imagine no one who plays a role that is more ideally suited to this discussion than Assistant Secretary Edwin S. Cohen. His background, as you may recollect, started in Wall Street and throughout his distinguished career he has continued to play a very active role in the formulation of the tax laws. I recollect my first professional involvement with Mr. Cohen occurred in connection with Tentative Draft Six and Seven of the Model Income Tax Code issued by the American Law Institute. Much of this material, in the preparation of which Mr. Cohen played a key role, may now be found in the Internal Revenue Code itself.

"Assistant Secretary Cohen also served as a member and counsel of the Advisory Group for the Ways and Means Committee in connection with proposed subchapter C revisions. This occurred in 1958, and since that time he has played, both as a private citizen and Treasury official, a very leading role in responsible formulation of the tax laws.

"Since his tenure in the Treasury, he has become involved with other subjects and has been called upon to be a monetary as well as fiscal expert. He has been at Secretary Connally's right hand in revaluing or devaluing—whatever is now happening—international currencies. I hope in connection with his remarks about philanthropy and taxes that we shall also have some opportunity to hear about what must have been a very exciting trip.

"It is a great pleasure to welcome Ed Cohen to this meeting."

LEONARD L. SILVERSTEIN
Attorney, Silverstein and Mullens, and Chairman, Friday Luncheon Session

CHAPTER III

TREASURY'S EXPERIENCE AND. VIEWS

Theodore A. Kurz
Attorney-Advisor to the
Assistant Secretary of the Treasury for Tax Policy

IT IS a pleasure to take part in your consideration of the impact of taxes on philanthropy. A glance at the program indicates that the morning has been devoted to the "Trends in Philanthropic Giving and Receiving as Affected by the Tax Reform Act of 1969," and this afternoon's discussions will deal with the "Effects of Tax Reform Act of 1969 on Role of Private Foundations." As your luncheon speaker, I feel very honored to be sandwiched in the middle of these two Gargantuan undertakings, with the opportunity to explore with you the area of organized, private philanthropy from the vantage point of the Treasury.

I think I ought to observe at the outset that any views or opinions I express today are solely my own and do not necessarily represent those of the Treasury. I will devote most of my comments to a few of the significant regulatory issues which we are presently attempting to resolve and to the general matter of the interpretation and administration of the charitable provisions of the 1969 act.

Background

In order to appreciate and evaluate the impact of the 1969 act, it is necessary to go back a few years to the more or less untarnished days of private philanthropy in this country. In 1960, when Dean Rusk was still the president of the Rockefeller Foundation, he gave a series of lectures in Claremont, California, about philanthropy in general, and about the virtues of tax exemption as the basis of our system of private philanthropy. He also talked about the problems faced by the 12,000 or so foundations of 11 years ago. These lectures make very interesting reading, less for what they said about the virtues of private philanthropy than what they did not say about its shortcomings and problems. It seems that the remarks of Dean Rusk in 1960 accurately reflected the overwhelming mood of the times that tax-exempt private philanthropy, but for a few overgeneralized and seemingly innocuous problems, had become an inherent part of our democratic system, and as such, was simply beyond reproach.

Nine short years later when the bubble burst and the foundation community was shaken by the congressional debate and ultimate passage of the 1969 act, it was abundantly clear that times had changed. There is probably little to be gained from debating exactly how and why this change came about. There are those who would argue that organized philanthropy had become too strong and too cavalier, and that a good dressing down was in order to curtail or at least contain this independent force in our society. There are others who would attribute the climate of the 1969 act to a growing distrust and suspicion of all philanthropic acts as motivated and controlled by private and sometimes clandestine economic benefit, rather than charitable intent.

Whatever the variety of factors which contributed to the passage of the 1969 act, there is no need to speculate about the specific charges which were ·leveled against organized philanthropy. One need only skim through the legislative history to get the appropriate flavor. Ultimately, Congress decided that certain of these charges merited strong, remedial legislation, the guts of which are now found in chapter 42 of the Internal Revenue Code.

I think it is important to note at this point that Congress excused a substantial segment of organized philanthropy from the private foundation provisions on the theory that organizations which receive a substantial part of their financial support from the public would somehow be responsible or responsive to the public. Thus, organizations which maintain the necessary degree of public responsiveness and supervision would be less likely to · respond to the abuses of private interests, especially where those

24

interests were in conflict with the public interest. Without passing on the wisdom or validity of this theory, I would simply note that the status of an organization as a public charity or a private foundation has now become crucially important and appears to be having a decided impact on those organizations which can arrange their affairs to qualify as public charities. I need not dwell on the advantages of obtaining public charity status under section 509 (a) of the Code. Organizations which are described in section 501 (c) (3), or are charitable trusts described in section 4947 (a) (1), derive a multitude of advantages from public charity classification such as exclusion from the 4 percent tax on investment income imposed under section 4940, exclusion from the restrictions and requirements of sections 4941 through 4945, and eligibility for the full 50 percent charitable contributions deduction under section 170.

For organizations which *are* subject to the private foundation provisions of the 1969 act, the impact thus far is anything but clear. To take the most general question first, it is simply too early to judge whether the long-term effect of the act will be to enhance or impede the flow and freedom of use of private philanthropic funds in this country. There are those who are currently arguing that the presence of the 1969 act itself has intimidated existing organizations, and prevented the creation of new organizations, to the degree that our system of private philanthropy has already been, and will continue to be, severely damaged. I have no idea what the basis is for these forecasts of gloom, but we are unable to substantiate them. While there can be no doubt that the foundation provisions of the 1969 act represent unprecedented regulation of philanthropic organizations, the foundation community appears to be adjusting to the new restrictions without extreme hardships. In the recent words of Robert F. Goheen, president of Princeton University and chairman-elect of the Council on Foundations, Inc.:

"The Tax Reform Act of 1969, despite its many complex and inhibiting provisions, still permits considerable flexibility, while safeguarding the public against abuse of the foundation privilege for personal gain. Those directly responsible for the foundations must themselves, however, carry the lead in upholding the essential public-purpose character of foundations while improving the quality of their work."

Perhaps it would be appropriate at this point to explore a few of these provisions and some of the regulatory issues they raise.

REGULATORY ISSUES

Classification of Public vs. Private Under Section 509

A major issue has been raised as to whether certain independent trusts which support public charities could themselves be public charities, even though they do not provide the public charity with a substantial amount of its support, as required by the so-called integral part test of the proposed regulations. T.I.R. 1111, issued a few weeks ago, provides for public charity status if the following conditions are met:

1. The entire trust must be devoted to a charitable purpose and a charitable deduction must have been allowed.
2. The trust must have been created before November 20, 1970 (which was the date of the proposed regulations which announced for the first time our interpretation of this section).
3. The trust must be required to distribute all its income to a designated public charity or charities in fixed shares.
4. The trustee may have no discretion to vary beneficiaries or their shares.
5. None of the trustees would be a so-called disqualified person, if the private foundation provisions applied.

Classification Generally

It has come to our attention that certain organizations are experiencing difficulty in assessing their status either as public charities or private foundations. This difficulty will continue until the proposed regulations under section 170 (b) (1) (A) and 509 (a) can be finalized, which we hope will be in the very near future. This problem becomes very real for organizations faced with the possible obligation to file tax returns, pay their section 4940 tax, and amend their charters in accordance with section 508 (e). Because these organizations have done everything possible to comply with the Internal Revenue Service procedures for determination of their status, they should not run the risk of incurring penalties or losing their exemption for failure to file timely returns or for failure to amend their governing instruments. Accordingly, the Internal Revenue Service has recently announced that these organizations would not incur penalties for failure to file timely returns, provided that such returns were filed, and taxes paid, within 90 days after publication of the final regulations, if the organizations were deemed to be private foundations. A similar grace period is being considered for the inclusion in a foundation's governing instrument of the section 508 (e) requirements, and this should be published in the near future. [This was done by temporary regulation, section 13.17, issued December 15, 1971.]

Section 170 and Concept of "Public Support"

A major issue has been raised as to the imposition of a 10 percent floor of public support before an organization may show, under all the facts and circumstances, that it is publicly supported, and thus a public charity.

A major problem involves certain specific organizations (e.g., museums, libraries, old-age homes) which were never thought to be abuse situations, which are not donor controlled, which perform primary (or active) rather than secondary (or passive) charitable services, but which have large endowments and high investment income, and therefore have traditionally neither received nor solicited contributions from the public. Many of these organizations have difficulty meeting the 10 percent test and, therefore, may be subject to the private foundation provisions, including the tax on net investment income and the mandatory distribution requirements.

This problem remains unresolved, although it is noteworthy that Senator Gordon Allott of Colorado has introduced a bill (S. 2851) which would explicitly exclude from foundation status homes which care for the elderly or the destitute.

Governing Instrument Requirements of Section 508(e)

Many states have enacted statutes to make the private foundation governing instrument requirements applicable to all foundations and charitable trusts. The Internal Revenue Service is ruling on such statutes as they are submitted.

Problems may occur if such a statute is later held unconstitutional. In such a case, the regulations will very likely protect an organization which had relied on such a statute and give it a reasonable time to take alternative measures, with no retroactive adverse effect on the organization's status.

Charitable Remainder Trust Regulations

The deadline to amend certain charitable trusts to conform to the regulations under section 664 is January 1, 1972. The deadline has been extended a number of times to give the Service an opportunity to formulate appropriate rules and to give taxpayers ample time and experience before they had to create such trusts "at their own risk." We have received many requests to extend the deadline again; this is being seriously considered, but no final decision has yet been made. [The deadline was extended to July 1, 1972, by T.I.R. 1120 dated December 17, 1971.]

We have also started a project to develop model forms and clauses which we hope to publish, and we also hope to publish rulings on individual instruments as they are processed.

As many of you know, new proposed regulations were issued in September, and there will be a public hearing on December 8, 1971. The notice says taxpayers may rely on the proposed regulations, and instruments need not be amended to conform to any changes made by the final regulations. This was done because of the need for certainty in an area still encumbered by a good deal of doubt.

For example, many protests have been received on the necessity for all of the regulatory governing instrument requirements to be included in the trust instrument. It has been suggested that these could all be incorporated into these trusts by reference, so that deductions would not be lost by failure to include all the requirements correctly. We are currently considering this as well as many other proposals in this area.

Proscription of Political Activities

Interestingly enough, the effect of the 1969 act on foundations seems to be interpreted with substantially different emphasis by lawyers than by some foundation managers. Most lawyers are immediately interested in the tax on investment income, the mandatory distribution requirements, the problems of classification, and the like, but not necessarily so for foundation managers. For example, I was speaking in California recently on the same program with the president of the Danforth Foundation. He remarked at that time that in his opinion, the key to the future of organized philanthropy in this country was really hidden in the Code provision which effectively proscribes the political activities of private foundations. The policy behind this provision is not altogether clear. Was Congress saying that it is improper for foundations in their work to express social concern and to be interested in various pressing social problems? When the foundation community was charged in 1969 with partisan political activity, was this tantamount to a finding that foundations must refrain from addressing the serious problems of our social order because, ultimately, these were political problems? There is reason, if we read the 1969 act carefully, to raise these questions. Section 4945 of the act, for example, subjects to tax any attempt to influence any legislation through an attempt to affect the opinion of the general public or any segment thereof.

The Treasury has already issued proposed regulations, and will soon issue final regulations, that interpret this language in a reasonable manner, intended to comply with congressional intent without impinging upon the broad social role of foundations. Thus, as one small example, the regulations provide that expenditures for examinations and discussions of broad social, economic, and similar problems are not taxable, even if the problems are of the type with which the government would be expected to deal. The regulations provide that the term "any attempt to influence legislation" does not include public discussion or communications with members of legislative bodies or government employees, the general subject of which is also the subject of legislation before a legislative body, so long as such discussion does not address itself to the merits of a specific legislative proposal.

INTERPRETATION AND ADMINISTRATION OF 1969 ACT

At this point I think it would be appropriate to make a few comments about the general matter of the interpretation and administration of all of the Code provisions affecting private foundations.

As for interpretation, the Treasury is attempting to write reasonable interpretative regulations under the new foundation provisions in an effort to carry out congressional intent with as little disruptive effect on the foundation community as is possible under this type of legislation. On January 6, 1971, the front page of the *Wall Street Journal* referred to comments by the president of the Council on Foundations, Inc., the membership of which is composed of a mixture of several hundred community, family, and corporate foundations of all sizes and types and from all areas of the country: " 'Thus far we've seen a real desire by the Treasury to make this law work,' says David F. Freeman, president of the Council on Foundations. The new law subjects foundations to unprecedented regulation, but a year after it became law, foundation circles find relatively little to complain about in the Treasury's proposed regulations interpreting the act."

Both the Office of Tax Legislative Counsel at the Treasury and the Legislation and Regulations Division of the Internal Revenue Service have been working night and day throughout 1970 and in 1971 in order to formulate regulations under the Tax Reform Act. I believe that the regulations which have already been published indicate the seriousness with which we are approaching our task and the unparalleled record which we have produced in explaining comprehensive tax legislation in record time.

With respect to the day-to-day administration of these provisions, I am of the strong belief that they must be administered in light of their special purpose and their individual structure as a group in the Code. Their purpose is not to raise revenue; they are designed to act as a guardian to insure that foundation assets will be put to charitable uses. In administering these provisions, a strict adversary position cannot automatically be taken. They call for an extraordinary degree of care and judgment in their application. We cannot assume that private foundations are subject to a presumption of impropriety in their dealings, or that it is the role of the Treasury Department to discourage their existence.

I believe that sanctions should be imposed only where appropriate, and that every effort should be made to carry out the congressional intent to benefit, rather than impede, charity. Each factual situation must be examined on its own merits and a threshold decision made as to whether it violates the basic intent and spirit of the provisions. If it does not, then the purportedly charitable activity should be allowed to continue, and the Treasury should not attempt to proscribe such activity by creating formalistic, unworkable, or unreasonable rules, through strained interpretations of the Code provisions.

By pressing for results which are too severe or are unreasonable in light of the underlying purposes of these provisions and not justified by a reasonable interpretation of them, we could seriously hamper the flow of charitable funds in this country. If this type of approach were to predominate, it would not be long before there would be sufficient pressure for a full congressional reconsideration of this area, which could result in losing the substantial benefits and safeguards of the long-awaited private foundation provisions of the 1969 act. I hope we can insure that these provisions will be interpreted and applied in the same spirit, and with the same kind of care and judgment, which I believe has been exercised in deevloping the very reasonable and excellent rules in the regulations.

CONCLUSION

By way of conclusion, I would just like to say that we at the Treasury are trying very hard to make the unique charitable provisions of the 1969 act workable for organized philanthropy. The regulatory and rulings processes have been marked by unprecedented communication and cooperation between the Treasury and attorneys from all over the country. We have every intention of continuing in this spirit, and I hope that as problems arise, you will continue to call on us, so that we may resolve together the many complex issues and unanswered questions raised by the act.

On balance, then, I would have to agree with those spokesmen of the Council on Foundations, and others, who have indicated that our system of private philanthropy has survived in spite of (although some would say because of) the 1969 act, and that the foundation community, while still stunned, is nevertheless alive and well. We at the Treasury are continuously sensitive to the state of being of private philanthropy in this country, and we are unanimous in our view that we must achieve a regulatory pattern for foundations that will give them the fullest opportunity to continue making their substantial contribution to all of us.

* * * * *

DISCUSSION

Chairman Arthur M. Hayes, Standard Oil Company (N.J.): Ted, thank you very much. You certainly did a wonderful job.

Mr. Robert Anthoine, Winthrop, Stimson, Putnam & Roberts, New York: Would you comment on the merger of private foundations?

Mr. Theodore A. Kurz, Attorney-Advisor to the Assistant Secretary of the Treasury for Tax Policy: The word merger is a little slippery, but I take it you are referring to section 507 of the Code, which is one of the sections under which we are presently developing proposed regulations, and all of you will shortly be able to examine and comment on the new rules which will govern such mergers. I should add that the provisions of section 507 (b) (2) and the regulations thereunder will also govern the transfer of assets from one foundation to another pursuant to any liquidation, redemption, recapitalization, or other adjustment or reorganization.

The only other comment I would make in general terms is that if any of you have problems related to section 507, or expect to have them, and want to go the route of merger, liquidation, reorganization, and what have you, the Service is geared up and is already issuing rulings with respect to these matters, even though we do not have final—or even proposed—regulations out. As a general matter this is a good point I think for foundation lawyers to remember.

Thus, just because you see no regulations in CCH or Prentice-Hall, it does not necessarily mean that the Service is not issuing rulings. There are a lot of rulings being issued under the private foundation provisions of the Code where most of the policy questions have been resolved but where no final or proposed regulations have yet been published.

President R. Palmer Baker, Jr., Lord, Day & Lord, New York: Ted, there has been a great deal of concern expressed about the drain of the 4 percent tax under section 4940 of the Code and some skepticism among the larger foundations as to whether the cost of their audit program quite justifies the drain on their income and the drain on charity. Is there any consideration being given at the Treasury and on the Hill to a change in the 4 percent tax?

Mr. Kurz: I would like very much to answer your question, and I think I could, but I know this is a topic on which Mr. Cohen will speak directly tomorrow. Let me just answer it in the affirmative. The 4 percent tax is getting a fair amount of attention both in the Treasury and on the Hill, although specific proposals for a change, as well as congressional reaction to a change, have not yet clearly emerged. I think that Mr. Cohen plans to cover this matter in detail tomorrow.

CHAPTER IV

THE TREASURY VIEWPOINT

Edwin S. Cohen
Assistant Secretary of the Treasury for Tax Policy

IT IS a great pleasure to be here even though I appear 24 hours late, which is a bit unusual even for me. My long-suffering and loyal wife is sitting immediately in front of me, and she is accustomed to my being five minutes or ten minutes or even a half hour late, but 24 hours goes beyond the pale. I have asked my children, if they feel so inclined after I am gone, to use as my epitaph: "He was worth waiting for."

I am not sure it will be true in your case. I shall try to make it so.

COMMENTS ON GROUP OF TEN ROME MEETINGS ON INTERNATIONAL MONETARY CRISIS

I shall comply with your request, Leonard, and make a few remarks about my trip to Rome. This was an exciting and fascinating experience on a matter of the greatest seriousness and urgency for all the nations of the world. It was an invaluable and interesting experience to be there when these momentous monetary matters were being discussed.

We who have had experience in the tax field in the United States are familiar with the intricacies of fiscal problems, and the day-to-day resolution of tax disputes, but we are not normally involved in the intricacies of monetary affairs, of trade problems (which are extremely complex and difficult to solve), of military burden sharing, and of other matters that are involved in the balance of payments positions of the major countries of the world, and particularly that of the United States.

I know Professor Bittker is interested constantly in broader problems of constitutional law and many other phases of the law, and I am sure that others of you go beyond the tax field on many important matters. It was a great privilege for me to participate in these wider interests.

I had been in Rome in May of this year discussing fiscal matters with my counterpart in the Italian government, the head of the Italian tax system, the Undersecretary of Finance, Mr. Machiavelli. It does seem to me that he has the most fitting name for a tax collector that I have seen throughout the world.

I might say that, from my own viewpoint, I think we have made significant progress. I take it as a very hopeful sign for the world. Though this is not necessarily true, I think it is an encouraging sign that the ministers and governors there assembled were unanimous in their desire and willingness to meet here in Washington two weeks from today. I think that indicates their desire to go on with the negotiations and to move them forward as rapidly as possible. Secretary Connally has expressed this hopeful appraisal of the situation. We do not know whether the next meeting will produce an agreement or not, but I am sure that all parties aspire to that end.

I see so many members of law and accounting firms here that I think I might mention that during one of these lengthy meetings it occurred to me that, as Secretary Connally said last night when he met the press, we must remember that this is not simply a problem of a relationship of other currencies to the United States dollar, but a problem of the interlocking relationships of each unit of currency to the others throughout the world. While we in the United States may see all these other currencies in relation to their value in terms of the dollar, individuals in Italy will see it in an entirely different light with respect to the relationships of other currencies to the value of the lira.

Other governments, particularly those within the Common Market, are even more concerned in some cases about the relationship of the value of their currency to that of another country within the Common Market than in its relationship to the value of the dollar. This reminded me of the process that occurs in a law firm where one has to decide how to divide up profits. If you

35

ask any member of a law firm what percentage he thinks he should have, if he is worth his salt he thinks that he should have a higher percentage than he is actually getting. And if you go around the table and ask everyone to name the percentage that he thinks he should have and then you add up all the percentages, they will come to about 183 percent. The remaining process is a very hard and difficult one of shoving that 183 percent down to 100 percent. This, I think, illustrates in a way some of the difficulty of making all of the interrelationships involved in the monetary settlement come out in a manner that meets with the agreement of all the parties.

In relationship to the arts, Mr. MacBain, this meeting was held in the magnificent Palazzo Corsini, and Secretary Connally held a press conference at the end of each day with quite a large gathering in one of the rooms of the palazzo. Overhead, there was a beautiful ceiling designed and painted by Raphael and other noted artists. It was a magnificent historical setting for a modern discussion of the monetary problems of the world.

Effect of 1969 Act on Philanthropy

Let me take up with you a few points on which I have been asked to comment from time to time about the effect of the 1969 act on philanthropy. I apologize for the fact that I have been unable, due to these other commitments, to have a prepared text today. But I do want to review with you several points in connection with the 1969 act as to which I think there is some misunderstanding concerning the Treasury position and the history of provisions in the statute dealing with philanthropy. Also, I would like to give you an insight into the first figures we have that deal with the contributions as they appear on the 1970 individual income tax returns, the data on which were handed to me just before I left last week for Rome.

Treasury Attitude Toward Tax Provision

Let me go back first to the 1969 act. We, of course, intended by the proposals that we advanced to the Congress in 1969 not to hem in, but really to encourage, philanthropy; but at the same time we tried to curb certain abuses that had become rather prominent.

36

In our proposals presented to the Ways and Means Committee on April 22, 1969, we built upon the work that had been so ably done by my predecessor Professor Stanley S. Surrey, who is here today, and Professor William F. Hellmuth, who so kindly stayed over to span the two administrations and helped so ably in this work. Our feeling when we presented these proposals was that we wanted to encourage the use of the tax laws for the purpose of stimulating philanthropic work and charitable giving, while not permitting abuses to continue. We sought, however, to make sure that to the extent that we had these benefits in the tax law, and therefore experienced reductions in tax revenue for the public, there was a public good that stemmed from these tax benefits. We wanted the good to be available to the public at large and not merely to the individual donor or to his private foundation. That objective is easily stated but difficult to attain; it is not easy to secure a balance in this cost-benefit relationship.

When we appeared before the Ways and Means Committee in connection with the 1969 act, we did not make a proposal for a tax on private foundations. We presented proposals with respect to self-dealing, with respect to the required payout or distribution, with respect to holdings of stock in closely held companies, etc., but we did not propose a tax. The Ways and Means Committee in its executive session decided to include in the bill that it reported out a tax of 7.5 percent on the investment income of private foundations. When Secretary Kennedy testified, and I presented a detailed version of the Treasury views, before the Senate Finance Committee on September 4, 1969, we proposed that the tax be set at a level of 2 percent.

If I may, I shall just quote briefly from that statement:

The provision of the bill on this subject which requires the most careful evaluation is the imposition of a 7½-percent tax on investment income, including capital gains, of a private foundation. We have concluded that a tax designed to raise revenue from private foundations cannot be justified once the other restrictions imposed on them by the bill have been enacted to ensure that their funds will be used solely for charity. That is, there is no reason to reduce funds available for charitable activities by a tax once their tax-exempt status has been justified in the first instance.

However, the Administration considers that it is unfair to require taxpayers in general to pay the increasing cost of administering the audit program for these organizations when such program is required to ensure that charity re-

ceives the full benefit of foundation resources. Thus, the Administration rec-
ommends an annual supervision tax of 2 percent of private foundation investment income. This will raise about $25 million per year in the long-run effect
(about $17 million in 1970), which approximates the estimated audit cost.

That was our position.

At the same time certain foundations and their representatives
were very strongly of the view that the tax, if there must be a tax,
should be one on the value of the property or the assets of the
foundation and not on its income. In the Senate Finance Committee executive sessions, those representatives prevailed over our
suggestion of a 2 percent tax on income, which was roughly a
quarter of the amount provided in the House bill, and the
Finance Committee imposed a tax of 0.2 percent on the net value
of the assets of the foundation. This rate of tax on assets would
have raised about twice the revenue that would have come from
our proposed tax on income.

On the floor of the Senate this was reduced to 0.1 percent,
which was roughly the equivalent in revenue of the 2 percent tax
on income we had recommended to the committee.

I proposed to those representing the foundation group that we
try to reach an understanding on a tax of 2 percent on income
before the bill went to conference, but I was unable to achieve
that agreement. Some persons thus continued to advocate a tax
on assets while the Treasury felt—for reasons that I will not
elaborate now, but which led us to conclude that the Treasury
would not be able to cope with the significant administrative
burden that would result from a tax on asset values—that we
much preferred the tax on income.

When we went before the conference committee, the committee
accepted our conclusion that the tax should be based upon income
rather than upon asset values. But in the compromise between
the House and the Senate views, the conference committee went
to a 4 percent, rather than a 2 percent, tax on income. I think it
might possibly have been that, had we all been seeking the same
objective, we could have come out with a 2 percent tax on income,
although I am not at all confident of that view. There were certain members of the committee who were strongly of the view
that there should be a revenue-raising aspect to the tax on founda-

tions. And this view, so far as I know, still exists in the minds of some members of the committees.

I think that the Treasury has not changed its mind as to what would be the proper tax. I still adhere to the view—and I believe my colleagues do likewise, although I have not personally discussed this matter with Secretary Connally—that we would be satisfied with a tax that would raise sufficient revenues to pay for the cost of auditing and supervision of the philanthropic organizations. Though we still hold that view, I am not at all sure that if the matter were presented to Congress today the result would be any different than it was before, because there are others who hold to a different view as to the purpose of the tax and do believe in some revenue-raising aspects. So, it may come out just the same if the issue is raised again.

History of Payout Provision

Secondly, with respect to the payout provision, we proposed in the spring of 1969 that, in addition to the then existing requirements for distribution of income and prohibitions against unreasonable accumulation of income, the minimum distribution should be 5 percent of the net value of the investment assets of the foundation. And I would say today that we still feel that that is a better solution than the final one reached by the 1969 act. We convinced both the Ways and Means Committee and the Senate Finance Committee of this, but on the floor of the Senate the percentage was raised from 5 to 6 percent and in the conference the 6 percent figure prevailed. We have recently stated to the Ways and Means Committee, and I think this is our position still, that we adhere to our previous view that a 5 percent payout is, in all the circumstances and especially in the initial stages of the operation of the new law, a sufficient requirement of a public charitable benefit from the assets of the foundation. Again, I would repeat, there are others who believe the figure should be above 6 percent; and in a democracy, in the Congress of the United States, we often wind up with compromises, as the 6 percent was a compromise, and one does not know how a compromise would emerge again.

39

Treasury Administration of Act

We have entered into the vast program of preparing the regulations under this important set of provisions in the 1969 act with a strong effort to get the regulations out in proposed form for the guidance of foundations and others interested at as early a moment as possible.

We have concentrated the resources of the Treasury and the Internal Revenue Service, particularly the Chief Counsel's Office, on this task. We have issued a major portion of these regulations and the remainder of them are near to conclusion. We would have said on August 15 that they were imminent. But the emergence of a new and important tax law in August of this year necessarily diverted much of the time and work schedule of the Treasury and the Chief Counsel's Office to the task of that legislation. I am hopeful, now that that legislation is about to be reported out by the conference committee, that we will be able once again to concentrate our energies on the winding up of the rule-making process in the private foundation area.

We have tried—I hope that you will feel—to talk to all of you who have had problems; to listen sympathetically to the desire of those who are interested in the charitable and educational field and are promoting the finest of philanthropic work. We are conscious of the problems that you have had in becoming adjusted to this bill. We have tried not to construe the law in a technical way, but rather to adhere to the broad purposes of Congress. This is not always easy to do because individual members of the Congress in reaching a compromise sometimes have different purposes in mind, and it is hard to know at times what is the intent of Congress as a whole in passing a particular provision. But we have tried to adopt, and we shall continue to adopt, a sympathetic approach to philanthropy and the work of private foundations in the philanthropic and educational field. We shall try to give particular recognition of the fact that during the phase-in period while the regulations are being worked out and the instructions are being developed and you are becoming familiar with these problems, we should be as lenient as possible. But I must say that we hope to remain ever faithful to the broad purposes of the Congress, and expect to carry out the law and to supervise it through the Internal Revenue Service with an augmented program which the funds from the tax will produce. We are happy that you have cooperated with us in making known your problems and your suggestions, and we hope we can continue to work together.

Effects of Act on 1970 Contributions

That brings us to the interesting question of what has happened since the 1969 act went into effect, for most purposes, as of January 1, 1970. There are no data as yet available with respect to private foundations alone. We do have data, however, just handed to me, hot off the computer, so to speak, as I left for Rome. I took it to Rome together with some comparable pages from the *Statistics of Income* of the Internal Revenue Service for the year 1968. Deductions are analyzed in the *Statistics of Income* in even-numbered years. So, we have to compare what happened in the 1970 returns with what happened in the 1968 returns to see what trends may have developed.

I would caution you that these 1970 figures that I am going to refer to today are from the preliminary data. In particular, the difference between the preliminary data and the final data is that some returns are filed late under an extension of time, and therefore are not in the preliminary data, but will come into the ultimate statistics when they are finally available next year and are published in the final *Statistics of Income* for 1970.

I was going to make the other cautionary note that I did these calculations myself on the airplane and in automobiles and between conferences, and I was none too sure of them, but I have had the opportunity this morning to have the figures checked at the Treasury, and I am told that they are correct. Therefore, I give them to you with greater confidence than I would have a few hours ago.

The first significant fact that emerges, I think, is that the dollar amount of charitable contributions deducted on individual income tax returns increased from $11.1 billion in 1968 to $12.9 billion in 1970, a rise of $1.8 billion in the two-year period, or about a 16 percent increase. During the same period, the total adjusted gross income on all individual returns rose some 14 percent, and the total AGI on returns with itemized deductions rose some 22 percent.

Though subject to infirmities in that there were changes made in the 1969 act regarding the personal exemption, the low-income allowance, the filing requirements for the returns, etc., and in that one has to take into account the factor of inflation and other aspects it does seem to me reasonable to conclude that the aggregate contributions moved up in 1970 over 1968 in the general range that might have been anticipated. It does not appear to me that overall the 1969 act has had any noticeable impact in holding down the aggregate amount of contributions flowing to charity as has been alleged from time to time by a number of persons.

Another interesting fact seems to emerge if one reviews the changes from 1968 to 1970 in the aggregate charitable contributions and the adjusted gross income level within different income groups. For this purpose I compare total contributions and total AGI in the income group above $10,000. A large proportion of the returns below $10,000 are standard deduction returns. So, I start with the level of $10,000, and I use the customary seven categories of income that were available on this preliminary computer run: in other words, from $10,000 to $15,000; $15,000 to $20,000; $20,000 to $25,000; $25,000 to $30,000—there are $5,000 jumps in those four groups—then $30,000 to $50,000; $50,000 to $100,000; and $100,000 and over. There will be some more detail in the ultimate statistics, but that is what is available in the preliminary run.

The interesting fact to me was that in all of these seven categories, except the last—that is in all of them except the income group above $100,000—both contributions to charity and adjusted gross income increased substantially. In other words, adjusted gross income and charitable contributions increased in all these groups between $10,000 and $100,000. But in the group with adjusted gross income above $100,000, we find that the aggregate AGI on the itemized returns—which represent substantially all of those returns—fell from $16.6 billion to $14.1 billion, a drop of about 15 percent in income of the group above $100,000; and the aggregate amount of contributions in this above-$100,000 income group fell from $1.89 billion in 1968 to $1.25 billion in 1970, a drop of 6 percent.

In other words, the income in this top income group dropped 15 percent, and charitable contributions in the top income group dropped 6 percent, but in all other income groups, the income went up and the contributions went up.

Again, let me caution you that we do not have in this preliminary run the returns of those who filed late under an extension of time. And in the final data it could be that these figures will go up, both on the income side and the contribution side, with respect to those above $100,000 of income. Yet, on the other hand, it does not appear likely that this $74 million drop in contributions in this group would be made up by the late filed returns, nor that the drop in income of $2.5 billion is going to be made up by the late returns. So, I would say the likelihood is that there was a significant drop-off in both income and contributions in the group above $100,000. I think this reflects what many of you believed and experienced, that the contributions from the top income group fell off in 1970. But the decrease in contributions in that group seems to have been less than the decrease in their income.

I think it is rather interesting—I had somebody check this this morning—that in the $100,000 or more group contributions as a percentage of adjusted gross income had dropped from 8.5 percent in 1962 to about 6.6 percent in 1968, and actually went up during the period between 1968 and 1970. Because their income went down by more than their contributions went down, the percentage of their income contributed to charity actually increased between 1968 and 1970.

You may ask why the adjusted gross income in the group above $100,000 dropped so significantly from 1968 to 1970 while in general incomes were rising in that period. The answer is pretty obvious, because as you look at the preliminary statistics that will soon be published for 1970, you will see that capital gains in general fell in 1970 to roughly half of what they had been in 1968 almost up and down the line in the income groups.

In the group above $100,000, the capital gains as reported— this is one-half of the long term capital gains—fell from $6 billion in 1968 to $3 billion in 1970, a drop of about $3 billion. So, capital gain, which is a substantial part of the income of the above-$100,000 group and which shoves many persons up into the above-

$100,000 group when businesses are sold or profits are realized, fell to a very substantial extent. This is reasonably a reflection of the course of the stock market. So, your high-income group had a substantial drop in capital gains and income, and their contributions to charity fell off.

One other point seemed to me to be significant. Although we do not have all the data yet, there are included in the preliminary data the data for nontaxable returns with adjusted gross income of $5,000 or more that show itemized deductions for charitable contributions. The number of such returns—that is, that paid no tax but had adjusted gross income of $5,000 or more—went up, but the dollar amount of the contributions went down from 1968 to 1970.

In 1968 the average contribution on a nontaxable return with income above $5,000 was $1,115, and it dropped in 1970 to $558, almost exactly half. Now, it is too early to tell why, but I would guess that the reason for this is the statutory change that eliminated the unlimited charitable contribution deduction. That change took effect in 1970 and provided that contributions may not be used as a deduction to reduce the taxable income to less than 80 percent of the adjusted gross income. You must have at least 20 percent left as far as the affected contributions are concerned.

The amount of contributions in this nontaxable group with AGI above $5,000 dropped $89 million on the preliminary returns, and it seems to be obvious that this had some effect in 1970. This $89 million drop in the deductions on the nontaxable returns with significant amounts of income is a small part of the $12.9 billion of total charitable contributions in the year 1970. But I think it did affect contributions to certain types of organizations that come from the very high income group.

Conclusion

It seems to me that the Congress made the decision—and the Treasury felt this way also—that while we wanted to sponsor philanthropy, and we have tried to continue the encouragement for charitable giving, we did feel that it ought not to be used in the future as a means of permitting a person to wipe out entirely, even though he is in a high income group, all his responsibility for contributing to the cost of the United States government.

This gives us something of a bird's-eye view, it seems to me. I think that there are certain noticeable effects, but I am happy to say that overall the level of contributions has been moving up and I hope it continues to do so in the future.

I would say one last word. The Treasury continues to remain extremely concerned and interested in advancing the cause of philanthropy and pluralism in our society. We shall continue to try to administer the existing law in an evenhanded way that will not thwart, but will actually encourage, the continued development of philanthropic work, but without abuses that have occurred in rare instances in the past.

We think that the time has come, with the first availability of data and shortly when we complete the remaining proposed regulations, to take another look see where we are going in this field, and review the effects of the tax laws and the role of government in promoting and supervising philanthropic giving. To that end, we hope to call upon persons from the public to advise with us in some group, the precise nature of which has not yet been worked out, to review the situation two years after the 1969 act and see what program or changes might be in order not only with respect to private foundations but with respect to public charitable organizations as well. We shall call upon the members of the public who have devoted so much time and effort in this great cause to assist in this work and help develop a program that will continue to sponsor philanthropy throughout the years ahead.

PART THREE

TRENDS IN PHILANTHROPIC GIVING AND RECEIVING AS AFFECTED BY THE TAX REFORM ACT OF 1969

"As chairman I have been asked to point out two or three superficial trends that have resulted from the 1969 act. One of course gives me great personal pleasure. The Program Committee Chairman said that I had something to do with the 1954 Code. My chief contribution, of which I have been accused many times, was that I changed all the section numbers. The section numbers that have been added in the Tax Reform Act of 1969 are even worse, I think, than the changes which we made in 1954.

"Moreover, we have also had to learn a lot of new terms. We now talk about unitrusts, charitable remainder trusts, annuity trusts and wills, public charities, private operating foundations, and private foundations. So, not only do we have a whole new terminology to learn but also all of the new sections and rules. There is one effect of all this, of course; it must reduce the federal revenue when the deductions are taken for lawyers' and accountants' fees in explaining these sections.

"But there are much more sophisticated trends which have developed as a result of these provisions, and these will be delineated by the speakers at this session."

Kenneth W. Gemmill
Attorney, Dechert Price & Rhoads, and
Chairman, Thursday Morning Session

47

CHAPTER V

EFFECT ON DONORS

ROBERT ANTHOINE*
Attorney, Winthrop, Stimson, Putnam & Roberts

TAKE your mind back to the last days of 1969. The President has just signed the 1969 Tax Reform Act into law. In New York City the snow is snowing, the wind is blowing, but somehow wagon after wagon weathers the storm and pulls up in front of the Museum of Modern Art and the Whitney Museum of American Art to disgorge a stream of paintings and sculpture. Strange and wonderful indeed—and directly attributable to the new tax law and to the alertness of the administrative directors of those museums.

Seldom is it possible to pinpoint so directly the impact of tax law upon human behavior. The 1969 act changed the law, effective January 1, 1970, with respect to the gift of "ordinary income" property to allow only the adjusted basis of such property as a charitable deduction. Those last days of 1969 represented the last chance—perhaps in a lifetime—for the creator of property such as paintings and sculpture to obtain the full fair market value deduction for the donation of his created work.[1] For gifts to public charities up to midnight on December 31, 1969, the creator

---

* The author is indebted to Glenn E. Coven, Jr., of the New York Bar for his valuable help in the preparation of the manuscript.

[1] The same opportunity was not available for the creator of literary properties because Congress had eliminated as of July 25, 1969, any deduction above cost by an author for a contribution of property containing his work product. The Tax Reform Act amended section 1221 to add to the exclusion from the definition of a capital asset a letter or memorandum, or similar property, in the hands of the creator or his donee. With a special swipe at certain persons who had hit upon the technique of accumulating papers bearing upon public events and then contributing such papers to charity, the amendment also excludes letters and memoranda prepared or produced for the taxpayer. For this type of property only, the effective date of July 25, 1969, was carried over to the provision under section 170 disallowing any deduction on a gift of appreciated property to the extent that the appreciation would be taxed as ordinary income.

was entitled to a fair market value deduction up to 30 percent of his adjusted gross income for the current year. Moreover, to the extent the property contributed had a fair market value in excess of said 30 percent, that excess was carried forward as if it had been a cash contribution and could be applied against 50 percent of the donor's adjusted gross income for the next five years. Hence the enormous incentive for immediate donations.

The carryover principle described above also applied to gifts of capital gain property to public charities and stimulated some late 1969 donations. Also, the new rules applicable to gifts of all appreciated property to private foundations and to transfers of property to charitable remainder trusts did not come into play until 1970 and hence led to considerable late 1969 activity. Since the Treasury maintains statistical data with respect to charitable donations only for the even years, we will never know whether the last minute rush in 1969 amounted to much statistically. However, on the "retail" level, from which vantage point I address myself to the impact of the 1969 law upon donors, it was indeed a frenetic period.

GENERAL RULES APPLICABLE TO DONORS

One of the most far-reaching changes made by the 1969 act was to fashion an entirely new set of ground rules for charitable giving by large donors. While these changes came in the form of a superstructure of apparently minor adjustments to the basic pattern of section 170, for the large donors the changes will have as great an impact as any of the changes made by that act. At the same time, small donors, those who customarily make cash gifts of a minor fraction of their income, are virtually unaffected by any of the new provisions.

One Favorable Provision

Turning away from the high adrenalin days of 1969 and to the more permanent effects of the 1969 act, in surveying the impact of that act upon individual donors I am able to find only one provision more favorable than former law—the increase in the general limitation for deductions to public charities from 30 percent to 50 percent of adjusted gross income (or the "contribution base" as it is now called). All other provisions of the act are unfavorable. Very little impact is expected from this change because so few taxpayers have given more than 30 percent of adjusted gross income to charity and because the additional 20 percent cannot consist of appreciated property. Indeed, the principal purpose of the provision appears to have been to ameliorate the gradual elimination of the unlimited charitable contribution deduction. By 1975 the 50 percent limitation will apply to the 100-150 persons who have been using the unlimited deduction and so some slight impact may be experienced.[2]

Retention of 30 Percent Ceiling for Gifts of Appreciated Property

I do not anticipate an increase stemming from the tax law in the general level of charitable giving by individuals because the old 30 percent ceiling of pre-1969 law has been retained unchanged for gifts of appreciated "capital gain" property to public charities. This ceiling within a ceiling is by far the most important for nearly all big donors.

The 1969 act does provide that a taxpayer can avoid the 30 percent ceiling on a gift of appreciated capital gain property and can deduct his gift up to 50 percent of his contribution base if he makes an election to reduce the amount deductible with respect to all gifts of property made during the taxable year by an amount equal to one-half of the element of appreciation contained in each such contributed property. Such an election may be useful to an individual receiving ordinary income taxable in the highest brackets who holds such a large amount of low-basis property that

---

[2] Prior to the Tax Reform Act, the 20 percent and 30 percent limitations on the deduction of charitable contributions did not apply to an individual who for the taxable year and at least 8 out of the 10 preceding years had made charitable contributions equal to 90 percent of his taxable income for the year, less his federal income tax for the year. The Tax Reform Act gradually eliminates this exemption from the ceiling so that beginning in 1975 the unlimited charitable contribution deduction will no longer exist. During the transitional years, the 90 percent threshold requirement is gradually eased to 50 percent while at the same time the percentage of the taxpayer's income that can be sheltered from tax through charitable contributions is gradually reduced to the 50 percent ceiling applicable to all taxpayers. It is interesting to note that the source of several of the changes affecting private foundations contained in the Tax Reform Act, particularly the definition of a private operating foundation, may be traced to the definitions contained in the unlimited charitable contribution deduction provision, which limits the types of charitable organizations deductions to which can be taken into account for the purpose of this provision.

it is more important to him to shelter additional amounts of ordinary income than it is to lose a portion of his deductions. Presumably there are few such individuals. The election device was originally designed to aid taxpayers making donations of only slightly appreciated property. Such individuals could, it was thought, make the election to forego one-half of the appreciation as a deduction in return for the benefit of being able to take those deductions up to 50 percent of their contribution base.

Because the election must apply to all property gifts made during the taxable year, however, it will rarely be of use since few, if any, persons donate over 30 percent of their contribution base in such slightly appreciated property. Furthermore, the election also applies to redetermine carryovers from prior years: contributions made in prior years are recomputed as though the election had been in effect in the year of the actual gift, and only the amount of carryover available had such election been in effect may be carried forward to the year in which the election is actually made. In short, it is likely that only a few contributors of property will be making this election in order to take advantage of the increased general ceiling.

Private Foundations

Retention of 20 Percent Ceiling for Gifts to Nonpublic Charities. The 1969 act contains for the first time a definition of a private foundation. Colloquially, prior to the 1969 act these were referred to as 20 percent charities to distinguish them from the public charities to which contributions by individuals could be deducted up to 30 percent of adjusted gross income. The distinctions are not the same in all instances but in general those foundations to which contributions would have been eligible for the 20 percent deduction before the act will be similarly treated after the act.

New Rules for Gifts of Appreciated Property. A significant new rule has been introduced for contributions of appreciated capital gain property: the donor's charitable contribution amounts only to the fair market value of the property minus one-half of the unrealized appreciation. This provision has benefited public charities since many donors have shifted their appreciated property gifts from private to public charities.

The foregoing statements require qualification because, as noted below, gifts to private operating foundations and to certain "conduit" private foundations are eligible for the much more generous limitations applicable to public charities.

Retention of 5 Percent Ceiling for Gifts by Corporations

The 1969 act made no change in the existing law which permits corporations to deduct charitable contributions up to 5 percent of net income. In the case of gifts of appreciated property by corporations to private foundations, the reduction from fair market value is 62.5 percent of the unrealized appreciation.

Gifts of Ordinary Income Property

The general rule with respect to ordinary income property was noted at the outset—if the property donated would produce ordinary income on a taxable disposition, the amount of the charitable contribution is limited to the adjusted basis of the property. Gifts to museums and public libraries of their works by creators have been few indeed since 1969. This new rule also prevents businesses from obtaining fair market value deductions for gifts of inventory and other property held for sale to customers in the ordinary course of trade or business. This change may prove to have some significance. In the past many charities such as relief agencies have greatly benefited from substantial gifts of inventory by manufacturers. However, it is difficult to assess the impact of such a change because of the presence of nontax factors that play a large role in the making of such contributions. Many businessmen, whether small retailers or large manufacturers, anticipate deriving indirect business benefits from the making of such contributions and while the change in the tax law has made these benefits more expensive, they remain as real as they ever were. In addition many corporations are impelled by social and humanitarian reasons to make substantial gifts of their manufactured articles—such as the gift of drugs and medical supplies.

The ordinary income rule will also apply to properties such as section 306 stock—preferred stock received as a dividend on common and transferred subsequently by the shareholder—and to capital assets held for less than six months.

53

Tangible Personal Property

The Tax Reform Act also increased the cost of donations of certain types of tangible personal property even though made to a public charity. Unless the property is used by the recipient charity for a purpose that is related to its exempt activities, the deduction by the donor is reduced by one-half of the element of appreciation in the contributed property. This provision was primarily directed at individuals who had used their captive private foundations as depositaries for unproductive assets.

The scope of the provision, however, is far broader. Thus, the gift of a painting to a university where the work is hung in the office of the president rather than used in a class on art history may not generate a full deduction to the donor. It has been reported to me that museums have failed to obtain contributions of valuable works of art because of the uncertainty in the operation of this provision. The regulations have not provided a great deal of assistance in answering such questions as whether the donee museum must display the painting or whether it must even retain it. Their example is of a gift of a painting to a university and concludes that a sale by it would be an unrelated use. What of interinstitution loans? Would the same be true for an art museum?

The regulations contain a provision intended to ease the donor's burden of proof in that he may either establish a related use or demonstrate that at the time of the contribution it was reasonable to anticipate that the property would not be put to an unrelated use by the donee. More is needed. Both counsel to the donor and the donee are confounded by this provision. The museum does not wish to be hamstrung with conditions as to utilization of the acquired property and the donor does not wish to jeopardize the fair market value deduction by granting to the museum less than all of the unrestricted rights in the property. It is to be hoped the final regulations will be rewritten to permit public charities greater flexibility and yet accomplish the statutory objective of preventing deductions for the full value of property not contributing to charitable purposes. The law in this area does discriminate between the investor in securities and the investor in works of art, but perhaps justifiably so in light of the differences in the natures of the properties and their respective markets.

MISCELLANEOUS PROVISIONS LIMITING DEDUCTIONS
FOR GIFTS TO CHARITIES

Short-Term Charitable Trust

Prior to the 1969 act the 30 percent ceiling could be avoided with relative ease by the creation of the so-called two-year charitable trust. Through this device, individuals were able to transfer substantial amounts of income-producing property to a short-term trust, the income of which was dedicated to charitable purposes, while retaining the reversionary interest. Although the donor was not entitled to an income tax deduction for the actuarial value of the income interest donated to charity, the income of the trust so paid to charity was not included in the grantor's income and hence was outside the 30 percent limiting provision. For transfers to such trusts made after April 22, 1969, the income of the trust will be included in the grantor's income. However, if the grantor is willing to postpone his reversionary interest for 10 years or more, the trust income will not be taxed to him.

Life and Testamentary Gifts Not in Trust of
Remainder Interest to Charity

A little noticed amendment to the estate and gift tax law has seriously interfered with some normal lifetime and testamentary dispositions of property. For such dispositions after 1969, with the limited exception of remainder interests in farms and personal residences, there is no longer for estate and gift tax purposes a deduction for the actuarial value of a remainder interest in tangible personal property left (not in trust) to charity where there is an intervening interest in a noncharitable person. For example, the testamentary gift of a remainder interest in a business building to a public charity will not qualify for the estate tax charitable deduction if an intervening life estate is given to a related or unrelated person. Similar rules apply to remainder interests in works of art given to museums. It is difficult to understand the policy behind these estate and gift tax provisions and they should be changed. (The income tax deduction is similarly limited but the change is of less significance because a deduction for the actuarial value of the remainder interest where the donor or related parties retained a life estate was eliminated by the 1964 act.)

Alternative arrangements may be available to satisfy the objectives of the parties where it is desired that the property in question be enjoyed by the private party for only part of a year, say, six months. Taking into account the new life estate-remainder tables which use new life expectancy data and a 6 percent interest factor, a gift or a bequest of a 50 percent undivided fractional interest in property to a charity and an outright gift of the remaining 50 percent interest to a family member may produce a better result than a gift of 100 percent of the remainder interest after an intervening life estate under the prior law. For example, suppose a testator owned a painting valued at $100,000 that he wished to bequeath to a museum subject to a life estate in his widow, aged 50. Even if the remainder interest were still allowed as a charitable deduction, the value thereof would be worth only $32,000. On the other hand, if the testator today bequeaths an undivided one-half interest in the painting to the museum and either bequeaths the balance outright to his widow or bequeaths the remainder interest in the other one-half to the museum subject to a life estate in his widow, the estate will be entitled to a charitable deduction of $50,000. Of course, under this arrangement the museum must be entitled to have possession of the painting for six months out of every year and the widow, whether she be the 50 percent owner or the life tenant of the remaining 50 percent, will be entitled to possess the work of art for the remaining six months.

Bargain Sales

In earlier days, fund raisers delighted in demonstrating to a prospective donor that he could actually improve his cash position by selling appreciated property held for less than six months to a charitable organization for an amount equal to his tax basis for the property as compared to an outright sale of the property and retention of the proceeds. Even where it was not possible to make money through the charitable contribution, the cost of a charitable contribution could be made nominal through the bargain sale device.

Under prior law a taxpayer making a bargain sale to charity was entitled to offset his full tax basis against the proceeds of the sale before he was required to report any gain. Thus, a taxpayer having property with a fair market value of $100 and a tax basis of

$20 could sell it to a charitable organization for $20, have no gain from the transaction, and a charitable contribution deduction of $80. For a taxpayer in the 70 percent bracket, the tax benefit from this deduction by virtue of offsetting the tax on other income amounted to $56. Thus, the net after-tax cost of the bargain sale was $24 ($100 less than $56 benefit from the deduction and less $20 received from the sale).

The Tax Reform Act now requires the taxpayer to allocate the basis for the property between the sale and the gift portions of the transactions. The taxpayer is thus treated as though he had made a gift of $80 of his securities and sold the balance while retaining the proceeds. In the above example the taxpayer would have a basis for the "sale" portion of the transaction equal to 20 percent of his $20 basis or $4 with the result that he would have a gain of $16 subject to tax. He is still entitled to a charitable contribution deduction of $80 although this gift is now subject to the rules concerning donations of ordinary income or appreciated capital gain property. The result of this change is that the after-tax cost of a bargain sale is increased by the amount of tax that the donor will be required to pay on the sale portion. (Of course, it is generally no longer feasible to make an outright gift or a bargain sale of ordinary income property or of capital gain property held for less than six months.)

While it is a popular refrain that the Tax Reform Act eliminated the bargain sale, computations demonstrate that it still remains a low-cost method for making to public charities a contribution of capital gain property held for more than six months— superior to either an outright gift of the property or a sale of the property and the contribution of the proceeds to charity. In fact, the more highly appreciated the property, the less significant is the change made by the Tax Reform Act. Hence, bargain sales to public charities may be expected to continue. (Such sales to private foundations by a wide category of persons connected with the donee would constitute "self-dealing.")

No Deduction for Contribution of Right to Use Property

The Tax Reform Act in effect bars any deduction for contribu-

tions of the right to use property. In the past, taxpayers might donate to a charitable foundation the right to use a portion of a
building owned by the taxpayer. The donor would be entitled to
deduct as a charitable contribution the fair rental value of the
contributed property without having to take into income any
actual or constructive rental income attributable to the property.
It is unlikely that this change will have a significant impact on
contributions to charitable organizations since the nontax factors
that motivated the gift in the first instance will remain. While
this change might have led donors of space to charge rent to such
charitable organizations, such a charge is now forbidden by the
provisions on self-dealing where the donor is related to the foundation.

Charitable Remainder Trust

Under the old law donors could create a trust with the income
to a private person for life and the remainder to charity and be
entitled to an immediate charitable contribution deduction for
the present value of the remainder interest. It was alleged that
trustees of such trusts in some instances invested funds in high-
yield securities that did not fare well over the long term with the
result that the charity ultimately received less than the amount of
the claimed deduction. The 1969 act introduced new conditions.
In general, to obtain an estate, gift, or income tax charitable deduction for such a gift in trust under the 1969 act, the trust instrument must either provide that a sum certain (not less than
5 percent) of the initial net fair market value of the property
placed in the trust be paid annually to one or more noncharitable
persons (the charitable remainder annuity trust)[3] or that a fixed
percentage (not less than 5 percent of the net fair market value of
the trust assets, determined annually) be paid out annually to one
or more noncharitable persons (the charitable remainder unitrust). However, this latter unitrust arrangement does permit the
payment to the noncharitable beneficiary of only the actual trust
income if lower than the said 5 percent; there need be no invasion

---

[3] The annuity trust permits only one contribution. Hence the frequent testamentary "pourover" of assets into an existing trust cannot be directed to this type of
trust; the unitrust is not so limited.

of principal to meet a mandatory 5 percent return. The value of the charitable remainder in such cases must be calculated on the assumption of a 5 percent return.

These new provisions have been known to antagonize creators of charitable trusts. Consider the person who planned to contribute $100,000 in trust with an annuity of $3,500 a year to a private beneficiary, remainder to charity. The donor is advised that the income beneficiary must receive a 5 percent return; he is forced to reduce the contribution in trust to $70,000 in order to obtain the charitable deduction and the charity receives less.

Another type of charitable remainder trust that is permitted under the new law is the pooled income fund. This is a trust maintained by a public charity to which two or more donors have made contributions of property. The donors or their designees enjoy lifetime income interests. This form of trust is commonly used by educational and religious organizations. The Senate Finance Committee Report refers specifically to this type of split-interest trust as one that should continue to qualify for the unlimited deduction for long-term capital gains set aside for eventual distribution to charity.[4] As enacted, the provision prohibits the donor or private income beneficiary from acting as trustee, prohibits the trust from receiving or investing in tax-exempt securities, and requires that the remainder interest be irrevocably contributed to the public charity maintaining the trust. It seems highly likely that this pooled income fund will continue to be a popular method for making gifts to schools and churches.

Charitable Income Trust

The 1969 act effectively eliminated any net income tax deduction for charitable income trusts by permitting the donor a deduction only if he remains taxable on the trust's income. The trust must also be in the form of a unitrust or annuity trust. A deduction will, however, be available for estate and gift tax purposes for the actuarial value of the income interest given to a charity and this deduction may prove significant in permitting property to pass

---

[4] United States Congress, Senate Committee on Finance, *Tax Reform Act of 1969,* Report to Accompany H.R. 13270 Together With Separate and Individual Views, Senate Report No. 91-552, 91st Congress, 1st Session, Washington: Government Printing Office, 1969, pp. 84-86.

largely free of tax to private beneficiaries upon termination of the trust. For example, assume the grantor contributes $100,000 in trust directing the payment of an annuity of $8,000 to a designated public charity for 23 years, remainder to his heirs. The deduction for gift tax (or estate tax) purposes will be $100,000 and hence there will be no tax payable upon the creation of the trust. If the trustee is able to obtain an 8 percent annual return on the principal, the amount of $100,000 will be available to the heirs on the termination of the trust.

GIFTS TO AND BY PRIVATE FOUNDATIONS

The new law provides deterrents to gifts to private foundations, to continuation of the existence of private foundations, and to the creation of new ones. With respect to contributions to private foundations generally, apart from the special categories noted below, it is true that the cash gifts can still be made up to 20 percent of an individual's adjusted gross income. The gift of appreciated property no longer is feasible, however, because the fair market value of the donated property must be reduced by one-half of the unrealized appreciation in computing the amount of the charitable deduction. The administrative and operating requirements added by the 1969 act, combined with the new donation rules, should result in a significant reduction in the amounts contributed to private foundations and in the number of new private foundations, and should lead to the complete dissolution of a substantial number of existing ones.

The subject of private foundations is complicated by the fact that there are at least five different types when viewed from the standpoint of an individual donor. There is the "garden variety" type described above. Then there is the "private operating" foundation, donations to which are treated as if made to a public charity. This is an organization that is directly involved in carrying out the charitable purposes for which it exists. A good example (unless and until it becomes publicly supported) is the Frick Museum in New York City.

A third type is the "full conduit" private foundation. This is a foundation that within two and one-half months of the end of its taxable year distributes an amount equal to all of its income for the taxable year plus an amount equal to the full fair market value as of the date of gift of all property contributed to the foundation during the taxable year. Individual gifts to such foundations enjoy the same deduction limitations as gifts to public charities.

Still a fourth type is the "partial conduit" private foundation— a creature largely of the regulations.[5] Contributions to this type are entitled only to the 20 percent deduction but with the wrinkle that appreciated property is entitled to a full fair market value deduction up to the 20 percent limitation if, within two and one-half months after the taxable year, the foundation has distributed an amount equal to the full fair market value on date of gift of that appreciated property.

The fifth type is a fascinating new branch of private foundation that has not yet received much attention and is still very much in the dark. It is described as a private foundation all of the contributions to which are pooled in a common fund which would qualify as a public charity but for the right of any substantial contributor or his spouse to designate annually the recipient (from among the described public charities) of the income attributable to the donor's contribution to the fund, and to direct (by deed or by will) the payment to such an organization of the corpus in the common fund attributable to the donor's contribution. To qualify, all of the income of the common fund must be distributable and in fact distributed to a qualifying organization within two and one-half months of the end of the taxable year and all of the corpus attributable to any donor's contribution must be distributable and in fact distributed to one or more qualifying organizations not later than one year after the donor's death, or after the death of his surviving spouse if she has the right to designate the recipient of such corpus.[6] This new provision ap-

---

[5] Treas. Reg. § 1.170A-9 (g) (2).

[6] Dispositions of this type in which the donor retains an interest such as a life estate or the power to designate beneficiaries leads to the inclusion of the property in the gross estate, followed by a charitable deduction for the amount so included. However, the charitable deduction is taken after first calculating the maximum marital deduction. The resulting increase in the maximum marital deduction (well understood for over 20 years) is sometimes heralded by the Treasury and even by some practitioners as a great benefit. However, in the absence of careful advance planning and subsequent execution, this so-called benefit can become a serious detriment; the devolution of property may take an unexpected turn and total family taxes may be higher because of the increase in the estate of the surviving spouse.

pears to have interesting potential. Indeed, this type of pooled fund, the type of pooled fund referred to above in connection with charitable remainder trusts, and community trusts[7] present fruitful avenues for charitable giving to be explored.

Within the past two years a number of private foundations have qualified either as operating foundations or as full conduit foundations. Considerable flexibility is provided for the full conduit foundation because there is no precise tracing of specific property —it is only necessary that a dollar amount equal to the fair market value of the contributed property on the date of the gift be distributed to qualifying charities within two ond one-half months of the end of the taxable year. Thus a private foundation can retain particular contributed properties and distribute others at then current market values if so desired.

Summing up, the provisions dealing with private foundations will surely result in the flow of greater sums of money to public charities. This will result from (1) the requirement that a private foundation distribute annually (by 1975) an amount equal to at least 6 percent of the average fair market value of its assets not devoted directly to actual charitable activities,[8] (2) the favored posi-

---

[7] While community trusts are not a new phenomenon, the proposed regulations (§ 1.170A-9 (e) (10) for the first time provide this form of charitable organization with a clearly defined status under the tax law. This treatment apparently became necessary when the Treasury Department determined to tighten the "facts and circumstances" test for the definition of a publicly supported charity within the meaning of section 170 (b) (1) (A) (vi) of the Code. While these proposed regulations have been criticized as unduly restrictive because of their questionable incorporation of various prohibitions that are only applicable to private foundations, the support definition of community trusts is quite liberal. Thus, during the first five years of its existence, a community trust will qualify as a publicly supported charity even though one person has contributed 90 percent of its assets. Even after the end of its tenth year, a community trust may receive up to 50 percent of its assets from a single person and all of its assets from no more than five persons. Furthermore, while the governing body of a community trust must be generally representative of the community, up to one-third of the governing body may consist of substantial contributors to the community trust or members of their families. While there are, of course, several technical requirements for the qualification of these organizations, the community trust appears to be a feasible substitute for a private foundation in many instances. Particularly in a relatively small community, the amalgamation of the charitable pursuits of a small number of families into a community trust may provide—depending upon the content of final regulations—many of the private foundation advantages to the donors with few of the penalties.

[8] See United States Congress, House Committee on Banking and Currency, Subcommittee on Domestic Finance, Staff, *The Fifteen Largest United States Foundations: Financial Structure and the Impact of the Tax Reform Act of 1969,* 92d Congress, 1st Session, Washington: Government Printing Office, 1971, 27 p. The Report states that the mandatory payout provisions of the new law will require estimated additional grants from the 15 foundations of $75,000,000 in 1972, increasing to $157,000,000 by 1975.

tion of the private foundation that follows the full conduit approach, (3) the incentive to dissolve existing private foundations, and (4) the incentive to individuals and corporations to make gifts of appreciated property directly to public charities.

COMPLEXITY OF THE CHARITABLE PROVISIONS

If during the taxable year the donor proposes to give cash and appreciated long-term capital gain property (apart from tangible personal property) solely to public charities, there should be no problem for the donor and no confusion about the tax consequences. The rules are essentially as they were prior to the 1969 act. Indeed, there is an actual improvement in that gifts of cash and non-appreciated property can be made up to 50 percent of the contribution base. Once there is any deviation from that simple pattern, however, a great deal of complexity is introduced. For example, where appreciated property is given to public charities and cash to private foundations in the same year, the donor may find his deduction for charitable gifts impaired by the peculiar workings of the deduction limitations.[9] An effect of this complexity has been to direct the flow of contributions to public charities

---

[9] The order of deductibility of charitable contributions is as follows:
   1. Cash and nonappreciated property contributions to 50 percent charities in the current year.
   2. Carryovers for cash and nonappreciated property contributions to 50 percent organizations.
   3. Appreciated property contributions to 50 percent organizations in the current year.
   4. Carryovers for appreciated property contributions to 50 percent organizations.
   5. Contributions to 20 percent organizations in the current year.
The foregoing computations are further complicated by the election available for appreciated property contributions to reduce the contribution by a percentage of the unrealized appreciation (50 percent in the case of an individual and 62.5 percent in the case of a corporation). That election pertains not only to the appreciated property contributed in the current year but also to all appreciated property carryovers. Furthermore, even though a current contribution of appreciated property is deductible only up to 30 percent of the contribution base, any excess in value above the 30 percent is applied against the full 50 percent contribution base, thereby eliminating deductions for contributions made in the current year to 20 percent organizations.
For example, assume that an individual's contribution base is $50,000. During the year he gave $2,500 in cash, and securities having a cost of $2,500 and a value of $22,500, to public charities and, in addition, gave $5,000 in cash to a 20 percent charity. The $2,500 in cash and $15,000 of the value of property given to public charities are currently deductible, and the $7,500 excess of the appreciated property above 30 percent of the contribution base can be carried over for five years. However, because the individual exhausted his 50 percent limitation, the gift of $5,000 in cash to the 20 percent charity is not currently deductible and cannot be carried over to any subsequent year even though only $17,500 of his $25,000 is currently deductible.

and away from private foundations, and in some cases to deter, temporarily, charitable giving generally.

The complexities inherent in the interaction of the new charitable provisions with other parts of the tax law remain to be explored. One situation that illustrates the need for countless hours of struggle, fasting, and prayer, and the talents of a cryptographer, is described in the Appendix.

Conclusion

Although the enormous complexity of the law is bound to remain, most of the present confusion and uncertainty should disappear as final regulations are gradually promulgated. The flow of contributions to public charities should continue unabated. The purpose of the legislation to diminish the role of private foundations will surely be realized. Hopefully, the present timidity in the grant-making process will vanish and charities, in addition to their important routine contributions to society, will perform the role, which government has wisely left to them, of allocating resources to experimental charitable projects and nourishing new ideas.

* * * * *

APPENDIX

A Case For the Curious

The holder of a qualified stock option exercises it and forthwith sells the stock at the exercise price to a public charity. Assume, for example, that the exercise price is $54 and that the fair market value of the stock on date of exercise is $60. Shortly after exercise, when the stock is still worth $60, the owner sells the stock to a public charity for his cost of $54.

The resulting bargain sale to charity constitutes a disqualifying disposition of the stock. Accordingly, the transferor will realize $6 of compensation income representing the difference between the exercise price and the fair market value at the time of exercise. (For those persons covered by section 16 (b) of the Securities Act of 1934, there is no problem because the seller-donor has realized no actual gain.)

With respect to the charitable contribution deduction, under section 170 (e) (1) (A) there normally would be no deduction because the transaction constitutes the sale of ordinary income property for an amount equal to its tax basis. However, proposed regulation § 1.170A-4 (a) provides that where income is actually realized with respect to a transfer to charity in the same year as the transfer, there will be no reduction from the fair market value of the property, even though it would have produced ordinary income on a sale, in measuring the charitable deduction. Accordingly, there will be a charitable contribution deduction of $6.

The fact that there is a charitable deduction allowable under section 170 brings the bargain sale rule of section 1011 (b) into play. Under that section, where property is transferred to charity at a price less than fair market value, the tax basis of the property must be allocated between the part donated and the part sold. However, in this example, the fact that $6 of compensation income is realized on the disqualifying disposition will result, pursuant to regulation § 1.421-6 (e), in an increase in the basis of the stock by the $6 of income. Thus, the stock transferred to the charity will be deemed to have a basis equal to its fair market value of $60 and there will be no allocation of basis under the bargain sale rule. Accordingly, up to this point, the transferor has realized $6 of ordinary income and has a charitable contribution deduction of $6—a complete wash (except that he has lost the benefit of his option).

The foregoing result is not changed by the minimum tax on items of tax preference because proposed regulation § 1.57-1 (f) (5) (i) provides that if stock acquired on exercise of a qualified stock option is disposed of in the same year, there will be no tax preference income. Accordingly, the complete wash effect does prevail!

It should be noted that the transferor will bear the risk of any decline in the fair market value of the stock between date of exercise and date of donation. Because the transfer to charity is not an arm's length transaction, the amount of the compensation income to the transferor is fixed at the time of exercise and will remain throughout as the difference in amount between the exercise price and fair market value on date of exercise. As the stock declines in value, however, the amount of the charitable contribution deduction will be reduced and the transaction will no longer be a wash. (The foregoing result assumes that a bargain sale will not be treated to any extent as a "sale" which would limit the amount of compensation income to the excess of the amount realized over the exercise price. An alternative analysis would fractionalize the transaction and so limit the amount of compensation income attributable to the sale portion. However, even under this analysis, the amount of compensation income attributable to the gift portion, while less than $6, would still exceed the amount of the deduction attributable to the gift portion in the event that the value of the stock declined.)

On the other hand, if the value of the stock increases before the donation date, the contributor will not be entitled to more than a $6 contribution deduction. Until the stock has been held for over six months, it constitutes ordinary income property. Notwithstanding the literal language of proposed regulation § 1.170A-4 (a) referred to above, the exception to the rule requiring a reduction from the value of contributed ordinary income property in computing the charitable deduction will probably be limited to the amount included in income as a result of the transfer. Thus, any appreciation in the value of the stock will not increase the amount of the deduction.

CHAPTER VI

EFFECT ON DONEES

Edwin D. Etherington
President, National Center for Voluntary Action

YOU MAY remember a 1968 cartoon which pictured two business-men over a drink at their club. One said to the other: "Confused? Of course I'm confused. I've got a son at Vassar and a daughter at Yale."

At about that time, the Congress was gearing up for the 1969 Tax Reform Act. The intention, of course, was to make matters less confusing for each of us and more equitable for all of us.

It is obvious enough that matters are at least as confusing as they ever were for the ordinary taxpayer. He does not have the advantage of reading all that legislative history. He does not get his hands on all those clarifying Internal Revenue Service rulings or on the opinions of tax court judges.

Now the experts who arranged this program have confirmed *their* confusion by asking someone who cannot even understand the preamble of a withholding statement to talk about the 1969 legislation.

Confused? Of course we're confused—perhaps even desperate.

Fortunately for me, the subject today is related not to tax code detail, but to broad public policy and to equity in the wide sense of the word. We are concerned with the likely impact of the Tax Reform Act of 1969 on donees—the agencies that depend on charitable contributions. Was the Congress ill advised, if not confused, about priorities when it acted in 1969? Do we now have a more equitable and sensible tax structure? Are we on the way to a better society as a result?

HISTORY OF CHARITABLE DEDUCTION

These questions imply that the Congress has always seen a relation between the federal income tax structure and private giving. But that is not the case.

The income tax between 1861 and 1872 had no provision related to private giving. Nor did the law enacted in 1913. The Congress did not then, and may not now, believe that equity—fairness—required that gifts to educational, religious, charitable, medical, or other independent agencies be deductible in the process of going from gross to net income.

But in 1917, the Congress changed its approach. Tax rates were up. There were fears that independent organizations might suffer from a reduction in the flow of giving. So the Congress decided that the value of gifts from individual taxpayers to agencies operated for philanthropic purposes could be deducted from income. The limit was 15 percent of net income.

The principle established in 1917 was that the cost of the gift to the taxpayer would always vary inversely with the donor's highest tax bracket because the deduction was from income. That principle is still in the law.

In the 52 years between 1917 and 1969, the only substantive changes in the law were in the direction of greater encouragement of giving. In 1935, the deduction was made available to corporations with a ceiling of 5 percent of net income. In 1952, the ceiling on deductions for individuals was lifted from 15 percent to 20 percent. In 1954, it went up to 30 percent, with some conditions on categories of gifts. In 1964, the restrictions by categories were eased and the "carryover" for gifts in excess of the ceiling was introduced.

Along the way, the standard deduction was introduced. The effect was to break the connection between giving and the size of the donor's income for millions of low- and middle-income people. The underlying assumption was that giving is so ingrained a habit that the loss of a tax advantage would not blunt the impulse of generosity.

The lessons I draw from this brief review of history are two. First, we cannot assume that the Congress sees or has ever seen the deduction as a matter of equity for taxpayers of any class. And second, we must recognize that the trend for 52 years was basically toward more—not less—encouragement of private giving.

EQUITY FOR RECIPIENTS

I do not intend to review the provisions of the 1969 act nor can I recite its dollars-and-cents consequences for independent sector institutions. My purpose is simply to suggest that the nation will be well advised to start its next consideration of tax laws related to giving from a new perspective—a perspective which emphasizes the matter of equity for the million or so independent agencies that count essentially on private giving for their survival.

Whatever abuses the Congress meant to curb in 1969, the plain fact is that a 4 percent audit tax on foundation income does not penalize the donor, or the trustees, or the administrative staff. The tax comes out of the pockets of potential grant recipients. The fact is that the cost of compliance with new accounting requirements, for those who choose to meet the burdens, is carried ultimately by potential recipients. The pity is that the discouragement of giving hurts not those who would have given but those who would have received.

Until now, the debate about the new requirements has centered almost entirely on foundation practices and on *giving*, as if giving can be considered as an isolated act of virtue—or self-fulfillment or tax offset—that is separable from the result.

That, of course, is absurd.

A careless financial reporter will sometimes write that the market is in decline because "everybody is selling." This leaves out the fact that there is a buyer for every share of stock that is sold. In the same way, giving *never* occurs in a vacuum. For every giver there is a receiver somewhere. And whereas the life of a donor is not radically disjointed by restrictions on his giving, the lives and ambitions of his recipients may be vitally and painfully and profoundly affected.

It is important, of course, to debate the rights of people to *give*. But it may be far more important to talk about the rights of the nation's voluntary agencies to *receive*.

ATTACK ON FOUNDATIONS

In 1969, the Congress was concerned about revealed abuses of

69

donor privileges. Gross self-dealing and other sour practices were described on the record. Then when the focus shifted to the major foundations, the agenda seemed to be distorted by concern over certain types of grants. One effect was the surfacing of latent prejudices against foundations and latent concern about giving as a tax loophole for the rich.

It is hard to find a political champion for the larger foundations. To people on the left, they represent masses of money not adequately subject to public control or influence. To people on the right, they are supporters of far-out, left-wing research and activities. There are very few people ready to argue for a balanced view.

The foundations, in short, were and remain good political targets but have no real political defenses.

But what are the consequences of a gradual erosion of foundation giving?

The distinguished Peterson Commission, after a careful study, warned us of "a charitable crisis" in the seventies.[1] Since then, Alan Pifer, the wise and able president of the Carnegie Corporation, has sounded the alarm in his annual report:

> . . . a high proportion of our private educational, cultural, health, and welfare institutions are heading into deep trouble. . . .The steady, unrelenting deterioration of their position has now, for the first time, raised doubts about the continued viability of our traditional system of shared responsibility between public and private endeavor.[2]

At lunch recently, one of the most generous and imaginative philanthropists in America told me he had been obliged to cut his giving in half largely as a result of the Tax Reform Act of 1969.

One of the best informed senior students of private higher education tells me that money for private charitable purposes is tighter than it has been at any time since the Great Depression.

These are opinions and signals. Still, no one can say what might have been. No one can say whether the Jonas Salk of Cancer research has been passed over in this cutback. No one can say which private college gave up or went public for lack of these funds.

---

[1] Commission on Foundations and Private Philanthropy, *Foundations, Private Giving and Public Policy*, Chicago: University of Chicago Press, 1970.

[2] Alan Pifer, "The Report of the President," *Annual Report for 1970*, New York: Carnegie Corporation of New York, 1970, p. 3.

We know that a substantial number of smaller foundations are liquidating rather than staffing to conform to the complex reporting requirements of the new law. But we do not know which prisoner may go without guidance, which retarded child may grope without help, which older person may waste precious time without comfort as a result of these liquidations.

The best we can do now—and also the least we can do—is think about some larger effects of the act on America's voluntary institutions.

To get the matter in perspective, it is right to observe that formalized philanthropy—most directly and seriously affected by the act—is comparatively a tiny business. There is only one philanthropist listed as such in the Manhattan telephone book. A large amount of capital is involved, but the gift dollars available each year do not represent a spending torrent on a comparative basis. If the annual income of foundations were wholly confiscated, the proceeds would pay the costs of the federal establishment for less than three days.

The act simply taxes these organizations a little and regulates them somewhat more severely than before. What, then, is all the fuss about? Why are we taking two days to review the act's possible consequences? Why is there a growing concern about philanthropy's future?

I think it is because we all sense that much larger issues are involved, that there is much more at stake than a few million dollars of foundation contributions, and that the reform act raises questions fundamental to an essential American tradition.

The Tax Reform Act of 1969 was important because it was perceived as an official, congressional vote of "no confidence" in private foundations; a vote of low confidence in some of the larger public foundations; and a vote of diminishing confidence in the nation's network of independent agencies. As such, it was a tremendous blow to the morale of the agencies in this sector.

Congress suddenly—perhaps somewhat impulsively—reversed a 52-year trend toward expansion of philanthropic prerogatives.

This action could scarcely have come at a worse time. It came just as the nation was beginning to rediscover the forgotten potential of private action on social problems. It came when the press had begun to sense the vast importance of the enormous network of independent service agencies, and to report their activities more extensively.

The action came only a year after the President of the United States had, for the first time in recent history, given official recognition to the tremendous potential of nongovernment action for the public good by establishing a Cabinet-level Committee on Voluntary Action and calling officially for the establishment of the private National Center for Voluntary Action.

It came at a time when the nation, discouraged by the results of a generation of massive experimentation with government programs, was becoming heartened by a renewed awareness of a neglected option to public problem solving. It came at a time when "reprivatization" was being discussed in the corridors of the White House as an alternative or supplement—depending on the subject—to further expansion of federal responsibility.

Finally, the Congress acted just when inflation and a mushrooming agenda of unsolved problems were already straining the slender resources of independent organizations.

In short, when voluntary action was most in need of reinforcement, it was at least indirectly rebuked.

Response of Independent Sector

Fortunately, the most profound and important effect of the Tax Reform Act of 1969 has been a kind of purposeful backlash. There has been, since the act, more intelligent soul-searching, more serious self-study, more strengthening of resolve than at any time since the thirties. It is a pity that it took an attack on the financial base of the independent sector to focus our attention on what we had to lose. But now, regardless of the reason, a sector of society that has suffered a full generation of benign neglect is suddenly a matter of widespread concern and debate.

Philanthropy, treated by some as if it did not matter very much, is developing a new determination to matter decisively.

But we are woefully short on the knowledge we need to make a case for independent action and for the private giving it needs. We have never taken stock of our nongovernment, nonprofit organizations with thoroughness and precision. It is alarming how little we know about a sector of society that is unique to America and crucial to the realization of American ideals.

We do not know for certain how many entities comprise the independent sector. Some experts estimate that there are a million, but no one knows for sure. We have no measurement of the resources they bring to bear on public problems. We have no inventory of the assets they control and no calculations as to the money and time channeled through these agencies.

We need to know what these independent sector agencies now do, how much they contribute to the public welfare, what kinds of services they deliver, how and to whom. We can hardly formulate wise public policies until we catch up with the facts. With the facts, we can consider what these entities *could* do.

My own impression is that independent agencies, taken as a whole, are grossly underutilized compared to their government or commercial counterparts.

Precisely because the contributions of the independent sector are not widely and clearly recognized and understood, our political leaders may doubt the capacity of independent action for problem solving. It is easier to depend on government with its relative power, including its power to tax and spend, than to speculate about capacity elsewhere.

The displacement of private action by public action in the last generation has often been the product of perceived necessity. But it has given rise to a vague national presumption that government can do anything it puts its mind to, and do it better than it might otherwise be done. Now there is reason to wonder whether we have carelessly assigned to government responsibilities that might better be performed privately. We must find ways to assess the *comparative* effectiveness of independent action on public problems. The task is to develop more certain measures of social performance, more sophisticated devices for deciding how responsibility can best be distributed among public and private agencies.

Can it be true, for example, that independent agencies are best thought of as entities that exist through tax loopholes? Can it be true that foundations are best viewed as creatures of a special privilege, to be subjected to extraordinary surveillance and restrictions?

I think not. Tax exemption should be viewed not so much as the extension of a privilege as the protection of a right. Tax exemption should stand as an affirmation that the public interest is better served if voluntary agencies have the first, rather than the last, claim on the citizen's dollar.

We tend to speak of voluntary agencies as if they had great power. But they have, comparatively, no power at all. They can try to persuade people to give. But this is a fragile prerogative. It clearly needs protection from the inexorable power of taxation.

We must also consider the right of independent agencies to be heard. We can agree that exempt money should not be used for partisan political purposes. But this proposition should not be taken to mean that voluntary agencies must suffer extinction in silence. It should not be taken to mean that Congress will be deprived of facts and insights indispensable to a rational decision-making process. If this is what we have done to ourselves through the 1969 legislation, we have selected too blunt an instrument to prevent unfair political activity. We are guilty of political overkill.

A closely related point is that voluntary agencies need to develop a new sense of community. These organizations have traditionally been much more aware of their differences than of their essential similarities. It seems, at first glance, that the Civil Air Patrol has little in common with the Teachers Insurance and Annuity Association, or either of them with the Salk Institute or the Groton School or the Ford Foundation. But these five and a million more are best viewed as parts of an integral whole, as specialized elements of a coherent sector of American society.

The individual pieces of the independent sector, like the pieces of a jigsaw puzzle, are often grotesque and meaningless by themselves. Many of the particular acts of independent institutions are absurd and indefensible. Why should we spend precious tax-exempt dollars to permit a psychologist to teach pigeons to play ping-pong?

But the issue is not ping-pong or even psychology. The issue is pluralism. The issue is whether we are to have a vital, responsive society, with multiple independent centers of initiative, or whether we are to suffer through sluggish and unresponsive centralization.

The debate must be about the total result, not about the funny little pieces that are sometimes a part of that result. The independent sector, like the commercial sector, must be seen as a whole.

The Tax Reform Act of 1969, to the extent that it dampened the philanthropic impulse, reduced giving, taxed resources that voluntary agencies desperately need, and rendered cautious a sector of society that needs a measure of audacity, was a negative influence on voluntary organizations.

But the reform act will be a positive influence if, as I hope, it prompts us to define independent action and its place in society with more clarity and force. The goal must be to quicken ambitions and improve performance in the independent sector.

It should be clear, from what I have said, that some of us believe the National Center for Voluntary Action can and should take the lead in organizing a major research effort to enlighten this subject. It is not something we will do impulsively or in a halfhearted way. It is a matter we will approach systematically and in depth or not at all. Right now, we are simply in touch with the problem, with some of the people who could be part of the solution, and with our own sense of deepest mission.

Ten years ago, it was fashionable to predict the disappearance of voluntary action. There are still a few people who believe that voluntary action is an obsolete instrument for effective social action and should be scrapped and forgotten.

I do not think so.

I think I can see the beginning of a great renewal of independent action—and with it a revival of spirit—in America. The challenge now is to help the process along in a serious and significant way.

CHAPTER VII

PUBLIC POLICY ISSUES AND FOUNDATIONS

Sydney Howe
President, The Conservation Foundation

I WOULD like to discuss an area that has been touched only briefly by preceding speakers, the area in which present tax law affects my organization most seriously. I have no law or taxation competence from which to address this knowledgeable audience. I am simply a working stiff who tries to operate an organization within the realities and technicalities that you know so much about.

Prohibition Against Influencing Legislation

What concerns me most is the Tax Reform Act's effects upon treatment of the public policy issues in which organizations like mine have always dealt and intend to continue to deal. Today, an organization like mine must perceive a very difficult line of demarcation between analyzing public policy questions, commenting on them, and telling the public about them, on the one hand, and, on the other, influencing public opinion toward the enactment of legislation.

For many years, the Conservation Foundation has been by law a section 501 (c) (3) deductible, tax-exempt organization. As you know so well, we may thus devote only an "insubstantial" part of our activities to influencing legislation. To define "insubstantial" is in itself virtually impossible.

In 1967 and 1968 we secured designation as a publicly supported organization. Then came the Tax Reform Act of 1969. After its passage we filed with the Internal Revenue Service as a charitable organization described in section 170 (b) (1) (A) (vi). We continued to believe that, on the basis of that earlier 1968 designation as a publicly supported charity, our status had not changed. (We operate without endowment, funded primarily by the grants of private foundations, secondly by government contract or grant work, and thirdly by individual and corporation philanthropy.) Late in 1970, just a year ago, IRS informed us that under section 509 of the Tax Reform Act we were not a private foundation.

But a hooker has come along, one with which we have to live until the rules change: Some of the private foundations which support our work have said that as long as they are funding our general operations across the board—meeting basic costs of maintaining our core staff and our offices and so on—we must pledge to them that we will behave as though we were a private foundation. Thus, we must behave just so until IRS issues new regulations which persuade our private foundation donors that we can again operate as a publicly supported organization eligible to engage in insubstantial influencing of legislation.

Our legal counsel does not rest easily with this situation, feeling that our income from private foundations should not so restrict us, but we do understand the unease felt by private foundation officers at this time.

Let me set forth some of our operational problems that are, I think, quite comparable to difficulties faced by any number of other institutions having staffs which study public issues and tell the public about them.

As you know, the prohibitions against lobbying are generally interpreted to mean that an organization like ours must be invited, in writing, by the chairman of a legislative committee to present testimony on potential legislation. In the milieu of Washington and probably most state capitals, the people who know something about a given subject, whether members or staff of legislative committees, or executive agency employees, or representatives of private institutions like my own, come to know one another and maintain a fairly lively dialogue. This communication is often important and productive. However, if an otherwise effective private organization is supposedly excluded from such dialogue on legislative matters, except by the written invitation of a committee chairman, the law is, indeed, a bit of an ass.

Another kind of problem arises in efforts to separate the executive branch, where lobbying is legal, from the legislative. When does an executive branch proposal become potential legislation? For example, when a large expenditure for the SST was first proposed in the President's budget, we considered that an executive action on which we could comment, and we did. But when the time came for congressional action on the same subject, we remained silent. We have (and had) no idea of the precise moment at which the SST sped beyond our proper ken, which simply illustrates the difficulty of dealing with this sloppy situation.

Our counsel advises that, when we testify by written invitation of a committee or subcommittee chairman in the Congress, we must not issue a press release on the substance of our testimony—as we did routinely prior to the Tax Reform Act. Perhaps such action would mean that we were influencing public opinion toward the enactment of legislation, but who knows? Of course, people from the wire services and other media men are always scouting around on the Hill. If our staff member who is there to present testimony happens to give a copy to a press representative, are we breaking the law? To two press representatives? Three?

Another aspect of this situation is raised by the work we are doing in community planning. We are conducting a series of demonstration projects, funded by a private foundation, in which we seek to resolve specific conflicts between preservation and development in about half a dozen locations around the country. If, in presenting our findings, we recommend that a local government enact certain ordinances or the like, to encourage either the preservation or wise development of land, are we breaking the law? To be sure, such recommendations can be implemented only by the local legislative body.

One conceivable means of handling some of these difficulties, says our counsel, would consist of carefully recording every hour of professional staff time spent, and justifying a full day's work by each staff member every day, on our institutional business. Then if a staff member goes to the Hill on his own initiative from four to five o'clock on a given afternoon, to lobby as an individual, we can show that he was not operating on "company" time. But this would be unmanageable.

RELATIONS WITH DONOR FOUNDATIONS

Let me also say something of dealings with private foundations that support organizations like mine. In the fall of 1969, a grant-receiving organization with which I am familiar was encouraged to seek new operating funds from a private foundation. The first indication was that the private foundation would make a grant for general purposes, and that an application for same should be prepared. The application was prepared, with careful documentation, and submitted. Then in the winter and spring following enactment of the new tax law—the winter and spring of 1970—the signals were changed. The applicant was told to prepare a new grant application showing that the funds would be applied to certain activities, earmarked to give the granting foundation assurance that tax laws would not be violated.

Then the granting foundation, after simmering for a while under the new tax law, had a change of heart. The procedure was changed again, and the applicant was told to prepare an application for general purpose funds! I cannot tell you how much staff time was wasted in this process, by both the applicant and the granting foundation. The grant finally was made, but this kind of gymnastics goes on.

In another instance, a private foundation, without clearance from a certain grantee organization, wrote a letter to IRS saying that the grantee conducts activities which might be construed as influencing legislation. IRS was asked if the grantor foundation, were it to support the grantee in such activity, would come a cropper with IRS. The grantee was irate, to put it mildly, and fearful of burdensome investigation.

TAX LAW PAMPHLET

We have tried to help smaller organizations face this difficult situation by publishing a pamphlet which, we hope, illuminates some of the problems. Many citizen groups around the nation interested in the environment have the same kinds of problems that we do, in their dealings with various levels of government. We have published, for them, a booklet called *Law and Taxation,* written by our counsel, Anthony Roisman, of the firm of Berlin, Roisman & Kessler. This is designed to help organizations know

79

how to operate in conformance with tax laws and to know when they enter gray areas. It is also directed to new organizations, as they adopt bylaws that will determine their freedom of operation and tax status.

In summary, the worst effect of present tax law upon us, and upon our kind of organization, lies in our constant concern that we may generate serious problems for ourselves or our donors, quite inadvertently. I have every confidence that we are behaving properly. Yet the time wasted and the anguish spent are really quite debilitating for an organization which tries to do a professionally responsible job of analyzing public policy from outside the bureaucracy. We are slowed down a lot, and I doubt that the nation gains by having private institutions thus restricted.

There are also some rather direct costs. I estimated recently that roughly half of our bills for legal counsel over the past year and a half have covered consultations on the Tax Reform Act of 1969.

CHAPTER VIII

FOUNDATION ACTIVITY IN PUBLIC PROGRAMS

JOHN J. KEPPLER

*Executive Vice-President, The Federation of Protestant
Welfare Agencies, Inc.*

I HEAD an organization that is a central planning and coordinating body for 275 social agencies, serving about a million and a half people and spending about $200 million. The member agencies raise their own funds. They serve the aged, children, youth, run institutions, run hospitals, and the like. It's the equivalent of a Catholic Charities or a Jewish Federation in a community. Generally speaking, we have not yet felt seriously the effects of the Tax Reform Act.

INCREASE IN GIVING

In the city of New York, the Salvation Army set a record this year, $8.6 million. If you look at the united funds or community chests across the country, they're up 5, 6, 10 percent in almost every location. Our chief concern is the one Mr. Howe just talked about, and I shall talk about it in a little different way.

In listening this morning at breakfast to the chairman of the Program Committee, I realized that the worst is yet to come, particularly in the way of legacies and also in the way of some of the things that we are doing that perhaps we should not be doing.

Personal income is up in the country and so are contributions. Even in our agency and our member agencies foundation grants are up, although not as much as we would like. The answer to many of our social problems in this country is changes in function for most of the voluntary agencies, and extension of services to all who need them. Many of them are doing this, as my own is, and this costs lots more money. We are living on our capital, which is very meager, at the rate of about $350,000 a year at this point, and so we need some relief. I am concerned about the ultimate effect of the act if it remains unchanged.

It seldom happens that the donor can ignore tax effects, but the other day an elderly woman, who is one of our favorite contributors, was talking about making a second gift in 1971. She usually gives to us in the spring, and she was considering a gift toward the end of the year. We were questioning whether, because of the fact that we had budgeted the use of capital against our deficit, she should not carry this over and give it early in 1972 as an incentive and an encouraging start. It would also be our golden anniversary year.

I was mentioning something like this and I said, "However, I'm not aware of what your tax problem is going to be." And she said, "Well, all my married life my husband did not permit me to give to charity, I could only contribute my time. When he passed away, I began to pay my way and I enjoy doing it." And she said, "Now, John, I'm as rich as Croesus. I don't care what the tax laws are."

Influencing Legislation

Prior to the Tax Reform Act, our agencies were very active in attempting to influence legislation. Obviously, informed lay opinion has a tremendous impact on legislators, whether it is at the local, state, or federal level. Our own federation, with 8,000 board members in the aggregate of 275 agencies, potentially possesses a good deal of clout. This impact is not only in terms of numbers but in the prestige of the people who are involved, and also the people who speak with a great deal of conviction about some of the ills of society and what can be done and what should be done.

Reform of Public Welfare

Some of you must be familiar with H.R. 1, which is an attempt to reform public welfare. People generally have lost confidence in the public welfare program. It has been said it is bankrupt, it is costly, it is demeaning and dehumanizing, and it fragments the agencies. We are very concerned about that, but we are also concerned because the voluntary agencies pick up the pieces where the public program falls short. Just by way of brief illustration, in New York City 60 percent of the children who become in need of foster care, and need to be placed in homes other than their own homes or in institutions, come out of public assistance families.

That means that these children were known to a caseworker and known to a supervising agency, and yet family breakdown and deterioration occurred to the extent that the family had to be broken up and the children had to be placed. So, we have a real stake in a strong public welfare program. Indeed the voluntary agencies probably cannot exist if the public program deteriorates any more than it has.

I shall not go into the details, but I will tell you this fact—which I am fairly certain that most of you are not familiar with—and that is that the total cost of H.R. 1 would be about $25 billion a year. I was led to believe that it would probably be half that, if even that much. But this is the result of aggressive research analysis by lay persons helped by professionals who have looked into the legislation in all its nuances and see this kind of revelation.

Actually for $4 billion more—I will not say only—we could have a children's allowance system in this country which would enable us to pay $50 a month to every child in the United States, regardless of his circumstances. For those families with children who did not need the $50 a month per child, the allowance would be recaptured through the income tax system. For those who needed it, it would replace much of the public assistance granted. And in most cases people who needed public assistance would not apply if they were sure of this income without a means test, without application, and so forth. Japan and the United States are the only two major industrial nations that do not have such a children's allowance. Most of them do not have it to this degree, that is, $50 a month; Canada is somewhere around $6 a month.

For $8 billion more than the cost of H.R. 1, we could have a negative income tax system instead of public welfare. We talked about it a few years ago.

For this $33 billion a year we could pass on to needy families the $600 exemption per dependent which they do not now get because they do not have sufficient income. In other words, a family of four without income would receive from the government

$2,400 and this would replace the public assistance allowance provided for in H.R. 1, which is $2,400 a year.

EFFECTS ON ACTIVITIES

I throw these out as illustrations of what we should be saying and what we should be doing in terms of what is happening to public programs. All of us I think could add illustrations as to other needs in the legislative area. Our counsel does not believe that the Tax Reform Act of 1969 is aimed at our federation. And we do not feel the kind of inhibition which Mr. Howe has expressed here. Different lawyers talk differently, obviously.

We are concerned, nevertheless, with some of the fears expressed by the foundations. We are lucky in that we do have a modest endowment. We have established a separate budget account of the expenses of all the staff, full- and part-time, who are involved in our efforts to influence legislation or public social policy, or administrative decisions, and this expense is being met from income from endowment. Consequently, the nervous foundations—and we have had several, not many—who are worried about eventually having to trace their foundation gift to our federation down to its final disposition, will not see their dollars going to support our legislative activity. I am not sure whether or not this kind of separate accounting will stand up. But at least it is an effort and it will be a talking point if the time comes when we have to show how far we had to go to continue to bring informed lay opinion to bear on the legislative process at our three levels of government.

I am also concerned about the effect on the elderly. We have been making substantial progress in organizing the elderly. And they have been notably effective in attending meetings, putting on confrontations and demonstrations, and receiving good press. Their purpose is to improve their lot, but the real purpose behind this is to make the elderly feel needed and useful and to prevent their further withdrawal from life so that they can continue to act and continue to be involved. But this is a concern to some of the agencies who are directly promoting this effort on the part of old people.

The other is Title 4 of the Social Security Act, which now permits a donation to a public official in a locality who can then obtain federal funds at least trebling the amount of the original gift. Usually the public official is the local commissioner of welfare.

This opportunity is being exercised initially by united funds or community chests across the country. It means that a united fund or community chest can take a portion of its total receipts or total funds in a given year and turn it over to the local commissioner of welfare and then sit down with him and plan how it might be spent. In the meantime, the commissioner can be preparing to approach the Department of Health, Education, and Welfare for a matching contribution of three times this amount, and in some cases it is as much as nine times.

There are some restrictions. First, the public official must look upon this gift as unrestricted funds. He must treat it as state funds. He cannot return the donation, plus the public matching, to the donor, and he first must look at community-based self-help groups as a priority.

Secondly, he may then allocate the funds with some accord with the donor's purposes—for example, day care in the community that is to be served.

I may cite to you by way of example that last year Milwaukee was able to take $380,000 of its united fund and through this negotiation with the local public welfare commissioner build this up to $7 million, all to be turned back for the expansion and improvement of services in Milwaukee.

Last summer I had a note from John Simon, the executive of the Taconic Foundation, who asked my interest and support of Senator Muskie's bill to amend the Tax Reform Act. I acceded and sent individual letters to each member of the House Ways and Means Committee and the Senate Finance Committee. I was surprised to get thoughtful letters, lengthy letters, from about half the members of each of these committees expresssing interest in reform of the act.

I realize from looking through your material that the Tax Institute of America is not an advocacy organization. I just wish earnestly that there was some way, other than through your public meetings, that you could bring to bear the knowledge, the acumen, that I have seen since I have been here.

CHAPTER IX

PROPOSAL FOR A NEW FUNDAMENTAL RIGHT

E. Hugh Luckey, M.D.

President, The New York Hospital-Cornell Medical Center

PHILANTHROPY in 1970 was reported to be $18.3 billion. This is an increase of 4 percent, in spite of the following disruptive factors during the year. First, 1970 was the opening year of the Tax Reform Act of 1969. Then in May, campus unrest boiled over when United States and South Vietnamese troops crossed over into Cambodia. Finally, the stock market was badly down until the last quarter.

Growing Apprehension

The mission of this panel is to study the effect on giving of the Tax Reform Act and indeed all of the foregoing would seem to have had a disastrous effect on giving—but it did not. And it makes one wonder what records might have been eclipsed had we experienced more stability. We spend a great deal of time and effort in promoting the habit of giving with donors. Maybe we have succeeded beyond our wildest dreams. I think not, however. The goose that lays the golden egg *can* be slain, and we who are responsible for the successful operation of private nonprofit institutions were thoroughly shaken by the Ways and Means Committee's tentative decisions in May, 1969, which threatened to seriously reduce, or remove entirely, certain long-standing donor tax incentives. We heartily supported the concept of regulatory measures to curb abuse, but we were equally anxious to preserve the traditional tax incentives which affect our very existence.

The New York Hospital-Cornell Medical Center, one of the world's major medical complexes, exists today because of phi-

86

lanthropy. It has depended upon major support from private sources for 200 years—ever since the inception of The New York Hospital in 1771.

It seemed inconceivable that Congress would jeopardize the traditional system of private support that annually saves the taxpayers millions of dollars in government subsidies which otherwise would be needed to finance our privately supported health, educational, and welfare institutions. Certain of the committee's tentative decisions, however, had deadly serious implications, and the great ground swell of institutional opposition ultimately gave Congress reason to pause. The resulting legislation was toned down and a number of restrictive measures revised, as institutions anxiously explained their apprehension during committee hearings which ran well into the fall. The provisions of the new bill were finally hammered out, however, and the new tax reform act was signed into law in December.

The Early Returns

Now, starting with January, 1970, what has happened during its first year? As indicated earlier, nothing particularly dramatic has occurred according to the best estimates available. Total philanthropy in 1970 increased 4 percent, which is about the same annual rate as in the past 10 years. A breakdown reveals that giving by individuals totalled an estimated $14.3 billion, an increase of 5.2 percent. Foundation grants amounted to $1.7 billion, up 6.3 percent. Corporate giving was originally estimated to be $900 million, with no increase over 1969, but preliminary figures recently released by the Internal Revenue Service put corporate giving in 1968 at $1.0 billion versus the original estimate of $865 million. This would seem to imply that $900 million for 1970 is a rather conservative estimate. Finally, bequests were estimated to be $1.4 billion for 1970, down a little from 1969.

Now, how were the funds distributed? As in the past religion received the greatest amount, $8.2 billion, up 3.5 percent over 1969. Education was favored with $3.05 billion, an increase of 4 percent. Health was up 6.0 percent with a total of $3.02 billion in 1970. Other recipients fared as follows: human resources, $1.26 billion, up 6.9 percent; the arts, $550 million, up about 3 percent;

civic causes, the fastest growing category, up 20 percent to $200 million; and foreign aid, about $600 million, almost even with 1969. All of these figures represent estimates of the American Association of Fund-Raising Counsel which, consistent with past years, has drawn upon its own records as well as those compiled by the various donor and donee service organizations.

It should be emphasized that even if 1970 *had* brought forth dramatic changes from previous years, the figures represent the results of only one year and could hardly be considered trends. The Commission on Foundations and Private Philanthropy, headed by Peter G. Peterson, has recommended that, within three years, the Congress should thoroughly reassess the impact of the new law on the creation of new foundations and the total level of giving to and through the foundations.[1] It would seem wise to extend this examination to all sources of philanthropy. Gifts and grants to our medical center, incidentally, were up 7.4 percent in 1970 which is consistent with the national results mentioned earlier.

Make it Easy to Give

I agree with the spirit of the new tax law and the need for many of its provisions. It remains to be seen, however, what the net effect is, and I am particularly anxious about the reaction of the individual donors who represent 78 percent of total giving, and also the foundations which comprise an estimated 9.3 percent. It is simply common sense to make it easy for people to help you, and the complexities of the new tax provisions in many cases require sophisticated tax assistance, not to mention the dampening effect of reduced incentives. As one astute member of the bar remarked: "It will strike most donors that many of these new rules tighten the strait jacket without reason, and we cannot expect many to slip into it, and those who do will try to wriggle out of it. The results will be disappointing for many charitable organizations and even disastrous for others."

Possibly this gentleman had in mind the following provision regarding the ceiling on charitable income tax deductions. The new

---

[1] Commission on Foundations and Private Philanthropy, *Foundations, Private Giving and Public Policy,* Chicago: University of Chicago Press, 1970.

law calls for a ceiling of 50 percent of adjusted gross income with a five-year carryover for gifts of cash and so-called ordinary income property. For gifts of long-term appreciated securities, long-term appreciated real property, and long-term works of art for a related use (so-called capital gain property) the ceiling is 30 percent of adjusted gross income, with a five-year carryover. Under an election, a donor can increase the ceiling to 50 percent of adjusted gross income by reducing the amount he is deemed to have contributed by one-half of the appreciation. Once making this election, he must similarly reduce his deduction for other appreciated property gifts made during the year or being carried over from 1970 and later years.

I hope Congress will simplify and liberalize some of these charitable deduction provisions as soon as possible, and in this case I feel the ceiling should simply be 50 percent of adjusted gross income for *all* gifts to public charities. Tax incentives should be increased rather than reduced.

THE HEALTH CARE CRISIS

In the field of medicine we are faced with a dilemma—many dilemmas. Health care is now considered the fundamental right of every citizen. This means we need lots more medical doctors, dentists, nurses, and other health professionals, yet our schools of medicine, dentistry, nursing, and health professions are in serious financial straits and running substantial annual deficits. A number are on the brink of bankruptcy. The medical centers where these schools are located are, at the same time, faced with a substantial increase in demand for patient care. Their teaching hospital affiliates are also running deficits as their once ample and efficient physical plants are now hopelessly obsolete, expensive to operate, and overcrowded with indigent patients whom curtailed Medicaid payments no longer cover. In addition, there are new community programs to finance, and increased supporting facilities and personnel are needed to keep pace with the expansion of its affiliated schools of medicine, dentistry, and nursing. Also, the university medical center is the major source of research and innovation in the delivery of health services—expensive activities indeed. Wage rates have been another major problem. Wage levels at medical centers have traditionally been well below the rest of the economy. Now as they are forced to catch up, they have had to contend with the additional problem of inflation.

While the problems are seemingly endless, these institutions have been simply magnificent in responding to the challenge of providing quality health care for all. But, additional funds must be obtained. Federal grants for medical education and research have been drastically curtailed in recent years, and grants for construction purposes, when available, are contingent upon the institutions' ability to secure substantial matching funds from private sources. The Hospital Survey and Construction Act of 1946, commonly known as the Hill-Burton Act, is worthy indeed, as far as it goes. But it has been a mere drop in the bucket as far as meeting national needs for hospital construction. New York Hospital-Cornell feels a strong sense of responsibility in helping to relieve the acute shortage of doctors and nurses, as well as devising innovative methods and facilities to reduce the high cost of patient care. Planning has been under way for more than two years for the expansion and renovation of its physical facilities so that it can play an even greater role in meeting these critical needs. The cost of this program, much of which will be a cooperative venture encompassing the entire community of medical institutions adjacent to it, will be in the range of $300 million, and the availability of major support from individual donors, foundations, and industry is of critical importance.

A Proposal

In conclusion, I propose that Congress establish a counterpart to the citizen's right to health care. It should be called *the fundamental right of every nonprofit institution to philanthropy.*

CHAPTER X

DISCUSSION OF TRENDS IN GIVING AND RECEIVING AS AFFECTED BY ACT

Moderator Leonard E. Kust, Cadwalader, Wickersham & Taft, New York: It will be our purpose in the panel discussion to elicit some comment from the panel members and audience with respect to the presentations that we have heard. This period of questions and observations from the floor has been one of the main contributions of our symposiums.

Mr. Kenneth W. Gemmill, Dechert Price & Rhoads, Philadelphia: I appreciate particularly the emphasis that Mr. Etherington put on fact gathering and the gathering of more information, particularly on the assets of foundations, the uses, the cost of compliance, and their activities and places. This is a thing I have been arguing for for a long, long time, but there really isn't enough factual basis to form some of the judgments which have been formed.

Mr. Robert Anthoine, Winthrop, Stimson, Putnam & Roberts, New York: Leonard, may I exercise a panelist's privilege and make a couple of comments that I didn't get around to in my scattershot a little earlier. I do want to note that having talked to a number of my colleagues in the larger firms in New York City, Palmer Baker is the only lawyer who has told me that his office has formed a single foundation since the 1969 act that is designed to be and remain a private foundation. My office did not participate in the creation of one, and I have talked to quite a few who said that no new private foundations had been formed in their offices.

On the other hand, as I indicated, there have not been thus far as many liquidations of existing private foundations as might have been anticipated, although I would not rule out that happening in a number of presently "conduit" foundations.

However, there are factors other than taxes which do bear very heavily on human decisions. We have several foundations in the office in which the name of the founder, now deceased, appears, and as long as his widow is on the board of that foundation, you can be sure that all gifts are going to continue to be made in the name of that foundation. I might add that I have not experienced serious difficulty with the problem of expenditure responsibility on the part of private foundation grants to other private foundations in this patricular instance, to date.

As an aside, I have seen a few human interest situations in which parental dissatisfaction with offspring may result in more money for charity: Parents say, "We won't leave any money to those no good so and so's," so the will is revised and charities benefit.

Finally I would say that if you really want to reform the tax system, adopt Bill Vickrey's cumulative lifetime income averaging.

Moderator Kust: Thank you Bob, for amplifying your remarks.

We shall now open the discussion to the floor.

Professor William Vickrey, Columbia University: I can't help remarking that when I hear these intricacies displayed by various members of the panel, I can imagine a sort of fiendish glee with which legislators and persons who are advising them in these matters erect ever more intricate solutions to the problems so that in subsequent years they can display their consummate skill in unraveling the problems they have set themselves. I would not say that they do this maliciously, but I think there is something about the legislative process that produces this effect, quite without malice, simply in terms of: "Isn't it wonderful we can produce this complicated law that nobody will understand but us!"

How can one get out of this situation where every time there is a tax reform bill, the volume of the Internal Revenue Code goes up by about 20 percent? It ought to be the other way. Reform ought to make the thing more consistent and hence fundamentally simple.

On another aspect, Mr. Howe was talking about the difficulties that various philanthropic organizations have in worrying about how far they can go in pursuit of their activities in ways which involve to some extent public action or public legislation. And here it seems to me that what we have done is really to bring in by the back door what to me is a clear violation of the constitutional provisions for freedom of speech and freedom of the press. It goes so far that it was recently suggested as a result of the 1969 act that possibly Columbia University should throw out the *Columbia Spectator*, the student daily newspaper, which enjoys a good many free privileges, including free working space in university buildings, because quite possibly the *Spectator*, in its usual journalistic activities, would have things to say about pending legislation, and if the *Spectator* said things about pending legislation, this would jeopardize Columbia University's tax-exempt status.

I understand that some form of legal action is being taken, but it seems to me that this is a totally unwarranted infringement on freedom of speech. The tax exemption may be a privilege, but if you give a privilege generally and then you withdraw that privilege from those who talk in ways which you disapprove of, I think that you have really seriously infringed on their constitutionally guaranteed freedom of expression. It amounts to saying that the Internal Revenue Service, which has no competence in this matter, is being set up as a sort of censor, not only a censor in the ordinary sense but a censor in the most invidious sense of prior censorship by implied threat.

I would like to see somebody get together the resources necessary to carry a case on this ground all the way up as high as necessary.

Moderator Kust: Thank you, Dr. Vickrey, for that provocative suggestion.

Is there any further comment on what Dr. Vickrey has brought on the floor from the panel or are there other questions?

Mr. T. M. Kupfer, Haskins & Sells, New York: I have a question for Mr. Howe. It's somewhat technical, but you referred to concern expressed by several private foundations which caused you to act as though you were a private foundation despite the fact that you have a letter which states that you're not a private foundation. Would you care to elaborate on what the concern of the other private foundations is?

Mr. Sydney Howe, The Conservation Foundation: I wish I were technically competent to do so. My understanding is that this rests heavily in the potential punishment of private foundation officers, should any funds they grant be used to influence legislation, even insubstantially. We hope this is an interim condition lasting only until IRS may decide, by regulations, that money passed from the private foundation to our kind of organization is no longer so encumbered when used in our operations. But this isn't clear yet. I wish I could be more technically responsive.

Moderator Kust: Bob, would you have some comment on that?

Mr. Anthoine: I have had the problem of the foundation directors on Mr. Howe's side of the matter, that is, seeking to obtain grants from private foundations, typically corporate foundations. I remember early in 1970 we wrote a lengthy opinion for the recipient to address to the private foundation that was prepared to make the donation if the donee qualified as a "public charity" under the law, so that the donor could avoid expenditure responsibility. It required going back into corporate history to develop the sources of income to find out whether it was publicly supported. Private foundations were willing then to make grants on the basis of lawyers' opinions without rulings from Washington.

Mr. Kupfer: Without trying to belabor it, I just understood that you had this letter that said you were not private.

Mr. Anthoine: Remember the concept of private was not in the law in 1969. There was no such thing as a private foundation. There were so-called public charities, so-called because contributions to them were entitled to the 30 percent deduction as distinguished from the 20 percent charities. The private foundation is a new concept under the 1969 act.

Mr. Kupfer: I understand that, but you can get another letter which he seems to have.

Mr. Anthoine: If he had a letter from IRS after the 1969 act which says it's a public charity, why worry about it?

Moderator Kust: I think this is an illustration of some of the confusion and complexity that we are living with.

Mr. Howe: Our counsel agrees with you, incidentally.

Mr. William S. Liming, Furman University: I direct my question to Mr. Keppler and Dr. Luckey, both of whom stated that their gifts are up. Are these current gifts or does it include so-called deferred gifts or trusts and annuities and this type of thing? Because I feel this is the area that is going to be affected in the future.

Mr. John J. Keppler, The Federation of Protestant Welfare Agencies, Inc.: In our case both are up. The current contributions are up. We have recently changed our purposes and expanded our program which has made us a much more attractive grantee and the foundations are responding to this. I should say this in all fairness. But outside of that, they are up over last year.

Dr. E. Hugh Luckey, The New York Hospital-Cornell Medical Center: I know that the nondeferred contributions were up. It is interesting, however, that the figures that have been compiled by the organization to which I referred indicate that the gifts through the route of bequests were down last year. That sounds as though a lot of people who made their wills last year died last year, if that's the case. The answer to your question is: I do not think there has been any significant trend that has been upward.

Mr. Liming: My concern was that the testamentary trust, for instance, won't show up until future years and so you really wouldn't notice that change now.

Moderator Kust: Is there not in your question and some of the data the problem of whether there has really been enough time to measure effects quantitatively. On the other hand, of course, the qualitative kind of comment on what the effect may be is always rather dangerous because no one has the whole picture. As Bob Anthoine indicates, he's at retail level and there he has seen some effects, but these may not be mainstream effects, and we shall have to wait and see what develops.

President R. Palmer Baker, Jr., Lord, Day & Lord, New York: It has been pointed out to me in conversations here this morning that perhaps a major factor in this acceleration of gifts which is noted in 1970—and which I think you may note to an even greater extent in 1971—is the fact that the executive group and the professional group—lawyers, physicians, and others—at high personal income tax brackets are a major source of gifts to public charities. Of course, this year there is a 60 percent earned income limited ceiling; it will be reduced to 50 percent next year. And while there are enormous complexities in the operation of that ceiling, my guess and observation is that it is accelerating gifts this year and it did accelerate gifts last year.

Moderator Kust: There is also another short-term effect that will have to be factored out in analyzing what happens, and this is that one of the policy objectives in the legislation was to divert giving from private foundations to public foundations. To the extent that this is in fact working in the short term, particularly the termination of private foundations, there may be some short-term increase in giving that would have to be taken into account in analyzing the full effects of the Tax Reform Act.

Mr. Anthoine: I find this happening not only through the operations of the conduit principle for the private foundation under which it is distributing substantial amounts to public charities within two and a half months after the end of the year but also generally in terms of more direct contributions to the public charities and less to the private foundations.

Dr. Luckey: Mr. Chairman, may I ask a question before we get too far away from it. Accepting what I have heard about inter vivos trusts, why would there be any problem or why would the tax law changes of 1969 have added an important deterrent in testamentary contributions to institutions?

Moderator Kust: I would answer just a part of that. In the small area that Bob Anthoine has already covered, where you want to reserve a life estate in connection with a testamentary bequest to charity, I don't suppose there should be any effect. Would you agree, Bob?

Mr. Anthoine: The effect would be, if anything, in the direction of the bequest going directly to a public charity. Bequests of closely held stock to the private foundation invoke the excess holdings provision. And if, although not a bequest of stock of a closely held company, it's a property that is not substantially income producing, the foundation must face the minimum income distribution provisions.

Mr. George J. Leibowitz, Library of Congress: I don't want to expand this discussion too much, but I think it worth while to highlight one other aspect that Mr. Anthoine touched on. Part of the sense of optimism, or pessimism, about the question of increasing or decreasing contributions of property is that, as Mr. Anthoine pointed out, there was a big flurry of contributions of appreciated property just before the end of 1969. I would like to ask whether we have any evidence, just after 1969, as to the decrease in donations of appreciated property—particularly so-called ordinary income property—that the charitable agencies experienced?

Mr. Anthoine: On the ordinary income property, powerful inferences flow from the very existence of the provision. But in terms of actual experience with artists' donations of their created works, I called the administrative directors of two museums in the city of New York, and they assured me that gifts of such ordinary income property have completely dried up. They are living at the moment off the fat of those enormous contributions made in the last few days of 1969.

Moderator Kust: I wonder if Dr. Luckey would have any information on this, because I think there are a number of manufacturers of equipment in the hospitals and health services area that have made a practice of donations of their products, which of course is very useful to hospitals. I wonder if that's still being done.

Dr. Luckey: It was never done. We missed out on that. We pay for it. And no cut prices either.

To go to the other question though, about 75 percent of the total private philanthropy which we have received as an institution over a period of years in which we studied this scheme was from appreciated property contributions. Unfortunately, I do not have the breakdown for 1970 showing whether there was any change in 1970 on this. I think it will be a very important thing to look at and see what happens.

Mr. Anthoine: In theory, there should be no change. After all, the rules generally speaking are the same. Gifts of appreciated securities are entitled to the full fair market value deduction up to 30 percent of adjusted gross income. It would be interesting to see whether psychological factors have entered into the question.

Mr. Leo A. Diamond, Austin & Diamond, New York: Mr. Etherington commented that for 52 years the Congress consistently enacted legislation which encouraged gifts of property to charity, and with that I cannot disagree. But I think it's also necessary to observe that it has not been all that quiet on the front. For ex-

97

ample, in the Revenue Bill of 1938, as Professor Surrey well knows, there was a real attempt by the House of Representatives to limit the deduction of appreciated property to cost basis. On the plea of representatives of the American Hospital Association and other similar organizations, that was finally dropped from the 1938 act.

True, that was an abortive attempt, but we know that that issue has plagued Congress all these years in one form or another. And whether the 1969 act was an overkill I don't know. But one thing I feel confident about, namely, that the day is over when there will be a deduction for fair market value generally, as in pre-1969, and in part that result is due to the fact that there was abuse by donors. So, our objective today and in the future, it seems to me, is to see how we—as knowledgeable and apparently sophisticated students of taxation—can try to work with that new policy instead of bemoaning the fact that the 1969 act is discouraging deductions of appreciated property.

The truth of the matter is that the public will make its adjustments. I, for one, for example, believe that if there were no deductions for many business expenses, business would finally adjust itself to that fact. While Congress may have overacted in the 1969 act, I think in large measure it's going to help weed out the hypocrites in our society who go around bragging how generous they are to charity at no appreciable cost to themselves. Furthermore, it's time we get rid in many ways of the so-called garbage organizations, many of whose names appear in that list that the Treasury puts out, that really serve no beneficial purpose. I'm not in any way minimizing the deleterious effects the 1969 act may have on the bona fide organization, but I think there is a real problem in getting rid of the cancerous and tumorous growths that we have in the whole situation with respect to charitable organizations. Whether the 1969 eruption was good or bad, I believe it was not illogical to come after 30 years of germination of an idea started, at least, in 1938.

Mr. Anthoine: Leo, we haven't really been addressing ourselves to policy here this morning. We have been talking about the impact of the law on donors and donees. I deliberately refrained from talking about policy because that was not my job. I understand that tomorrow morning the subject matter is policy—what the law should be and what changes should be made in existing laws. I share a good many of your concerns, including the situation with which the law students at Columbia always had great difficulty—a footnote in the casebook had a clipping from *The New York Times* demonstrating how an individual could actually make money by giving property away!

Mr. S. P. Goldberg, Council of Jewish Federations and Welfare Funds: I am associated with the Council of Jewish Federations and Welfare Funds, one of the major Jewish philanthropic organizations in the United States.

I would like to make three very brief observations on the discussion which has taken place. First on the question as to whether giving is really going up, I think we are the victims of an optical illusion. The price freeze has not yet become so frozen that we forget what the actual rise in the price level has been in recent years. The amounts which have been quoted regarding the average rises in philanthropy in recent years are quite close to the average rise in price levels. This has taken place in a period when the needs of our inner cities have been growing. On balance, in terms of real dollars, in terms of constant dollars, I think it would be fair to say that we are not doing very well in keeping up with the trend.

The second observation I'd like to make is that people who are concerned with administering philanthropic enterprises are generally not lawyers or accountants, but rather have competence in the area which they administer. The Tax Reform Act has forced many of them to turn to their lawyers. When they do so, they find diverse opinions, some of which have been reflected in the discussions today. They are confronted with forms which allegedly are simplified but which are extremely difficult to understand. An agency, for example, which considers itself a social welfare organization may find that it's classified under 501 (C) (4), tax exempt but not tax deductible. Terminology in the welfare field and legal terminology just don't match. This need to match reality with legality is a challenge for some of the people who have competence in the field of legal research.

My third comment is of a similar character. The whole notion

99

of "substantiality" as a test of legislative activity is not something which arose with the Tax Reform Act of 1969. It has been around for a long time, and the attendant confusion and lack of clarity have been around for a long time. I know that there have been some cases in which there was some adjudication of "substantiality." But IRS doesn't go along with these interpretations or with any other consistent interpretation of "substantiality," but prefers an ad hoc approach. That leaves the administrators of welfare organizations high and dry.

Under these circumstances, the Muskie bill becomes something which is very important. I've heard it described by some people in the philanthropic field as a bill of rights for philanthropy. If this effort could get bipartisan, across-the-board support, perhaps it will be the answer to some of the major questions which have been raised regarding the legitimacy of activities of agencies concerned with public policy affecting the tax-exempt areas in which they operate.

PART FOUR

EFFECTS OF TAX REFORM ACT OF 1969
ON ROLE OF PRIVATE FOUNDATIONS

"Prior to 1969, it was alleged in many instances that private foundations, without the benefit of public scrutiny, were able to operate autonomously in diverting all or part of their funds from philanthropic purposes without adverse consequences. As we know, the 1969 Tax Reform Act was largely intended to forestall these activities which were inherently inconsistent with a preferential tax status. The new law, in effect, requires foundation management to examine its activities and, if necessary, to restructure its operations. Failure to comply with these complicated and comprehensive provisions of the act will cause the imposition of severe sanctions which, in the least, will be expensive and in some instances even catastrophic.

"Our discussion this afternoon logically centers on the effects of the 1969 Tax Reform Act on the role of the private foundation. At a time when there is a need for more innovation, more understanding, and clearly more money in so many vital sectors of our society, we are concerned with the short-term problems and the long-term aspects of bringing the private foundations under the blessings of tax regulation.

"Our first speaker has indicated in a prior conversation that this is a relatively new problem, that we have to face up to the reading and interpretation of the law, which few can understand and nobody can predict the results of. While I agree in part, may I read this very short passage from Chapter 5, Verse 7, of the Book of Daniel:

> The King cried aloud to bring in the astrologers, the Chaldeans, and the soothsayers. And the King spake, and said to the wise men of Babylon, Whosoever shall read this writing, and shew me the interpretation thereof, shall be clothed with scarlet, and have a chain of gold about his neck, and shall be the third ruler in the kingdom.

"It's not a new problem."

B. KENNETH SANDEN
CPA, Price Waterhouse & Co., and
Chairman, Thursday Afternoon Session

CHAPTER XI

OPERATIONAL EFFECTS

RUTH C. CHANCE
Executive Director, Rosenberg Foundation

THIS SESSION is an attempt to gain perspective on the operational effects of the Tax Reform Act of 1969 on its special target—private foundations. You will not find me as serene as Mr. Wadsworth, nor as objective as Mr. Surrey, whose brilliance in the tax field is so well documented. I am simply the harassed executive of a moderate-sized foundation which day to day must live with the act.

In a preliminary meeting Mr. Surrey, the moderator of the panel that will follow these initial statements, has urged us to separate the short-term effects of the new law from the long-term ones. It will be difficult to accommodate him, and in my judgment it is premature and speculative to do so. A great deal will depend on the final form of the regulations to be issued by the Treasury Department. (Nearly two years after the law became effective we still do not have the key regulations on the harshest section of the law.) Beyond that, enforcement of the law and regulations will to some extent hinge on a more subtle factor—the mood and temper of the times. Critical social and educational problems remain legitimate areas of concern for foundations, and in periods of great controversy it is prudent to assume that society's tensions will be reflected in its attitudes about institutions dealing with those problems. And the way in which laws are enforced will be affected by these attitudes. It is therefore hazardous to predict long- and short-term effects.

Some of the congressional discussion which preceded passage of the Tax Reform Act of 1969 created an atmosphere of distrust and suspicion of private foundations. There have been today and will be other speakers who will find this a legitimate reaction. I can therefore leave the cheering to them and say that abuses in the foundation field existed and needed correction. But individual private foundations which have for years attempted to be meticulous both in program and financial matters have few weapons with which to counter this atmosphere of distrust and hostility. We are all massed together in the public mind.

NUMBER AND SIZE OF FOUNDATIONS

A very large number of organizations fall within the now almost pejorative category called "private foundations." The recently published 4th edition of the Foundation Directory, certainly the most authoritative and respected publication in its field, estimates that there are about 26,000 foundations in the United States. But the Directory lists fewer than 5,500 of these, because it eliminates all whose capital fund is less than $500,000 or who make grants totaling less than $25,000 a year. In other words, nearly four-fifths of the organizations which come within the act's definition are small and usually too obscure to have much known about them.

The growth of foundations was probably quite reasonable and orderly from 1900 through the decade of the 1930's because tax laws then did not offer the favors which later made philanthropy sometimes come out second to other concerns of estate or tax planners. As congressional action made the mechanism of the foundation a more valuable instrument in such planning there was a dramatic increase in the number of foundations established during the decade of the 1940's and a special surge during the 1950's. Perhaps 90 per cent of all foundations were created after 1940. The overwhelming majority are small, but all have the substantial privileges that attach to foundation status, including the potential of becoming perpetuities. Since a great deal of this activity took place in the state in which the Rosenberg Foundation, of which I am the executive officer, is located, I am keenly aware that most of these are unstaffed, and frequently unknown and difficult of access. One thing we need from scholars of philanthropy in universities, government, and foundations is a more penetrating classification system or taxonomy which takes into account the impetus given to the creation of foundations by tax and other laws. This might have provided a more equitable basis on which to draft legislation. Several years ago Alan Pifer, President of the Carnegie Corporation, in a notable essay began to explore this problem in an effort to classify foundations and relate them by class to responsibilities and privileges. We can hope that others are engaged in the same kind of task. But here it will simply be noted that the thousands of organizations which meet the definition of the statute are of great variety, that most are small, and that an overwhelming number have no staff. Most have no association with the one national membership organization through which foundations cooperate, and which has the potential to be at least a minimum standard setter.

What are the effects so far of the Tax Reform Act of 1969 on the 26,000 organizations which, although created out of different motives and having different missions, have now been lumped together to become the objects of extensive government regulation?

Description of Rosenberg Foundation

I have been asked to speak about a California foundation of moderate size. Yet with capital of about $13.5 million, its assets probably place it among the 500 wealthiest in the country. But for perspective, let me remind you that none of the 12 largest foundations is located west of the Mississippi and that one-third of all foundation assets are in these 12. While the Rosenberg Foundation operates in the most populous state in the nation and one of the most troubled (it is commonplace to look on California as the laboratory in which others can view shudderingly an unpleasant future), West Coast philanthropic resources are sparse as compared with those east of the Mississippi. Only a few foundations in California have any staff. And by staff I mean typically one "professional," a secretary, and a part-time bookkeeper. The burdens the few foundations with an open door carry in California are therefore heavy.

The Rosenberg Foundation is in its 36th year. On his death in the early 1930's the donor left most of his wealth to establish this philanthropy. No relative of his is a member of the board of directors, on which nine well-known citizens serve without pay. No member of the board profits financially from his relationship to the foundation. Its investment portfolio is diversified. No director is either a substantial contributor to the foundation or the owner of as much as 10 percent of the outstanding stock of a corporation in which the foundation has a 10 percent or greater interest. The return on the foundation's capital is respectable if not sensational. For a number of years the payout has exceeded the requirements which will go into effect in 1972.

By its charter this foundation can invade capital and has done so in 13 of the last 14 years to give support to California programs for children and youth. To make my point, this relatively small foundation has, I believe, none of the problems that led to the Treasury Report of 1965[1] which identified and proposed remedies for many of the problems associated with some foundations.

EFFECT OF 1969 ACT ON PRIVATE FOUNDATIONS

Now for observations on the effect of the new legislation.

Private Foundation Dollar Debased Coin

The private foundation dollar has in some respects become a debased coin. It does not have the value of money from other sources, because it is marked money that now by law carries certain consequences for both the grantee and the foundation. One of our new routine but time-consuming tasks is to warn our applicants either that their favored status as "public charities" may be jeopardized by a grant, depending upon whether they can continue to meet the statutory formula, or that a grant may determine their initial status, often to their disadvantage. For example, most private foundations of the "venture capital" type are willing to finance the establishment of new agencies where existing organizations either are not yet ready or cannot appropriately undertake a new function. If a single, private foundation is the only source of support for a new section 501 (c) (3) entity the consequence is

---

[1] United States Congress, House Committee on Ways and Means, *Treasury Department Report on Private Foundations,* Committee Print, 89th Congress, 1st Session, Washington: Government Printing Office, 1965, 110 p.

usually to cause the recipient to become a private operating foundation within the meaning of the new law. Our more sophisticated grantees attempt to better their status by trying to get other "untainted" money to free them from the burden that comes from not being classified as a public charity. And private foundations making grants to those which are not "public charities" take on the as yet obscure duties which attach to what the Tax Reform Act terms "expenditure responsibility" with its possible penalties on the foundation itself, the members of its board of directors, and some of its staff.

Private Foundations Downgraded

The law's favoring of some categories of section 501 (c) (3) organizations over others has led to subtle divisions among exempt organizations. The downgrading of private foundations gives new and preferred status to those organizations that can claim to be "public" as defined by the statute. Although there is a good deal of mythology in this distinction, it encourages the more fortunate part of the exempt field to be silent or to dissociate itself from the private foundation category when that appears advantageous. But many private foundations can bear as close scrutiny as their more fortunate "public" colleagues. Private foundations have, in effect, become the stepchildren of the philanthropic field. Yet foundations, whether public or private, are the product of the American capitalistic system which most of our lawmakers enthusiastically defend. Whether their money comes from a number of sources or one, typically both public and private foundations result from the generosity of wealthy people. And it is probable that as inroads are made on one part of the 501 (c) (3) field they will appear in others and that long-term strength among voluntary exempt organizations may well depend upon their facing the issues together.

As every tax lawyer knows, estate and tax planning ideas are being revised as the implications of the Tax Reform Act of 1969 became clearer. Combining the payout provisions of the act with the restrictions which discourage the creation of new private foundations could mean that the entire institution will erode over a period of time. Whether private foundations should be perpetuities is philosophically debatable. But if the effect of the act is finally to make private foundations time-limited, thought should be given to how to encourage responsible replacement of them in each generation. What is at issue is whether a diversity of private grant-making entities should be encouraged if their purpose is truly philanthropic, or whether power should be increasingly centered in a few, mainly of the "public" kind, which, it is assumed by the act, can be disciplined by public opinion if they move too far ahead of it.

Administrative Costs Increased

Rising administrative costs are a troubling result of the Tax Reform Act. Moderate-sized foundations which have tried to operate decently will still find that bookkeeping, clerical, and auditing costs, attorneys', investment counsels' and consultants' fees will rise. Candidly, I should say that the legal and auditing back-up needed should not come from struggling young lawyers or CPA's. The complexity of the act and the specialization required to advise nonprofit organizations suggest the wisdom of employing law and accountant firms large enough to have this expertise. Since nationally known firms place unabashed value on their services, increased administrative costs inevitably result. But any foundation whose files bulge with attorneys' opinions that their clients are—invariably—"public charities" and not "private operating foundations" will forgive my snobbish resort to the large firms. And having advice from these prestigious sources is not exactly a handicap during a federal audit.

Foundations in the "venture capital" category are going to have to analyze what minimum capital is necessary to justify these larger operating expenses. Yet the statute makes mergers among private foundations a ticklish matter in which the total capital of each could be forfeited.

Change in Day-to-Day Operation

The day-to-day operation of a foundation such as Rosenberg has changed. Much more time goes to desk work and to what used to be routine matters. The primary function of foundations is to make grants, and for those foundations that encourage innovation, the essence of good staff work is to be in the field exploring new ideas and the capability of applicants to test them. The foundation with a small staff now is less accessible to applicants and much more time in interviews is given to examining formalities. The past decade has seen the development of a far greater range of applicants than before, including many inexperienced ones from low-income minority communities. Often they—as well as organizations of young people who are typically impatient about delays—do not understand the process or significance of acquiring 501 (c) (3) status. While private foundations are, of course, free to make grants to any organization whether 501 (c) (3) or not if the proposed use of the money falls within permitted philanthropic activities, the now wary foundation manager knows that the as yet uncertain duties that attach to "expenditure responsibility" under the new law must in such cases be assumed by the foundation. Just how burdensome these duties will be depends upon the content of the final regulations and on the way in which they are administered. In the meantime the government's Cumulative List of Exempt Organizations must have sales of best-seller proportions as foundations check out the status of their applicants.

Grants Restricted to Public Charities

Beyond restricting grants to 501 (c) (3) entities many foundations will not accept applications from organizations that have not filed form 4653 to determine whether they have the more privileged position of being "public charities" within the broader 501 (c) (3) classification. In a period of great social pressure many applicants with worthy new ideas and from groups that need recognition are eliminated from consideration for grants by perhaps the majority of private foundations of which I have personal knowledge. For these foundations the merit of an application depends first upon the proposer's legal status. This makes the most favored applicants (aside from churches) government agencies or long established "traditional" voluntary ones, both of which often need the nudge of new organizations to encourage shifts away from obsolete or peripheral activities. The ironical result of the law is therefore to make likely the reinforcement of outmoded activities carried on by the "safer" public charities. The irony goes even further. Perhaps the easiest grant a private foundation can make is an unrestricted one to a "public charity." Earmarked grants to give this group the leverage to change make more demands under the new law on use of foundation staff's time than do unrestricted grants. And there is no way of measuring the cynicism and frustration which are developing among minorities and others who find barriers in their paths as they approach foundation doors, nor the social loss from investments in outworn enterprises. Incidentally, we could and do spend a great deal of time simply helping individuals and groups understand the technical and legal hurdles set up by the Tax Reform Act, but in a section of the country which is on the depressingly unbalanced end of philanthropic resources uses of time have to be weighed.

Relationships With Grantees Altered

Foundations which are willing to continue to fund new organizations that cannot now get clearance as public charities must experiment to find ways of giving technical assistance without infringing unduly on the freedom of these grantees. Somehow a balance must be struck between protecting the donor foundation so that it can meet its expenditure responsibilities under the new law without monitoring projects to the extent that grantees feel they have lost control of their programs. This is a delicate, time-consuming problem. (I should note parenthetically that often the most difficult grantees from which to extract reports are those most favored by the statute and for which the burden of expenditure responsibility is not placed on the grantor.)

It is not surprising, then, that some changes in relationships are developing between foundations and their applicants. Foundations which used to respond in a friendly, welcoming manner to new applicants who had promising ideas now may take a more cautious approach as they explore first the formalities connected with legal status. And if a grant is finally made, the pleasant letters which used to confirm the good news have now often been superseded by forms and contracts. If these are couched in the formidable language of the statute, uneasy recipients may well turn to their own attorneys for advice before signing. We try to soften the blow in a final paragraph which, after all the technical language, assures the grantee of our sincere pleasure in supporting the project.

Trustees' Vulnerability

The law's possible penalties on individual trustees because of the taxable expenditure provisions of the act raise as yet unanswered questions about whether this will limit interest in serving on the boards of private foundations. The question is especially pertinent at a time when foundations are beginning to consider a far wider range of economic and ethnic representation on their boards. The proposed Treasury regulations appear to be moderate, given the law, but again some experience is needed before answers are clear.

SUMMARY

In summary, it is not easy at this point to separate the early shock effects of the Tax Reform Act from its longer term impact. The mood and reasoning of some members of Congress was instructive. A variety of philosophies, motives, interests went into formulation of the act. Is it a first step to be built on even more harshly later, or will there simply be minor corrections? Foundations have read the message in different ways, with perhaps the larger number deciding that "it's better to be safe than sorry" as they enter on a period of caution. The proposed Treasury regulations have shown such moderation as is consistent with the terms of the law, and the Internal Revenue Service, as it audits, is developing understanding of the new burdens of administration the act imposes. These burdens came at an unfortunate time when all foundations that have open doors are receiving requests in unparalleled numbers, and when government support has been cut back drastically. Foundations' responses have been slowed down as they try to cope with new requirements and limitations.

Can we live with the act? Of course we can. But as in ecology the central question is the quality of the life to be led. Are the formalities, the prerequisites, the technicalities to be our major concern as safety is sought, or are we to put our minds on ways in which the comparatively small amount of money foundations have can help the country through a transforming period? We need a few years of experience before we can begin to give you better answers.

CHAPTER XII

PROGRAM ACTIVITIES

Homer C. Wadsworth
President, Kansas City Association of Trusts and Foundations

IT CAME as something of a shock to many of my friends and colleagues in the foundation field to discover during the proceedings leading to the Tax Reform Act of 1969 that they were neither loved nor undersood. It is a bit much to expect to be loved in such times as these, however meritorious our aspirations if not always our achievements. It is to be hoped that we shall be understood, however, and the burden for achieving this is clearly on the foundations alone.

It is too much to expect that a constituency for the foundation idea will spring from the grateful few who receive foundation aid. The truth is that their numbers are far fewer than the petitioners who receive gracious letters, telling them in carefully chosen words that we have nothing but praise for their projects.

Diversity Among Foundations

It is good for the soul to confess, however limiting it may be to my effort to deal with the subject at hand, that we know all too little about the effect of the Tax Reform Act of 1969 on the activities of private foundations. The universe we deal with is a rather large and diverse one. There are about 22,000 private foundations in this country, holding assets of about $22 billion and spending about $1.6 billion per year. They represent about 9 percent of all private giving. These figures are a bit deceptive, however, inasmuch as more than two-thirds of all foundation assets are controlled by about 200 foundations. More than 12,000 foundations each give away less than $10,000 per year, suggesting

that the majority of all foundations are simply incorporated channels for private giving. No one really knows what is going on in
the thousands of places and among the innumerable people given
the responsibility of coming to terms with the new requirements
of law. All that can be said in the aggregate is that much more
systematic attention to this matter is desirable, preferably on a
highly critical review basis.

The scurrying about necessary to present some sort of face to
the Congress in 1969 did turn up a few facts of considerable importance, thanks especially to the Peterson Commission report.[1]
Private foundations control a very small and declining proportion
of the nation's total wealth. Peterson found that the percentage
of the nation's financial wealth held by all foundations declined
from 1.5 percent to 1.35 percent between 1958 and 1968. It is a
reasonable guess that a further decline will soon be noted as the
facts come to light. It could hardly be otherwise, considering the
provisions of the new law that limit tax deductibility on gifts of
appreciated property. It is also pretty clear that a good many people prefer not to tangle with the red tape and the surveillance
over expenditures made that the 1969 act now requires.

Even Congressman Patman should be able to sleep soundly at
night: the foundations are not about to take over the country,
nor any considerable part of it.

The foregoing may suggest to you what I consider to be entirely true: that a high percentage of all foundations in this country, although not the largest pools of money, are largely unman-
aged and therefore distribute their funds on the basis of limited
information about the world of philanthropy. This is not totally
bad: all too much of our lives are rather carefully regulated, in
one way or another, and some of the programs that people favor—
especially those of a religious character—are clearly outside the
purview of government sponsorship. It does mean that all of the
rhetoric about foundations as the spearhead of new knowledge
and the growing edge of innovative effort is to be taken with the
usual grain of salt. Most foundations are rather on the timid and
prosaic side and given to a view of charity quite out of step with

---

[1] Commission on Foundations and Private Philanthropy, *Foundations, Private Giving and Public Policy*, Chicago: University of Chicago Press, 1970.

the startling developments in public welfare over the past 25 years. The critics who have written and spoken about "timid billions" are far more accurate than those who see foundations as the moving spirit of the new left in American politics.

FOUNDATIONS CAN LIVE WITH 1969 ACT

On balance I think it safe to say that most experienced foundation people, trustees as well as managers, are inclined to the view that the 1969 act can be lived with comfortably. It brought to a screeching halt the practice of a small minority more interested in business matters than charity. It tightened public reporting, fixed reasonable requirements for payout, and clamped the door shut on the use of foundation funds for partisan political purposes. I know of no one working in the field today who finds these features of the act objectionable. It is a bit hard to keep up with the paperwork, and some of the provisions of the law are far from clear, especially those regulating our contact with public officials and our support of programs that might lead in time to legislative proposals. We are a bit scared at the amount of money that we must spend to comply with the provisions that make us responsible for the way grantees use funds given, and for legal and accounting expense. Presumably the Treasury is quite aware that they have added to our costs in this respect, just as the excise tax has simply removed funds from channels that flow normally to legitimate educational and charitable agencies.

I think it only fair to say that the application of the 1969 act to date has created less difficulty than was expected. It could not have been otherwise, taking into account that the fundamental right of foundations to be established and to operate for unlimited time in the future was unimpaired by this legislation. Foundations exist to serve public purposes through voluntary interest and effort. As such they deserve to be under constant surveillance, to be subject to criticism at every turn, and to be held accountable. To be curbed a bit, and especially along lines that simply confirm previous law and all good practice over the past 75 years, is hardly to be persecuted.

The excise tax is excessive for the purpose intended, and its passage does open up the possibility of similar tax programs in many states at their wit's end for revenue to meet pressing needs.

These matters are clearly secondary, however, to the need for review of the whole question of what sort of incentives in the tax law may be necessary to enable philanthropy to keep pace with the demand for money, and to cope with the unhappy fact that giving lags behind the need for such. The real question here is whether as a people we really wish to support a multifaceted system of social services and education. If we do we must provide greater incentives than we now possess to encourage private giving. If we do we must encourage some way in which to make this system moderately efficient, and some way to relate philanthropic effort to the enormous and also many-pronged effort of government at all levels, and on every subject area that commands public attention.

I believe that the foundations of the country have quite a bit of homework to do in this regard. A foundation created to serve national interests must reflect in its board composition and in its mechanics for assessing need a good sense of balance. This is a matter of assuring good geographical representation. It is also a matter of deliberately seeking out the segments of our population not now a party to counsel in such quarters. The Peterson report called our attention to the fact that only 4 of the 25 largest foundations in the country have boards considered to be fairly representative of the country at large. One-half of the trustees of these 25 foundations are Ivy League graduates, according to Peterson. Catholics, Jews, Negroes, labor, and young people are largely missing, leading Mr. Peterson and his colleagues to note that "these boards lack the kind of diversity that could enlarge their perceptions about the raw surge of American life."

An orderly network of communications between those who work with foundations at national levels and those who carry on comparable responsibilities in regional and community settings is highly desirable. They each have much to give to the other; they each lack at this time the greatly varied perspective that comes with familiarity with setting and with people—and it is only through support of people once discovered that our best results can be obtained. I think it also of considerable importance that national and local parties join together to prepare both trustees and managers for their responsibilities, and to take some necessary steps to interpret the foundation idea to the great mass of our people largely in the dark about such matters and therefore inclined to view the whole enterprise as a tax dodge of the rich and near-rich. It matters a good deal what the average American thinks about foundations. If he does not think at all, and if he has no way of encountering the fundamental ideas upon which generous provisions of the tax law are based, he will jump all too easily to the conclusion that we would be better off without foundations.

GROWTH OF COMMUNITY FOUNDATIONS

It is reasonably clear that the requirements of the 1969 act have forced many foundations to take stock of what they are doing and why for the first time in their histories. It is likely that many of these groups will pour their assets into community foundations where such agencies exist, and that many new ones are likely to be created in the period just ahead. This is a healthy sign, for the community foundation is a sound instrument for carrying out philanthropic purposes efficiently and well. The preservation of many of the special privileges given community foundations in the law are more than amply justified by the remarkable record of these agencies over the past 50 years or so, and they are clearly destined to bring a larger measure of careful scrutiny and sophisticated planning into local philanthropy.

There are likely to be many other instances in which the nature of the instruments involved, and the responsibility vested in named trustees, cannot be delegated to community agencies. In such circumstances it appears to me that federation of the interests of cooperating trusts and foundations is highly warranted as a means of conserving funds spent for management to meet the requirements of the law and to assure competent advice on project proposals. I commend to your attention our own experience in this regard in Kansas City over the past 21 years, and I shall be glad to review our experience with any of you who may have special interest in this matter.

PROPOSAL FOR ADVISORY BOARD ON PHILANTHROPIC POLICY

It is always a bit dangerous to prescribe what the world needs most, apart from love and its many elements. The philanthropic world, however, needs more than anything else some point of focus for its efforts, some orderly way of assessing its role in the scheme of things, some central point from which the elementary facts of life can be disseminated with confidence that they are as true as any such facts can ever be. I am much persuaded that the major recommendation of the Peterson Commission in this respect was entirely sound, and I regret that it has been given such scant attention. Peterson proposed that an advisory board on philanthropic policy be appointed by the President, subject to Senate confirmation. He suggested that this board be the responsible body for continuing review of all regulations having an influence on private giving. He suggested that such a body could have a close and regular eye on the interface of government policy and practice with private philanthropic practice. He proposed that such an advisory board be jointly financed by both public and private sources to assure its independence.

This proposal is not unlike the role performed by the Charities Commission in Great Britain.[2] I think it altogether likely that the problems in this field will grow more complex rather than less so as government moves into more and more fields in response to public clamor. For example, should any of the current proposals now before the Congress providing for extending the role of government as a third-party payer in medical affairs be enacted, we shall confront instantly a major overhaul of the financing of hospitals and the training of medical personnel to meet strikingly new conditions. It is highly desirable that private philanthropy continue as in the past to play a large and significant role in research and in building systems of delivery of medical care and all the rest. It is unlikely that this will be done wisely and well unless there is some common center of focus to bring attention to the new problems that will arise, and to seek appropriate ways of relating private policies in the main to the mainstream of the government's efforts in this field. We lack such a focus now, and we should create one and promptly. This seems the least we might do to give shape and purpose to efforts that now spend about $18 billion every year, are capable of generating a great deal more

---

[2] Comment of H. V. Hodson, former Rector of the Ditchley Foundation, Oxford, England, in letter to author:

I suggest you are off-beam in likening your proposed Presidential advisory board on philanthropic policy to the Charities Commission in Britain. The Charities Commission is essentially executive, entrusted as it is with the administration of the Charities Act 1960 and in particular with deciding (subject only to the Courts) on the charitable nature of applicants for registration on the Register of Charities. In so far as it is advisory, it advises the charities themselves.

under appropriate circumstances, and involve the voluntary effort of an estimated 55 to 60 million citizens every year.

One very good reason for moving on this front promptly is to provide suitable guidelines to all of us, including officials of the Treasury Department, on the ends that may legitimately be sought by all philanthropic endeavors, including foundations. The 1969 act requires that representatives of the Internal Revenue Service come up with their own estimates in this regard, even though it is doubtful that the Treasury is about to claim a high degree of expertness for its people in coming to judgment about the wide range of programs served by private giving. I expect the Treasury to be tough in review, and I expect to give evidence of good management and supervision. I think the Treasury would be greatly helped in carrying out its tasks if it could look to an experienced and properly staffed advisory council to delineate the main objectives sought through private philanthropy, and the relation of these efforts to the programs of government as well. The present system requires that the agent be both judge and jury, and this seems to be quite as unfair to him as it may be from time to time to harried foundation people asked to explain what they do and why.

Regulation of Foundation Programs

This line of thought brings to mind a very touchy subject, this being the right of foundations to sponsor programs that stimulate criticism of government policies and practices. It seems to me that we must live with our pretensions as a democratic people in coming to issue with this question. If what is produced is in the public domain and is itself open to rebuttal, and on a no-holds basis, then it seems to me that what foundations do in this connection is not only sound, it is also utterly wise and completely necessary if we are to have a well-informed general public. If we do not have ways of building critics into our system we shall surely destroy it by smothering it in a morass of regulations that cover everything but the essential points.

It is my hope that the Treasury will take a rather experimental view of the problem of regulating foundations. Foundations serve best when they are free to make mistakes: there is no alternative to occasional error when you are betting on people with ideas that may or may not pan out. What is important is that the decisions made be honest ones, and that they be made after due consideration of the particular circumstances presented by the proposals in hand.

A somewhat comparable observation can be made about the matter of requiring that foundations assume expenditure responsibility for other than public charities receiving support. Maintaining a reasonable surveillance is one thing; overwhelming a grantee with reporting requirements is quite another. This is especially true of the newer agencies that are always springing up in response to urgent need as viewed by their sponsors, and especially programs that are directed toward improving the lot of the disadvantaged. I would hope that a few years' experience would bring all parties to a recognition of the simple fact that it often pays to make an honest effort along some lines, even though the prospects for success are only on the slim side. Moreover, foundations serve best when they give maximum latitude to recipients to do their own thing, subject only to true accounting and to notice of changes in program or interest that may be indicated as a project moves through its various stages of development.

Much can be said about the problem of complying with the requirement that foundation officials abjure all programs calculated to influence public opinion and therefore have some bearing on legislative actions. I am inclined to feel that we can safely assume that all activities in the public forum are acceptable except those which are directly connected to partisan political activity. Many of my colleagues, however, being perhaps of less daring turn of mind, think quite otherwise. There is a marked tendency these days among foundation people to play it safe, to duck programs that might raise sticky questions when the time comes for review of the year's work by IRS agents. I know of no way to do a decent job without having some kind of influence on public opinion, quite apart from lobbying and grassroots campaigning and the like, and to stick our heads in the sand on this one is to do a great disservice to society and to run from the obligations that go with the special privileges given all foundations. I am in the midst of reviewing a study project designed to bring light on a tangled problem of school finance in my home state—a project clearly advanced by parties hoping to persuade the legislature that it is hardly in the public interest to permit most of our school districts to shortchange our children by closing out the schools before the current school year is over. Our contribution is likely to be in underwriting the cost of independent study of the whole matter, hoping that the facts and suggestions that come from such a study will have a very profound effect upon an unsteady public opinion on the matter at this time. If this be heresy, so be it. Leavenworth is a pretty nice town, and I hope that some of you will pay me a visit should it be necessary.

A final word on this subject seems to me quite in order. It is worth noting that the Tax Reform Act of 1969 was the first major modification of the national tax structure in more than 50 years. Consequently, a rather extended period of confusion is more normal than otherwise. Perhaps the truest mark of this singular fact is that most of the regulations necessary to administer the act are not yet approved.

But there is a more important fact that we must keep in front of us as we think of this matter and of the role of the private citizen in his nation's affairs. This is the uptight generation—confused, bewildered, and divided, unable to resolve how best to deal with the cancer of race; with the question of how to finance local services, most of them being about a step from bankruptcy; with a rapidly changing world condition of uncertain dimensions. About the only thing certain is that tomorrow will not be like today, any more than today is much like yesterday.

In such a period it seems to me that we must have the courage and good sense to think anew about what sort of country we want to put together, and what sort of country will seem to the young worth preserving. While we are at it we might give a bit of thought as well to how the ordinary citizen as well as the giver of large gifts makes a connection with events that gives him the impression that he is playing his proper role and playing it as well as he should. This is really what philanthropy in America is all about, for in the light of cold facts it becomes apparent that quite average people as well as those of considerable means dig into their own pocketbooks for about 80 percent of all the money that supports private efforts in this country. If it were any other way there would not be as much prospect for the future as there really is.

CHAPTER XIII

LEARNING TO LIVE WITH THE
TAX REFORM ACT

Howard R. Dressner
Secretary and General Counsel, The Ford Foundation

I KNEW I was in the right place yesterday when I walked into the lobby and saw the sign, "Welcome to the Conference on Aging." I won't reveal my age before the Tax Reform Act, but the number of years I have aged since then is considerably more than the two years—23 months—that have elapsed since its passage.

My assignment today was to make some brief and informal observations about our experiences to date under the act, and I welcome the opportunity to speak generally and extemporaneously. Indeed, given the many technical conferences in the past two years on the meaning of the new provisions, I am especially glad to stray for a moment from legal interpretation and analysis.

Lots of people used to have different views of foundations from those they have today. I remember when Mitchell Sviridoff, now the Ford Foundation's Vice President for National Affairs, who had come to New York City to run the Human Resources Administration, left the city administration to join the Ford Foundation. The *New York Times,* in an editorial, chided him for leaving the urgent problems of city government to go to an "island of serenity."

I have lived on that philanthropic "island of serenity" for the past eight years and can testify to the inexactness of the description—both before and after the Tax Reform Act.

Ruth Chance mentioned in her remarks earlier today that the act's definitions have made private foundations the low men—

or women, as the case may be—on the charitable totem pole. I don't know precisely where the Ford Foundation stands on the totem pole, but for the moment at least, since we are still a rather conspicuous foundation, interest in the way we conduct our activities under the act is probably fairly high. So I will address some of my remarks to our own experiences in the past two years.

The title given to our panel discussion today is: "Assessment of Present and Anticipated Capacity of Private Foundations to Fulfill *Expected* Philanthropic Functions in the Light of the Tax Reform Act" (underscoring supplied). Expected by whom? Both of the previous speakers indicated that views about what foundations do, what people perceive them as doing, and what people *expect* them to do, may be quite different. So, what foundations actually do may leave some people in a state of absolute ecstasy and others in a state of some despondency. But certainly the title of the panel discussion should at least serve as a reminder that there is a great variety of "expectations" vis-à-vis foundations.

NUMBERS OF FOUNDATIONS

Mr. Wadsworth and Mrs. Chance called our attention in each of their talks to numbers—numbers which are helpful to us in understanding the dimensions of the foundation field. We should remember, for example, that according to the most recent publication of foundation data only 32 foundations have assets over $100 million in a field which numbers more than 25,000 foundations. In the Foundation Directory, the cutoff point for listing is $500,000; and only 5,500 foundations are listed. Thus the great majority of foundations are relatively small. In the aggregate, foundations grant perhaps $1.5 billion a year, and though I cannot recite the exact figure of current annual expenditures of the federal government, there is clearly a vast gulf between the two numbers. Indeed the total assets of all foundations do not exceed $26 billion.

One other statistical note about the field may be of interest. In the entire foundation community, my understanding is that there are only some 1,500 full-time professionals, although I suspect that number will grow as the administrative requirements of the Tax Reform Act become more fully understood. I might add that a good number of that relatively small cadre of professionals are working in a relatively small number of the larger foundations where program choices and decisions rest heavily on extensive staff work.

At the Ford Foundation, we receive between 75,000 and 100,000 pieces of mail a year. A good deal of that mail contains requests for support. I do not here even try to cite the number of telephone calls, face-to-face presentations, and so forth, but one of the things that has struck me over the years I have been with the Foundation is that the overwhelming majority of applications for money that come to us are meritorious and worthy of philanthropic support. They come from people who are doing or planning to do worthwhile things, and with more money might be able to do them better. The problem of course is that all the money in the entire Foundation would not begin to meet the total needs.

(Just so you know that our mail is far from monotonous, I must mention a letter I recently received from a someone who described himself as a professional adventurer, asking whether we could provide funds which would enable him to travel to the Middle East to swim the Suez Canal between the military forces stationed on the banks. He said that such an enterprise would do much to enhance the whole world of professional adventurers, a field that hadn't been developed as fully as he thought it should be. Maybe we should have made that grant, but we didn't.)

FORD FOUNDATION EXPERIENCE WITH ACT

We have lived with the Tax Reform Act for one year and 11 months, and I can testify that to live with it is not necessarily to fall in love with it. But I can also say that the Ford Foundation has been able to continue its regular programs and activities and as far as we can tell, we shall be able to continue our work in full compliance with the letter and spirit of the law.

When the Act was first passed, I remember a round-the-clock nonstop "professional adventure" in my own office because we reviewed 1,500 ongoing grants that the Ford Foundation had made to assure our officers and trustees that payments under commitments already made would not violate the provisions of the Tax Reform Act. On the basis of that review, it was our judgment—reinforced by the view of outside counsel on a small number of grants in question—that we did not have to cease and desist on a single one.

It is important to remember that many leading foundations, including the one which I represent today, expressly supported the main Treasury recommendations of 1965 and 1968 which dealt basically with financial abuses and the need for disclosure, and the record will show strong expressions of support for remedying what we at the Ford Foundation and others considered to be such abuses. We wanted that to happen, and we were supportive of those ends.

I shall come back later to things that we did not wholly support and that to this day we are not fully reconciled to. As I have said, we shall be able to continue our work at the Ford Foundation, but that does not leave us without concerns.

For example, it is far from certain that smaller foundations will be able to continue to perform "expected" philanthropic functions.

COSTLY EFFECTS

We have lived with the act long enough now to know that it is costly. It is costly in staff time; it is costly in the allocation of energy; and it is costly in dollars. But we are not yet in a position to quantify that cost with any precision. Let me give one or two examples.

Two years ago the Ford Foundation did not have a general counsel. Today it has one. He is supported by an in-house legal staff. The administrative burdens on every side of us are heavier than they have ever been, not only in the comptroller's office where you would expect them to be heavier, but—because of all the reports, all of the detail that now has to be provided—by every program officer. It is a serious question, a question which Stanley Surrey in a sense has raised for us. Is there a difference between the increase in the costs to a business of dealing with extensive and detailed regulation and the costs to a charity? I submit there is a difference when one takes into account the sharply limited resources available to charity.

We can also sense the increasing burdens in other foundations. Hardly a day goes by that my fellow lawyers and I are not asked questions by staff members of other foundations without comparable resources to obtain technical assistance.

Robert Anthoine referred several times this morning to the incredible complexity of this law, and his metaphor was "fog." You can imagine the "ceiling zero" feeling of a non-lawyer, dealing in an area which a distinguished member of the tax bar describes as incredibly complex and very foggy.

Concern With Grantor-Grantee Relationship

Let me tick off a few more of the kinds of changes that are occurring every day of the week—changes we can deal with because we are fortunate enough to have the resources and the people to deal with them. We are concerned with the traditional grantor-grantee relationship which Homer Wadsworth adverted to. The grantee in the traditional view was a wholly independent recipient of funds. The provisions of the Tax Reform Act now bring the grantor-grantee relationship dangerously close to a contractual relationship. We still say "a grant is a grant is a grant"— that it is not a contract—but when I look at the kinds of grant letters I am signing these days, I become increasingly concerned about the traditional grantor-grantee relationship.

The specter of our turning a public charity into a private foundation is also with us a great deal these days. We have to be sure that in helping we are not "misshaping" the recipient to the point where we need to say, you had better be in touch with a competent lawyer before we make this grant, lest the size of the grant change your organization from a public charity to a private foundation under the provisions of the act. Ruth Chance covered this classification jigsaw puzzle earlier, and I shall not linger on the subject.

Need for Charitable Funds Rising

All these things are happening, mind you, at the same time that charitable demands and social needs are rising everywhere around us. We do not need foundation spokesmen to tell us that there is a real concern, a gut concern, about the environment. There is a grave concern about rising population in the world. And we are far from solutions in the central cities. Where will the money come from to support promising innovations in these problem-ridden areas? At the same time that inflation continues to erode the philanthropic dollar, private foundations will pay a 4 percent excise tax on their investment income. In concrete terms, for example, on February 15, 1972, the Ford Foundation will pay to the United States Treasury something in the vicinity of $10 million. In total, the foundations are likely to pay a tax of nearly $40 million.

In a very real and painful way, many worthy and important charitable organizations attempting to meet urgent needs in the society will be deprived of that sum. If we step back for a moment from the thousands of words in the fine print of the regulations, I think really what is at stake here is not the future of private philanthropy but the future of the society in which we live. What kind of society do we want?

Certainly among the choices for a society is one in which government alone does the lion's share of the thinking and the acting. Most of us, I take it, favor a somewhat different route. We believe that government has no monopoly on wisdom, and we want to preserve the right to speak freely and certainly to speak back to government. Preserving and sustaining the strength of the private sector, then, is crucial, and any substantial drain on philanthropic funds must give all of us concern.

CONCLUSION

The Tax Reform Act? First, most of us will learn to live with it, although I doubt that many of us will learn to love it. Second, living with it for the past two years has convinced me that it is helping us to understand ourselves better than we have ever known ourselves before. (That may even help us to learn to love it a little.) Third, we must as good citizens not only live with the act but live up to it. On the basis of our experience to date, I have no doubt we can do that—at a cost—without fundamental changes in programmatic content. Fourth, we must also as good citizens continue to point out that any tax on charitable funds is, in effect, a tax on the recipients of charitable funds. And finally, a word about public disclosure. Foundations fully support the disclosure requirements of the act. Certainly we believe in accountability for private foundation programs and activities. But the 1969 experience should have taught us that full disclosure on accounting forms will not be enough. Clearly we must do an increasingly better job of public explanation.

CHAPTER XIV

EFFECTS OF ACT

JAMES L. KUNEN
Executive Vice President and Secretary,
Eugene and Agnes E. Meyer Foundation

THERE is really very little that I can add to Mr. Dressner's eloquent statement. I think it is certainly true, so far as our foundation is concerned, that we can live with this act and we are living with it. It has not caused any major change in our programming. It has caused us a lot of pain and suffering. It has caused us to add to our staff. It has increased our space requirements. It has added to our audit fees. It has added to our legal fees. I do not think that that is going to go away. But I think we shall be able to live with it and I am not overly distressed.

PROBLEM OF ADMINISTRATIVE COSTS

The trouble is that we, like most smaller foundations—relatively small foundations compared to Ford and Rockefeller—are caught in a kind of squeeze. These are not the kinds of problems that we could not handle on a routine basis with an appropriate staff. In other words, if I could add four or five people, I would not have any concern about this problem. I would have one person handling one aspect of the tax act, another doing a series of investigations and reports, and somebody else doing another thing. We are caught in a squeeze because neither we nor the IRS like administrative costs to go up too high. So, therefore, people like Ruth Chance have to slug it out all by themselves, and this is where we are really caught in a bind.

The requirements of the act are manageable. If we had no problems about the amount of money we spend on administration, we could move with considerable ease and comfort. That is the kind of situation that we are in.

The reason why I do not think this situation is going to correct itself in the future is that the problems which we face are not the kinds of problems to which you can give an A, B, or C letter. Take the question of what kind of an organization the recipient is, under the new act. You cannot just throw them into certain categories and say one falls in this, another falls in that category. Each individual organization has its own peculiar set of circumstances around it. We have to think about each particular application before we can come to any kind of conclusion.

The problem is we cannot do that, because we cannot make the determinations as to the nature of the organization—whether it is a private operating foundation—unless we have all the information that is necessary to make that kind of determination. We cannot get that kind of information from many of the organizations we do business with. They do not know themselves. We tried right after the tax act to make our own determinations to see if we could come to some reasonable judgments, and we found that it really was not feasible to do that. Why? Because 100 percent of your time, as Ruth Chance indicated, would have to go into that kind of determination. If we cannot increase our administrative staff, if we cannot increase our administrative costs in relation to our net income, then we are going to have a continuing problem. But I think we shall be able to live with it perfectly well, and it certainly is not going to make any major change in the nature of our operations.

Diversion of Foundations From Current Social Problems

What it will do, of course, is to divert us. It will divert us from the pressing problems that we ought to be paying attention to. And in the discussion this afternoon I think there has been some recognition of what those problems are.

Take a city like Washington, for example, which is where our foundation functions. Every city has its own peculiar set of problems. They are all being subjected to rapid social change of one kind or another. Washington's problems, as most of you already know, are those of the nation's capital. It is a monument city.

There is not any major industry around to provide corporate wealth for giving. The main industry is government.

We have a town where the school kids are 92 percent black. We have a town in which the population—I think this figure is reasonably close to the census data—is 76 percent black. Middle-class and wealthy whites have fled out into the suburbs.

The consequences of this relate to housing needs, relate to welfare problems, relate to the quality of education from pre-school on up to the university level and graduate schools—the admission, for example, of minority students to graduate schools, law schools, dental schools, and medical schools.

They relate to all sorts of problems that the government is not and should not be expected to handle all by itself. In the first place, the problems are very new and they require a series of different kinds of approaches to see which ones really work. I do not think anybody really knows the answers to these problems. I have not seen any answers with respect to any of these fields in any city or state in the country.

The foundations have a degree of flexibility in this respect. For example, like all other cities, we have a problem with increased drug use, not only on the part of the black population but also among the middle-class whites these days. As far as I know, nobody has come up with a very clear solution to that problem. For example, is methadone maintenance the appropriate treatment or is there something else when it comes to heroin? We need some kind of experimentation with this whole business.

There is the problem of public advocacy—a whole new system of approaching social issues and social problems. Many organizations have been formed both in terms of legal advocacy and in terms of environmental advocacy. There are whole new areas of experimentation in dealing with the new social problems that we are facing. These all need to be supported.

The whole complex of urban living today, together with the rapid rate of social change, are problems that require at this particular moment in time the greatest degree of flexibility and experimental approaches. As Howard Dressner said, it is precisely at the time when we are under these pressures that we have to face the burden of taxation. I do not think any of us has ever been concerned with those aspects of the tax act that deal with self-dealing or the reasonable payouts, etc. But the tax levy is expected to raise some $55 million this year from foundations whereas the IRS budgeted $19 million for its total tax-exempt operations; so, a question can be raised about the relationship between the tax revenues and the funds required to supervise the IRS operation.

INHIBITING CREATION OF FOUNDATIONS

Those problems really do not bother us. The real problems are the kinds that Ruth Chance was talking about. To my knowledge, very few, if any, new private foundations—not operating foundations—have been formed since the passage of the tax act. I think there is something to be said for regulations that in certain respects limit the growth of what was rapidly becoming a kind of social fad, especially for those small foundations that never would have an opportunity to have any kind of professional staff.

On the other hand, of course, it will inhibit the creation of perfectly legitimate foundations which simply are not going to take a chance, particularly now that it involves this highly controversial and complex area with the kind of risks that are involved.

Even more significant is the fact that private operating foundations are the ones that are not going to get the funds from the private giving foundations because they are risks. First of all, they tend to be the newer ones dealing with the kinds of problems I outlined a few minutes ago. It is too hard to deal with their operations. It is too hard to deal with the problem of expenditure responsibility. So the question really is, will the act work in a way to inhibit what may be at this particular juncture in our social history the very important experimentation in connection with problems we have never faced before.

To summarize, I am inclined to agree with Homer Wadsworth that we can live with this law and regulations. Sure, we can. And it may be that within the course of time our concerns will disappear. Certainly they will diminish. I think, however, we shall have the administrative problems to deal with, and the very serious inhibiting factors against the experimental organizations handling social problems.

CHAPTER XV

DISCUSSION OF EFFECTS OF TAX REFORM ACT
ON PRIVATE FOUNDATIONS

Moderator Stanley S. Surrey, Harvard Law School: This part of
the program is to provide perspective on the operational effects of
the 1969 act, in contrast to the morning discussion which dealt
with the volume and direction of private giving.

The morning session indicated, as I heard it, that there was no
real effect from the 1969 act on the volume of giving to public
charities. Of course, it would be strange if there were an effect on
such giving, since the act was not planned to have any effect on
giving to public charities and Congress was careful to see that the
act would not have any such effect. So the morning's discussion
did not disclose anything essentially new.

Private foundations are, however, different. The act was planned
by Congress to have an effect upon private foundations. In a sense
that is what it was all about. Therefore, the question we are discussing this afternoon is: What are these effects on the operational
activities of private foundations, and are they good or bad?

In seeking an answer to this question, we must move beyond the
simplistic view, sometimes heard this morning, that the response
that philanthropy is involved is somehow a magic talisman that
prevents any scrutiny of the question at all. Certainly Congress rejected that view in 1969. The work of philanthropy is not a shield
against questions. That is a fortiori so when we are dealing with
the private foundation, which is an organization unique in our
society in that people can establish themselves as trustees of public
funds.

This doesn't mean that this unique organization is to be subject
to restrictions of any kind or that foundations are fair game for
any legislation or restrictions that do not have any solid public
policies behind them.

I. DISCUSSION BY PANEL

This panel is here to indicate what is the balance sheet of the 1969 act on the operational effects, both the internal operational effects on the problems of running a foundation and then the effects on the programs of foundations and the activities and purposes which foundations would like to accomplish in this world.

Could I just put a few questions here and then see where we come out. I am placing the 4 percent tax to one side because it is obviously costly. With respect to the administrative costs of running a foundation under the rules of the 1969 act, everyone seems to say they have increased. But the administrative costs of running the Harvard Law School have also increased tremendously with the same student body, simply because the problems are much greater. Do you put a special emphasis on administrative costs of foundations because you say you fear the scrutiny that IRS will give and therefore are really incurring unnecessary costs in preparing for that scrutiny? If so, what is the solution for that situation?

In other words, at this stage do we need some well-organized study of what it really costs to run a foundation in the modern world, so people have a realistic sense of what a well-run foundation is, and what responsible administrative costs are, so the government has an awareness of what is involved? Would that be some way to help prevent this squeeze between costs and fear of IRS scrutiny?

Mr. James L. Kunen, Eugene and Agnes E. Meyer Foundation: I think that a study of that kind was made recently, wasn't it, under the auspices of the Rockefeller Foundation, investigating a lot of the administrative problems of running a foundation? I think that may yield some data. But there are two problems. The foundation whose administrative cost is the lowest is not necessarily the best run. In fact, you may find it precisely the opposite. The second is that with respect to any foundation's particular philosophy or method of operation, who in government is going to make the determination of what is the best operation?

We have always felt in the past—when I first came into the foundation 15 years ago—and we still do feel that we have a moral duty not to be spending public trust funds on administrative expenses. We ought to be spending them on experimental programming. But I don't know how the government can help us unless they can say we understand your problem; we understand that the tax law is placing an additional burden on you; we want you to do a good job, because there is no point in making lousy grants; you might as well make good ones, otherwise you are really wasting public trust money.

Mrs. Ruth C. Chance, Rosenberg Foundation: What about that? Professor Surrey, what is a well-run foundation? One of the problems is that the government may push us into the mold of government granting. It is the only pattern they know, after all. I have the feeling that what they like to see is more forms, closer scrutiny of what grantees are doing, more rigid budgets so that they can measure expenditures against specific items. We are just as apt to tell a grantee that if it would achieve the purpose of a project better by shifting money within a budget all it has to do is convince us that that's a good thing to do and we'll permit the shifts.

We'll know a lot more when we get the regulations. But I believe that the relationship between grantor and grantee is undergoing changes because of the law, and that to me would be a problem.

Moderator Surrey: Let me perhaps narrow some of the questions and I think also develop an interesting agreement. You said that the programs you wanted to carry out you are still carrying out; so, everything you wanted to do you can still do. But then you said that the ability to handle experimental programs was defeated, and I wasn't quite clear why that was. It didn't seem to be due to any operative restrictions on the programs. I gather it was rather because maybe some new foundations won't come into existence which might have helped in some areas, and I gather because you are diverting, at the present time at least, time and energy to operational aspects. Those were the reasons rather than any substantive restrictions on program activities.

Mr. Kunen: The third reason is that most foundations won't enter these fields, under the present policy.

Moderator Surrey: They won't for what reason?

Mr. Kunen: Because they are afraid of the risks in handling this problem, if they don't get the right kind of reporting done from the recipient organization.

Mrs. Chance: It's involved in the law. Many of the best experimental new things come out of organizations for which we have expenditure responsibility. And if you do not have the time to give to exercise expenditure responsibility—and that is a very time-consuming thing so far as we can see now—then you are going to think in the back of your mind when you look at that application, "This is another one which I would have to monitor, check up on, and find out about, and I don't even know what I have to find out yet."

Mr. Howard Dressner, The Ford Foundation: Trustees are fiduciaries. They have important concerns and responsibilities. The men in those posts recognize the importance of accountability. To pick up your point: In a foundation like ours, or Rockefeller or a dozen others, we are in a position to introduce grant recommendations and, after the most careful checking, provide assurance that they conform to the Tax Reform Act of 1969—that there is compliance.

If you move out of the foundation that has resources of these kinds, then the executive director is faced with a new quandary. He can do one of several things. He can struggle endlessly to try to figure it out himself—and remember he's dealing with a law of considerable complexity—or he can engage outside counsel —proficient outside counsel—adding to the cost; or he can play it safe, thereby saving the administrative costs; he plays it safe simply by not recommending this or that proposal to the trustees.

As a consequence, some very important things are going to go undone, unrecommended to trustees.

Moderator Surrey: Let me ask if you and Mrs. Chance seem to be saying the same thing. The problem of exercising expenditure responsibility lies at the heart of this. My question is: What restrictions would you eliminate? There are really two separate questions. One is: Are you questioning the ultimate substantive restrictions that Congress adopted on what foundations should or should not be doing with their money? I don't think you are, because you say that at least the programs you want to carry out substantively you can carry out and are carrying out. Or, are you saying that the problem is that somebody—which happens to be you—has to exercise responsibility for this and this will inhibit that somebody?

Mr. Dressner: We are not yet ready—it's too early—we are not yet prepared to answer your question with any specificity. We are still learning. Proposed regulations have been issued but no final regulations. We still have some months of experience ahead of us before we will be able to say there are 3 or 5 or 10 administrative requirements in this act that are really unnecessary, that do not help the Congress to achieve its purpose.

Mr. Homer C. Wadsworth, Kansas City Association of Trusts and Foundations: I should like to make some observations that I consider to be on the hopeful side. In recent months I have visited a number of cities in the Midwest to talk with people who have trustee responsibilities for private foundations. The new tax law has forced them to think carefully about how foundation funds might best be used. It has also led them to think of various ways of putting together small foundations, either as a part of a community foundation or as a federation of trust and foundation interests, to secure good staff service and to keep overhead expense to a minimum.

I consider this a good sign for the future. The aggregate of foundation spending is relatively small—about 9 percent of all private giving in the country at this time. It is important, therefore, that foundations have a sound rationale to guide their efforts, and that they think clearly about good management of money and of programs sponsored. The consequence is likely to be that a good deal of foundation money that heretofore has been given only casual review will now come into control that considers carefully the terms of the law, but also the best possible way in which to put such money to work. The result, given this estimate of future developments, seems to me to be all to the good.

It is my judgment that those of us who happen to be involved in various forms of philanthropic endeavor other than private foundations should be having a careful look at the way in which many of our voluntary agencies now function. The overhead expense of foundations is but a pittance of the large amounts now spent by the very large multimillion dollar national charities for management and promotional activities. In many instances it is a bit hard to see how dollars given actually flow to people in the form of services, or in support of research activities designed to improve our knowledge.

I believe that a careful review of such matters is on the horizon, and that the time is now for those concerned and interested to take the steps necessary to put these several houses in good order.

Mrs. Chance: I'd understand your first remarks better if I knew whether your organization has been characterized as a public foundation. Are you regarded as a public charity?

Mr. Wadsworth: No. We're a 501 (c) (3), Ruth.

Mrs. Chance: But are you private?

Mr. Wadsworth: Our member trusts are private foundations. What we are now proposing to the Treasury is classification of the Kansas City Association of Trusts and Foundations as a community foundation.

The underlying thought is to give us as flexible an instrument for service as possible. Our present member trusts, and perhaps others to be added from time to time, simply purchase service from the association to review, monitor, and evaluate projects under consideration. If the association is classified as a community foundation it may receive gifts for custody, assuming in the process the responsibility for carrying out the wishes of donors within the terms of the law. Since the board of directors of the association is broadly representative of the community at large, and a majority of its directors have no trustee responsibilities nor employment with the bank that serves as corporate trustee, it would appear that the association is in a position to request such classification.

The point of our effort is to create useful ways of serving the community interest, bearing in mind that different people may prefer to render their assistance in quite different ways. The services of a community foundation may be most appropriate in many cases, just as the retention of private control coupled with professional services may be the best answer in other circumstances.

As to the purposes served by such a combination of services, I think it best to recognize that we live in rather dangerous times. There are risks involved in using philanthropic funds creatively— the risk of loss on programs that miss fire; the risk of projects that run counter to conventional wisdom. It is well to know that risk-taking is quite as normal to a good foundation operation as it is in a business enterprise.

Mrs. Chance: On that one Howard Dressner once referred to the foundation he represents as being a switchboard of information. I could spend all of my time in free consultation with un-staffed foundations, some of them quite large, in the western United States. But we just don't sell our services.

Moderator Surrey: I just want to comment on one thing that you said. You seem really to raise the question that a number of organizations with very large funds may not all along have had the requisite staff to justify themselves and their existence.

II. DISCUSSION FROM FLOOR

Professor LeRoy Dunn, Trinity College: As I listen to the comments by foundation representatives reflecting upon the lack of clarity in the IRS regulations and the performance criteria under the new act, it remains unclear to me as to what principles would be acceptable to both parties as a basis for the issuance of such regulations under the Tax Reform Act of 1969.

Moderator Surrey: I believe the panel was talking about that earlier. What they were saying, if I can interpret, is that they are not yet ready to suggest whether any of the substantive restrictions, apart from the 4 percent tax, that the Congress was seeking are wrong, or whether the operational rigors that are imposed could in any way be alleviated.

Mr. Dressner: One of the things that fascinates me about the discussion surrounding the Tax Reform Act—Homer Wadsworth referred to it earlier when he said there is so much more here than the auditors and the endless section numbers and regulations and all the rest of it—is the frequent failure to perceive the difference between partisan politics and the political process. I have yet to find anything that any American citizen does that isn't a part of the political process. Cancer research is one of the most debated issues in our country and will continue; so, where is the "apple pie" that isn't a part of the political process? It doesn't exist. Any subject is a political issue if you and I think differently.

Partisan politics is another thing. Of course foundation dollars should not back candidate Jones against candidate Smith. But when we get to that fine line between public education and the "political process"—and it is a fine line—we are faced with a far more difficult question.

Moderator Surrey: Let me just ask this question: What do you want to do, get into politics or out of education? In other words, do you say that there should be no line?

Mr. Dressner: I say there should be a line. But that does not mean it is easy to draw.

Moderator Surrey: Then what you are saying is that in the future there will be problems that people don't properly appreciate regarding the difficulty of locating that line. Isn't that right?

Mr. Dressner: There may be.

Moderator Surrey: It is a line with which we have lived for many years and which we have to keep, unless you can find some other way.

Mr. Dressner: But, Stanley, the search for the line is not over and may never be.

Moderator Surrey: But the world won't come to an end just because we have that problem. You seem to be giving the impression that somehow there's a great new cloud over you because as a country we are going ahead and trying to develop the line between education, which we are willing to support publicly, and politics which we don't feel you should be engaged in.

138

Mr. Kunen: May I comment? Our concern was first aroused by the very spirit that seems to pervade the act. It was a spirit which when it was finally written into the legislation seemed to say, "We're damned suspicious of you because we think you may be trying to overthrow the government, or else trying to maintain the status quo too much." We didn't know which side to respond to. But there is a brooding air of suspicion that runs through the legislation which is fortified by the serious penalties placed on the managers of foundations and on the trustees.

What really is involved is the way the law is written. When you combine that with the overriding spirit, with some of the punitive provisions, and with the rigorous adminstrative requirements of the legislation, we're very uncertain as to how we are going to fare. I think this is really what the problem is.

Mrs. Chance: I think Jim has said it exactly. The atmosphere of the act, the very vulnerability we see ourselves as having, the penalties imposed by the act tend to put us in a state of uncertainty extending even to abeyance. When society lives in the state of tension that it's in now and is as divided and polarized as it is, many things are regarded as political which at other times might be considered educational.

Moderator Surrey: I think these comments are helpful, and there may be many who feel that Congress should have gone into the program area. On the other hand, the task of making this very difficult decision you describe has always been present in the charitable area. It's something we have to live with if we are going to have the private support of philanthropy in the United States.

Lawyers perhaps captured the wrong tone in their language and in the whole complex structure of placing sanctions in the law which is, as I gather, a cause of many of the problems.

President R. Palmer Baker, Jr., Lord, Day & Lord, New York: Yes, Stanley, my question really goes to that and to you and the panel. I was taken, Homer, with your relaxed point of view as to the importance of the lawyer. Really what you say is that there is a tendency to put this problem in the hands of the lawyers which is not where it belongs. It's a question of foundation judgment. I wonder whether the foundation would be so concerned about the expenditure responsibility rules if their trustees and their managers under advice of the lawyers were not so terribly afraid of making a mistake and having a substantial personal liability as a result. And I wonder whether that isn't the area of the act where constructive change could be made and yet still maintain the necessary line that it seems to me the expenditure responsibility rules under the proposed regulations leave off.

Mr. Wadsworth: I agree that some constructive changes in the law are desirable, if for no other reason than to clarify what is really meant by expenditure responsibility. My earlier comment derived in considerable part from an extensive experience as a member of a school board for 14 years. I found it an irresistible temptation on the part of most of my colleagues to refer to counsel every sticky and complicated question that arose, presumably on the assumption that lawyers could come up with magic to straighten all things out. This seems to me an illusion of a high order, and more frequently than not a way of sidestepping responsibility. There is no merit in backing away from the hard questions, even though all we have to deal with them is the best judgment we can muster on the basis of the facts at hand. This is not to diminish the importance of having highly competent counsel. It is rather to assert that difficult issues are not settled by shifting the papers about from office to office.

A few comments need to be made about the relationship of the Tax Reform Act to program activities. I think that it was inevitable that the Congress deal with this aspect of the matter. Many foundations tend to be rather clubby affairs, and somewhat deliberately removed from the heat of public opinion. If people don't know anything about you, they have a right to conjure up any conclusion that suits their interests and their needs.

All of us, whether we like it not, have always been involved in the politics of non-politics. This does not mean that we are partisan in any sense; no sensible person in any foundation has been involved in supplying funds for partisan affairs. But if he knows his business and is doing his job, he is well aware of the political process and mindful of its impact upon our life. The chances are that with all the ambiguities of the act as it relates to these particular sections it is still a rather nice thing to have those who are tempted to spend their dollars in politics clearly prohibited from doing so. It is a little hard to identify the public interest with using foundations as blinds for political effort.

On balance it seems to me we must remember that looking at things from the standpoint of the country as a whole, it is well that the Tax Reform Act has knocked out a number of abuses. The right to establish a foundation and to serve the public interest through private effort is a very unusual privilege and one that must be handled in a highly responsible way. It is only sensible to know that most people are rather suspicious about money and about people who have money, no matter who they are or what they are doing with their money, or how decent their statements of good intentions. This is perhaps more normal at this time than at any other. Indeed, judging by the suspicious way in which the general public now views all tax proposals, suspicion about money in other people's hands is rather endemic.

Moderator Surrey: Our time has come to an end. I want to thank the members of the panel for their contributions and for a very interesting and informative period.

PART FIVE

SUPPORT OF PRIVATE PHILANTHROPY
THROUGH THE FEDERAL INCOME TAX LAWS

"The subject of our session this morning is 'Support of Private Philanthropy Through the Federal Income Tax Laws.' The specific topics to be covered are the propriety and vitality of federal income tax deductions for private philanthropy, and possible alternatives to a federal income tax deduction to support and encourage private philanthropy.

"One of the points that I hope will be covered in the discussion period is the questionable reliability of quoted statements by philanthropists that their gifts would be about the same if there were no tax deductions at all. Human beings being what they are, these self-serving statements are quite understandable, but, in my experience, quite inaccurate. Also, in my view they are quite unintentionally damaging to the cause of both philanthropy and a viable tax structure.

"It is my recollection that I have seldom sat down to advise on tax matters in estate planning with a substantial donor who did not make an additional gift he would not otherwise have made if there had been no tax deduction. As I mentioned in my paper on this subject published recently by the Tax Institute of America (April-May, 1971, issue of *Tax Policy*), I am convinced that the Congress and the Treasury should stop relying on these unreliable opinion surveys as a justification for further eroding the deduction for charitable contributions.

"Also, I would hope that in the discussion this morning serious consideration will be given to the deterioration in our education and culture that would result if prospective donors are able to say: 'The government has eliminated the tax deduction and we really can't afford to give anything at all.' "

JOEL BARLOW
Attorney, Covington & Burling, and
Chairman, Friday Morning Session

CHAPTER XVI

THE PROPRIETY AND VITALITY OF A FEDERAL INCOME TAX DEDUCTION FOR PRIVATE PHILANTHROPY*

BORIS I. BITTKER
Sterling Professor of Law, Yale University

THE SUBJECT assigned to me for discussion is the propriety and vitality of a federal income tax deduction for private philanthropy. At first blush, the question of the deduction's "propriety"—the legitimacy of governmental aid to private philanthropy—has been so frequently debated that one wonders whether anything new remains to be said. As to the deduction's "vitality," one might say briefly that even in the darkest legislative days of the private foundation, a few years ago, there was no disposition to abolish the deduction for charities as a whole; and that the changes that were in fact enacted do not really undercut the basic principle of the deduction. Still, the deduction has encountered stormy weather in academic circles in recent years,[1] and even though these clouds are

---

* Copyright © 1972 by Boris I. Bittker. This paper is part of a larger study by the author, in preparation.

[1] C. Harry Kahn, *Personal Deductions in the Federal Income Tax*, National Bureau of Economic Research Fiscal Studies No. 6, Princeton: Princeton University Press, 1960, pp. 46-91; Paul R. McDaniel, "Alternatives to Utilization of the Federal Income Tax System to Meet Social Problems," *Boston College Industrial and Commercial Law Review*, 11 (June, 1970), 875-82; Edward H. Rabin, "Charitable Trusts and Charitable Deductions," *New York University Law Review*, 41 (November, 1966), 912-37; Stanley S. Surrey, "Federal Income Tax Reform: The Varied Approaches Necessary to Replace Tax Expenditures with Direct Governmental Assistance," *Harvard Law Review*, 84 (December, 1970), 381-94; Stanley S. Surrey, "Tax Incentives as a Device for Implementing Government Policy: A Comparison with Direct Government Expenditures," *Harvard Law Review*, 83 (February, 1970), 705-38; Michael K. Taussig, "Economic Aspects of the Personal Income Tax Treatment of Charitable Contributions," *National Tax Journal*, 20 (March, 1967), 1-19

not yet any larger than a man's hand, the organizers of this symposium may have been watching them with care.

There are usually three counts to the indictment brought by critics of the deduction, viz., that a charitable gift is a personal and voluntary expenditure by the taxpayer that should have no impact on his tax liability because the tax should be based on "net" income; that deductions, even assuming they are to be allowed as a device to encourage philanthropy, are ineffective because they do not distinguish between gifts that need an official incentive and those that would be made in any event; and finally that, assuming we can get over these obstacles, deductions vary in value with the taxpayer's marginal tax rate and hence inure to the benefit of upper income taxpayers in violation of the progressive rate schedule. These objections to the deduction as it exists today have led to proposals to curtail it sharply, or to eliminate it entirely. The abolitionists sometimes suggest that the deduction be replaced by a system of matching grants for charitable contributions.

Before discussing the three basic criticisms of tax deductions that I have briefly summarized—which might be labelled "impropriety," "inefficiency," and "inequity"—I should like to say a few words about matching grants as a substitute for the deduction of existing law. If a system of matching grants is not feasible or would generate grave side-effects, I suspect that there would be little enthusiasm for a repeal of the tax deduction, no matter how strongly these theoreticians·are convinced of its impropriety, inefficiency, or inequity. Conversely, if matching grants would be the functional equivalent of the deduction as we now know it, producing substantially the same results, one might accept the change with equanimity, even if the theoretical objections to existing law are unpersuasive.

(hereafter cited as "Taussig NTJ"); Michael K. Taussig, "The Charitable Contributions Deduction in the Federal Income Tax," Ph.D. dissertation, M.I.T., 1965 (hereafter cited as "Taussig MIT"); William S. Vickrey, "One Economist's View of Philanthropy," in Frank G. Dickinson, Editor, *Philanthropy and Public Policy*, New York: National Bureau of Economic Research, 1962, pp. 31-56; Melvin I. White, "Proper Income Tax Treatment of Deductions for Personal Expense," in *Tax Revision Compendium*, Compendium of Papers on Broadening the Tax Base Submitted to the Committee on Ways and Means, House of Representatives, United States Congress, Washington: Government Printing Office, 1959, Volume 1, pp. 370-71. For a general review, with an extensive bibliography, see Lawrence M. Stone, "Federal Tax Support of Charities and Other Exempt Organizations: The Need for a National Policy," in University of Southern California Law Center, *Major Tax Planning for 1968*, New York: Matthew Bender & Company, Inc., 1968, pp. 27-78.

After commenting on the matching grant device, and on the criticisms that have led it to be proposed as a substitute for the deduction of existing law, I will set out my own affirmative views on the "propriety and vitality" of the deduction. Each of these subjects—matching grants, the three-count indictment of the deduction, and its affirmative defense—deserves more extensive examination than I can give it in the time allotted to me; and I ask your indulgence if I traverse the ground rather rapidly and totally neglect some of the interesting landmarks.

Matching Grants

At the outset, I should like to call attention to the fact that proposals for matching grants accept the contention, made by proponents of tax deductions for charitable gifts, that it is wise public policy to encourage the creation and growth of philanthropic institutions. Sometimes the premise is that they are doing socially essential work that otherwise would have to be carried on by governmental agencies, but that can be performed with more imagination, diversity, flexibility, or economy by private groups. More recently, the idea has gained ground—fed by concern over the citizen's alienation in a bureaucratic society—that independent centers of power with a large measure of private control should be encouraged, even if their functions would not be picked up by governmental agencies in the absence of private support. In keeping with either, or both, of these rationales, proposals for matching grants have as their core the concept of private choice: the grants are to go to institutions designated by private persons in a particular way, i.e., by putting their money on the line. Matching grants thus would be independent of whatever programs might be instituted as part of the government's regular expenditure budget to support education, science, arts and humanities, the poor, etc. These budgeted expenditures may embrace some of the same charitable institutions as the proposed system of matching grants, but the latter will go to organizations selected by private choice, manifested by private gifts, without federal screening, designation, or approval.

I begin with this point because the critics of tax allowances for charitable contributions often imply, even when they do not explicitly assert, that there is no justification for private control over the use of "governmental" funds. I will return to this strain of thought later; suffice it to say at this point in the discussion that those who wholeheartedly espouse this view, which is by no means irrational despite the counterarguments that persuade me to reject it, should be no more enthusiastic about matching grants than about tax allowances. For this reason, I am not sure whether they support matching grants as a desirable measure of social policy, or only as a temporary expedient, to be eliminated as soon as the public can be brought around to the view that "government" funds should be controlled solely by public officials.

Turning now more directly to the substitution of matching grants for the tax deduction of existing law, I foresee a constitutional obstacle, perhaps an insuperable one, to the inclusion of churches and other religious organizations (which in 1962 received more than 60 percent of itemized charitable contributions) in the grant system. In the most recent relevant Supreme Court decision, to be sure, a divided Court upheld federal grants to church-related colleges and universities for the construction of buildings and other "academic facilities" under the Higher Education Facilities Act of 1963, against a claim that the aid violated the establishment and free exercise clauses of the First Amendment.[2] The prevailing opinion, however, stressed several features of the construction grants that could not be embodied in a program of matching grants to churches. Thus, the enabling legislation explicitly forbids any grant for facilities "to be used for sectarian instruction or as a place for religious worship," a restriction whose violation will trigger a recapture of the facility's value, proportionate to the federal contribution to its cost. To the Court, a dedication of the facilities to secular purposes was so essential that a statutory provision permitting the recapture restriction to expire at the end of 20 years was held to be too lax, and was excised by the Court on its own motion. Even with this expanded safeguard, the legislation had to face the argument that the secular function of church-related colleges is so entangled with their religious mission that federal aid to the former inevitably advances the latter. The Court responded to this contention—simultaneously distin-

---

[2] Tilton v. Richardson, 403 U.S. 672 (1971).

guishing the case of federal aid to church-related elementary and secondary schools, which was held improper in two companion cases—by saying that "college students are less impressionable and less susceptible to religious indoctrination" than younger students, and that the "predominant" mission of the colleges in the case before it, though church-related, was "to provide their students with a secular education."[3]

Unless the sedulously narrow rationale of *Tilton v. Richardson* is relaxed to the point of nullification,[4] I see no constitutional future in a matching grant program that includes churches and other clearly religious organizations. It is barely possible that some of their social welfare activities could be split off sufficiently to gain a separate constitutional status for matching grants to these functions, but this would entail some excessively nice distinctions. (Do the Salvation Army's soup kitchens relieve secular—or religious—hunger?) Moreover, a federal effort to distinguish between the social welfare and religious functions of churches might reflect, or be perceived as reflecting, an intolerable bias against churches that openly avow their missionary purpose and in favor of those that are more subtle in their statements or activities.

Aside from the constitutional barrier, there would be a formidable political barrier to a system of matching grants that includes the churches. The struggle over public aid to parochial schools has produced some legislation, to be sure, but these results responded to concentrated pressure in communities with parochial schools that were near financial collapse, where it was possible to argue that the right of parents to send their children to religious schools—itself a constitutionally protected right—was jeopardized by their obligation to support the public schools as well. There is

---

[3] See Lemon v. Kurtzman, 403 U.S. 602 (1971) (Rhode Island and Pennsylvania statutes aiding parochial schools unconstitutional); see also Walz v. Tax Commission, 397 U.S. 664 (1970) (state property tax exemption for church property constitutional); Board of Education v. Allen, 392 U.S. 236 (1968) (loan of publicly purchased textbooks to parochial school pupils constitutional).

[4] It is barely possible that the Court might swing around to the view that the "entanglement" of church and state, one of its concerns in *Tilton v. Richardson,* could be avoided by grants containing no restrictions or rights to scrutinize or demand reports on the use to which the funds were put, so that a no-strings-attached "direct expenditure" would have the same constitutional status as the "tax expenditure" upheld in *Walz, supra* note 3. While not inconceivable, this rationale would mean that the more the state endeavored to prevent its funds from serving religious ends, the more it would approach an unconstitutional "establishment" of religion!

no such pressure for matching grants to churches; the potential recipients seem satisfied with the tax deduction of existing law, and Congress is not likely to substitute grants for deductions merely to improve the elegance of the Internal Revenue Code. Hard as it would be, then, to enact a system of matching grants that included churches, it would be equally difficult, in my opinion, to enact a system without them. Nor do I foresee as a compromise the enactment of a matching grant system for secular charities, and perpetuation of tax deductions for churches. Deadlock, i.e., preservation of the status quo, is the more likely outcome.

A related problem, which would also contribute to a political deadlock, is that a system of matching grants would hardly coincide with tax deductions in the pattern of benefits conferred on charitable institutions. It would be difficult to devise a formula for matching grants that would produce, even in the aggregate, the same amount of revenue that charities owe to the tax deduction, and it is almost inconceivable that this could be done for particular charities or even categories of charities.[5] If the rich now give to private universities and the poor to churches, for example, and the deduction is repealed, the post-repeal pattern of charitable receipts would depend on whether these groups respond differently to loss of a tax deduction, and on whether their post-repeal gifts will be matched dollar-for-dollar, or in a more complex fashion related to the size of the donor's income. If universities, hospitals, museums, community chests, foundations, churches, and others will be differentially affected by the change, there will be no

---

[5] McDaniel, *op. cit.*, says on p. 880 that any nontax substitute for the deduction of existing law must assure educational institutions of support equal to "that which they can reasonably anticipate from the present tax expenditure system." Unless this one class of recipients is to be singled out, it would seem that every other class would similarly be entitled to preserve its status quo ante. It is hard to envision a single formula that could do this, without giving some groups more than they had before. Efficiency, what crimes are to be committed in thy name!

Perhaps inefficiency is to be avoided by conforming the matching grants to a redefined Pareto-optimum (viz., every group is to be as well off, and none is to be better off) with a set of formulas, each exquisitely tailored to its own charitable category. The model that comes to mind is percentage depletion, where we give each industry a different percentage, accurately reflecting its economic risks, technological level, and political clout. Although I myself do not share the distaste that has been expressed at the appearance of college presidents before congressional committees (Surrey, "Federal Income Tax Reform," *op. cit.*, pp. 389-90; Stone, *op. cit.*, p. 76), those who think that lobbying is undignified might pause to consider whether a matching grant system, whether it uses one formula or several, would pit every charity against every other one, bringing about a donnybrook of quite new turbulence.

united front in favor either of repealing the tax deduction or of substituting a single formula as its replacement. The poker game will also be affected by the fact that some charities are more likely than others to qualify for direct federal aid apart from matching grants, and by the possibility that this independent source of assistance will shrink if a system of matching grants is substituted for tax deductions. If an all-powerful computer *could* devise a formula for matching grants that would restore the pre-repeal status for both donors and donees, I would hail it as a modern miracle; but would then go on to wonder if this feat of ingenuity should not be likened to the businessman who, fearful of an investigation by the Antitrust Division of the Department of Justice, instructed his secretary to burn his correspondence with his business competitors, but first to make copies for the files.

Perhaps, then, I am merely making a virtue of necessity by suggesting that matching grants would in any event be a poor substitute for existing law. My concern is that a system of matching grants would not preserve the large degree of institutional and donor independence that is now respected by the statutory provisions of the Internal Revenue Code and by the Internal Revenue Service's administration of these provisions.

When a donor takes a tax deduction for a charitable contribution, his privacy is an inextricable part of the more generally protected privacy that is accorded to federal income tax returns. Thus, an attempt to breach it—for example, on the theory that deductions are equivalent to expenditures, and that the public is entitled to know who is controlling the destiny of these hypothetical public funds—would be seen as a threat to the privacy of everyone's tax return, whether he makes charitable contributions or not. By contrast, a promise of privacy embodied in a matching grant system, not yet sanctified or steeled by history, would not be protected by a similar umbrella; and might well be swept away by a revival of McCarthyism, aided perhaps by a philosophic claim (already explicit in some proposals to substitute grants for deductions) that secrecy is incompatible with democratic values. It may be that some proponents of matching grants see their vulnerability to disclosure as an advantage, but I do not.

A closely related threat to the independence of donors and

donees is the intrusion of official concepts of right and wrong into the administration of a matching grant system. No public program is immune to either open or covert attempts to foster one set of values and discourage another, but the definition of exempt organizations by section 501 (c) (3) of the Internal Revenue Code and the administration of this definition by the tax authorities have been relatively free of bias. This freedom is fragile, of course, and it would be fatuous to assert that it will last so long as we stick with tax deductions, but will be lost forever if we shift to matching grants. Professor McDaniel assures us that "a direct federal grant or loan program can be drafted and operated as simply, and with the same degree of freedom from governmental control as a tax expenditure."[6] I am reminded—not unfairly, I hope—of William Butler Yeats' story about the Irish peasant who was asked if he believed in leprechauns. "Well, I've never seen one," was the reply, "but it stands to reason." The issue, after all, is not the drafting of a verbal formula promising independence, but its effect in real life. Acknowledging that a dogmatic conclusion is not warranted, I must say that I have very little confidence that a system of matching grants could be administered without administrative and congressional investigations, loyalty oaths, informal or implicit warnings against heterodoxy, and the other trappings of governmental support that the tax deduction has, so far, been able to escape. It is of course true that some recipients of charitable contributions (e.g., colleges and universities) are heavily dependent on other types of federal assistance, and that these may be encumbered by restrictions; but recent experience with federal scholarship programs shows that private institutions, deriving a degree of independence from their endowments and alumni contributions, are better able to resist such threats than institutions that depend entirely on public appropriations. Whatever may be said, therefore, in favor of matching grants as a substitute for tax allowances in such other areas as tax-exempt state and municipal bond interest,[7] the device is no panacea.

---

[6] McDaniel, *op. cit.*, p. 874.

[7] Thus, Professor Surrey's proposal for federal financial assistance to states and municipalities as compensation for repeal of section 103 (a) (exempt bond interest) has much to commend it. See Surrey, "Federal Income Tax Reform," *op. cit.*, pp.

"Impropriety"

I should like now to consider whether a tax deduction for charitable contributions is somehow inconsistent with the basic presuppositions of income taxation, one of the claims made in support of its repeal. Another way of putting this assertion of "impropriety" is that "horizontal equity" is violated if A and B, having the same amount of adjusted gross income, pay different amounts of federal income tax merely because A has made a charitable contribution. (I will discuss later the assertion, growing out of the progressive rate schedule, that "vertical equity" is violated if X and Y give the same amount to charities but get divergent tax benefits merely because X is in a higher adjusted gross income bracket than Y.) The assertion of unfairness when A's tax liability is lower than B's solely because A has made a charitable contribution is based on the premise that the taxpayer's income tax liability should be based on the amount available to him for consumption expenditures, taking no account of how he chooses to spend his money, coupled with the premise that a charitable gift is a consumption expenditure. "Tax logic," we are told, requires gifts to charities to be classed with wine, women, and song; to permit any of these to be deducted violates the Haig-Simons definition of income.

I have had occasion elsewhere to discuss at length the limited usefulness of this definition, sometimes described as "the comprehensive income tax base," and, tempting as I find any occasion to paraphrase my earlier remarks,[8] I will refrain from doing so here. I will instead content myself with asserting that even the most enthusiastic proponents of a comprehensive income tax base have themselves found a spate of occasions and reasons for departing from their ideal. This should be no surprise: when the proponents of a bleakly dogmatic theory confront life, they almost always get cold feet and withdraw to the comforting warmth of more familiar

---

371-81, and articles there cited; see also Henry C. Simons, *Federal Tax Reform,* Chicago: University of Chicago Press, 1950, p. 34.

[8] Boris I. Bittker, Charles O. Galvin, R. A. Musgrave, and Joseph A. Pechman, *A Comprehensive Income Tax Base? A Debate,* Branford [Conn.]: Federal Tax Press, Inc., 1968, 127 p., reprinting articles in *Harvard Law Review,* 80 (March, 1967), 925-85; 81 (November, 1967), 44-67; (March, 1968), 1016-43, with additional material.

terrain. As Holmes said, the life of the law has not been logic; it has been experience.

The no-deduction-for-consumption school of thought is no exception to this custom. Proof can be found in the very area that we are discussing. Thus, condemnation of the existing tax law for distinguishing among taxpayers merely because they use their money for different forms of consumption is often coupled with advocacy of matching grants by the government to charities that have been selected by the "private choice" of taxpayers. But a matching grant to A's charity, if nothing goes to B's mistress, also distinguishes among taxpayers by reason of their expenditures: A has been given an economic lever that is denied to B, solely because he spends his money differently. To use the economist's terminology, the price to A of enriching his favorite charity by $2 is reduced, by the matching grant, to $1; but if B wants to give $2 to his companion, it will cost him the full $2. Depending on whether the advocate of matching grants is a puritan, an idealist, or a utilitarian, his rationale for matching the taxpayer's charitable contributions but not his expenditures on wine, women, and song will be that charitable gifts are more "worthy," "selfless," or "beneficial to society." The adjective does not matter; what is important is the basic premise of the matching grant approach that some consumption expenditures should be rewarded or encouraged, and others not.

Yet, advocates of matching grants persist in telling us that it is a perversion of the Internal Revenue Code, but not of the national expenditure budget, to distinguish between one consumption expenditure and another. The burgeoning theory that tax deductions and direct expenditures are functional equivalents leads to some extravagances,[9] but none is more ironic than this idea that social objectives that are tolerable in one system are inconsistent with the other. It may be, of course, that tax deductions are less "efficient" than matching grants would be, but that is a very long

---

[9] See Boris I. Bittker, "Accounting for Federal 'Tax Subsidies' in the National Budget," *National Tax Journal*, 22 (June, 1969), 244-61; Stanley S. Surrey and William F. Hellmuth, "The Tax Expenditure Budget—Response to Professor Bittker," *National Tax Journal*, 22 (December, 1969), 528-37; Boris I. Bittker, "The Tax Expenditure Budget—A Reply to Professors Surrey and Hellmuth," *National Tax Journal*, 22 (December, 1969), 538-42.

way from saying that logic requires the "tax expenditure" system to treat all consumption expenditures the same, while the "direct expenditure" system, simultaneously and perforce, makes distinctions among them.

Returning now to A and B, who have the same amount of adjusted gross income, but choose to spend their money in different ways, I have no difficulty at all with the proposition that society can rationally distinguish between them. Whether this is done by giving A a tax allowance for his charitable contributions, by matching his gifts with smaller, equal, or larger amounts of government funds, by erecting a monument to him in the nation's capitol, or merely by assuming without official action that virtue is its own reward, is a matter of judgment, not of logic.

"INEFFICIENCY"

Turning now to the second count in the indictment of tax deductions for charitable contributions, the charge is that they are inefficient because such a large fraction of charitable gifts would be forthcoming in any event that the incremental contributions stimulated by the deduction are too small to justify their cost. Whether the criterion of "efficiency" should be the sole standard, or even a major one, in judging the deduction is a question to which I will return later in this paper; for the moment, I will accept the criterion as profferred by its proponents.

The major basis for asserting that the deduction is "inefficient" is a 1965 doctoral dissertation by Professor Michael K. Taussig, summarized by him in a 1967 article in the *National Tax Journal*.[10] Noting that the deduction increases the taxpayer's disposable income and hence his ability to make charitable contributions and other expenditures at the same time that it reduces the net cost to him of charitable gifts, Professor Taussig sought to separate its "income effect" from its "price effect." The distinction is important, because repeal of the deduction could be coupled with a subsidy or an offsetting general rate reduction to produce the same "income effect" (i.e., increase in aggregate after-tax income); thus, it is only the deduction's "price effect" (i.e., the reduction in the "cost" of making a charitable contribution by the amount of

---

[10] *Op. cit.*

tax saved by the deduction) that can be regarded as a genuine incentive.[11] Using a regression analysis of the adjusted gross income, deductible contributions, and marginal tax rates shown on the 1962 Treasury Tax File, and crosschecking the regression analysis with a series of ancillary studies, Professor Taussig concluded that "the incentive effect of the deduction for charitable contributions is, in the aggregate, weak."[12]

This conclusion is often quoted or paraphrased, but the commentators who build on it seldom quote the warning which immediately follows this conclusion in Professor Taussig's commendably cautious article: "At this point, there is no need to repeat all the qualifications of this result spread amply throughout the body of the paper."[13]

Professor Taussig does, indeed, sprinkle qualifications throughout the body of his article:

. . . Unfortunately, the tax-return data used in this study allow only a poor approximation of the ideal income measure. . . . The omission [of many

---

[11] Taussig MIT, pp. 93-94:
The quantity measured will be the difference between what is actually given (as reported on tax returns), and what would be given under the hypothetical situation in which the individual's tax liability and disposable income gross of contributions were held constant by simultaneously removing the deductibility provision and paying a lump-sum subsidy [presumably exempt from tax] exactly equal to the tax equivalent (marginal tax rate × deductible contributions) of the individual's deductible gifts. If this latter requirement seems too unrealistically strict, remember that the equivalent result could be brought about by at the same time removing the deductibility provision and very carefully designing a general tax reduction that brings about the same result as the lump-sum subsidy described above.
[12] Taussig NTJ, p. 16. To be more explicit, Taussig found no statistically significant incentive effect in income classes below $100,000 of adjusted gross income (consisting of two classes, viz., $0 to $25,000, and $25,000 to $100,000); only for incomes above $100,000 was an incentive effect reflected by his analysis. In absolute terms, the $2.5 billion of revenue lost by the deduction in 1962 is said by Taussig MIT, pp. 185-86, to have accounted for as little as $57 million of charitable contributions; in Taussig NTJ, p. 17, the estimate is 2 to 3 percent of total giving (i.e., $150 to $225 million, of an aggregate of $7.52 billion).
[13] Taussig NTJ, p. 17.
The policy recommendations in Taussig NTJ are quite bland, suggesting a disinclination to put much weight on the study's findings, viz., "the incomplete results cited in this paper do tend to lend some support to recent proposals to place a 3 percent floor under deductible contributions"; "a more effective policy mix would be a tax credit of from 50 to 75 percent, combined with a 3 percent floor and the present 30 percent of AGI ceiling." (I do not understand the rationale of the ceiling; the study does not suggest that the most generous givers are unresponsive to an incentive after they reach 30 percent of AGI.) With the mild proposals of Taussig NTJ, compare Taussig MIT, p. 198; after discussing a 3 percent floor on a tax credit: "This author would favor the alternative of doing away entirely with the present deduction. . . . The basic simplicity of outright repeal of the deduction is very appealing. With one simple stroke, the personal income tax could be transformed into a much better tax. Such a step would seem to be an indispensable part of any worthwhile general tax reform."

items] . . . impairs the reliability and usefulness of results . . . more sophisticated concepts . . . could not be used in our analysis. (p. 5)

. . . Some difficult problems in the reliability of these results need careful
discussion. . . . (p. 6)

. . . the difficulties involved in constructing this variable adequately from
the items available on tax returns. . . . (p. 7)

. . . the possibility that the incentive effect [of the deduction] is masked
by the more significant variance associated with different tax schedules must
be acknowledged. (p. 8)

. . . Unfortunately, . . . the problem of the proper treatment of capital
gains . . . introduces biases that cannot be satisfactorily removed. . . . The
estimates of income elasticities in these high income classes are certainly
biased. . . . Estimates of the marginal tax rate elasticities may also be biased.
. . . (p. 8)

. . . it seems a fair, if discouraging, judgment that the findings are sug-
gestive but of weak reliability. . . . [various factors] all tend to cast doubt on
the validity of the estimates of the incentive effect. . . . (p. 9)

Beyond the problems already discussed, any estimate of the total incentive
effect drawn from regression analysis results is open to the objection. . . .
(p. 9, n. 13)

Assume, for the following calculations, that all deductions in the personal
income tax other than the contributions deduction are "true" expense items
and serve the purpose of properly refining the concept of net income. Ad-
mittedly, such an assumption does not stand up to close scrutiny. . . . (p. 13)

. . . Two points should be clearly recognized before reading too much
significance into these results. . . . (p. 14)

. . . This assumption is . . . badly out of date. . . . For lack of a better
guess . . . , the same assumption is reluctantly repeated here.

. . . This assumption is open to criticism, again on the grounds of realism.
(pp. 15-16, n. 16)

The evidence presented in this paper, even if it were not subject to many
serious qualifications, is not as good as we might like for policy decisons. . . .
(p. 19).

Taussig does not attempt to estimate the cumulative effect, in
amount or even in direction, of these limitations, but it is hard to
see how they could do much to *reduce* his low estimate of the deduction's efficiency, unless we are to believe that it had no effect
whatsoever or that it actually discouraged donors.

The process of pruning and discarding Taussig's reservations
when citing his study to support such major policy recommendations as repeal of the tax deduction and its replacement by a system of matching grants is reminiscent of the Pentagon Papers,
which illustrated the same tendency to ignore anything that cannot be quantified, and then to eliminate any qualitative reservations about the naked numbers as prior studies are summarized

and then summaries of the summaries are passed on to the policy makers. The same latitudinarian use of evidence is reflected by the frequent citation of studies by Kahn and Vickrey, as though they were independent and cumulative buttresses to Taussig's conclusions, though Taussig himself, after describing their studies, concluded that "no useful information presently [as of 1965] exists on the allocation or incentive effect of the contributions deduction."[14] One is tempted to suggest, paraphrasing the title of a recent book, that this mode of analysis is characteristic of those wonderful folks who gave you Viet Nam.

My conviction about the risk of building too heavily on Taussig's study is buttressed by the fact that two subsequent studies traversing the same ground, published in 1968 and 1970 by Professor R. A. Schwartz, of New York University, conclude that "corporate giving [to charities] clearly appears to be price elastic" and that the same can be said of contributions by individuals.[15] Professor Schwartz's studies (finding price elasticities "considerably greater" than Taussig's) confirm the conventional view that a taxpayer who can transfer $1 to his favorite charity at a cost to himself of only 50 cents will be much more inclined to make the gift than one who must lay out a full $1 to transfer that amount. There may be weaknesses in Schwartz's methodology or statistical base, but I know of no effort by the critics of the tax deduction to point them out.

Indeed, even those who profess faith in Taussig's conclusions seem simultaneously to accept the conventional view that the deduction has a powerful incentive effect. At any rate, I do not see any other explanation for the fact that they continue to describe the deduction as a vast governmental "subsidy" to charitable institutions in the teeth of Taussig's conclusion in 1962 that the deduction reduced federal revenue by $2.5 billion, but increased

---

[14] Taussig MIT, p. 87. See also *ibid.*, p. 60 ("weak and inconclusive") and p. 151 ("Vickrey's conclusion of marked regressivity seems extremely dubious").

[15] R. A. Schwartz, "Corporate Philanthropic Contributions," *The Journal of Finance,* 23 (June, 1968), 479-97; R. A. Schwartz, "Personal Philanthropic Contributions," *Journal of Political Economy,* 78 (November-December, 1970), 1264-91. Schwartz's articles, like Taussig's, contain many caveats; but I have not quoted them here; since the authors of the policy recommendations that I am discussing have not taken any account of Schwartz's work, they cannot be accused of disregarding his warnings.

charitable contributions by only $57 million.[16] The same dollar of public money, after all, cannot be both a windfall to donors and a subsidy to their donees.

"INEQUITY"

I should now like to discuss the question of "vertical equity," illustrated by X and Y, who give the same amount to charity but get different tax allowances for their gifts because X has more adjusted gross income than Y and hence is subject to a higher marginal tax rate. It is asserted that X is thereby given an "upside-down" subsidy, because his deduction is "worth more" than Y's. In advancing this argument, the deduction's critics accept the theory that it subsidizes the donors, although, as I have pointed out, they sometimes prefer the theory that the subsidy goes to the donees.

The first point to be made about this disparity between X and Y is that it may be entirely harmonious with—indeed, required by—the criterion of efficiency that is usually put forth with equal fervor by those who criticize "upside-down" subsidies. Suppose, for example, it falls out that low-income taxpayers customarily put a dollar a week in their church's collection plate, and would not be influenced by changes in the tax system to increase or decrease their gifts, but that high-bracket taxpayers are very responsive to tax allowances.

On this set of behavioral assumptions or findings, the criterion of "efficiency" would dictate the elimination of tax allowances for low-income taxpayers and the preservation or liberalization of the allowances for high-income taxpayers. To maximize efficiency in this instance, then, we should not narrow the gap between X and Y, but broaden it. I need not go this far, however, to make the point I have in mind. It is that "efficiency" and "equity" are separate criteria, which are quite unlikely to coincide in their operational consequences.

Moreover, I find it ironic that not so long ago, some of my colleagues in the income tax business were arguing that tax preferences, including the personal deductions, must be extirpated so

---

[16] Taussig MIT, pp. 185-86.

that progression in the rate schedule could be moderated, or even replaced by a flat rate.[17] Having been denounced as an obstructionist in that campaign, I am now confronted by the assertion that these deductions must be repealed because they keep us from getting, rather than getting rid of, progression. And—unless I am the victim of combat fatigue—the new battle cry seems to come from some of the same soldiers who used to fight under the old banner. A second irony in this new-found passion for progression is that it is often coupled with specific proposals for replacing the tax deduction with matching grants for higher education, while little or nothing is said about grants to churches. Since it is quite clear that education is the favorite charity of the rich, while religion is the refuge of the poor, the matching grant concept seems to be lopsided, or even—shall I use the ultimate calumny?—"upside-down."[18]

However fickle its own advocates may be, however, I should like to grapple directly with the assertion that a deduction for charitable contributions is inconsistent with "society's judgment that [the federal income tax] should be progressive."[19] To begin with, this description of "society's judgment" seems to confuse hopes with reality. ("If wishes were horses, beggars would ride.") The qualifications and exceptions with which the Code is riddled belie the claim that we have made a strong commitment to progression *as such,* or that the differential impact of tax deductions is a shameful betrayal of a national ideal. What Congress has enacted is a progressive structure *with deductions;* you cannot hold up one as the authentic voice of the people, and condemn the other as a craven surrender to special privilege. (If put to a vote, would naked progression command more support than the charitable

---

[17] See Galvin, *op. cit.;* see also Boris I. Bittker and Charles O. Galvin, *The Income Tax: How Progressive Should It Be?* Washington: American Enterprise Institute for Public Policy Research, 1969, 184 p.

[18] Professor McDaniel, for example, proposes dollar-for-dollar matching grants for taxpayers giving more than 10 percent of their income to charity, with a sliding scale of less generous grants if the ratio of contributions to income is less than 10 percent. Since the 1962 ratio of contributions to adjusted gross income was less than 5 percent, on average, for all AGI classes below $200,000 (Taussig MIT, Table 3), this formula for matching grants might be even more regressive than the tax deduction of existing law is accused of being.

[19] McDaniel, *op. cit.,* p. 870.

deduction?) A rate schedule that is itself the product of compromise and judgment—born of experience rather than logic—
cannot be turned into a standard by which the "logic" of deductions can be judged. With equal if not greater warrant, one might
argue that the durable and central features of the Code are its deductions, and that progression is secondary and expendable.

I would myself prefer a more progressive rate structure than
Congress has seen fit to enact, but I see no inconsistency in simultaneously favoring deductions or other allowances for a variety of
specified expenditures, misfortunes, transactions, and other events
in the life of the taxpayer. Given a need for additional revenue,
for example, I would much prefer an increase in progression rather than a repeal of the deduction for charitable contributions.

Approaching the problem from a different angle, I know of
nothing in "tax logic" or in the theory of progression that requires
the top marginal rate on taxable income to be 70 percent rather
than 80 percent or 60 percent, or that requires today's rates to be
maintained for the indefinite future. Since there is nothing sac-
rosanct about the width of any given income bracket, the marginal
rate applicable to it, or the number of percentage points between
one marginal rate and another, I can see no valid objection, in the
name of progression, to the modest step of cutting the marginal
and effective rates for a selected group of taxpayers (viz., charitable
donors), by granting them a deduction for their contributions.
This need not entail *any* narrowing of the gap in effective rates between rich and poor taxpayers, since the loss in revenue from the
deduction can be recouped by increasing the rates on the very
same adjusted gross income classes that enjoy the deduction. To
illustrate the point with a simple example, assume a reformed
Code with no personal deductions; with only two classes of taxpayers, those with zero to $10,000 of adjusted gross income, and
those with over $10,000; and with rates of 14 percent on taxable
income up to $10,000 and 70 percent on taxable income above
$10,000. The introduction into this hypothetical state of affairs of
a deduction that would be employed *solely* by the rich (e.g., for
contributions to private foundations), would not necessarily alter
the disparity between the effective rate on rich taxpayers and that
on poor taxpayers—because the revenue lost by the new deduction

could be recovered by increasing the marginal rate on income over $10,000.

As respects the charitable contribution deduction of existing law, there is still another point to be made in refutation of the claim that it is inconsistent with progression, viz., that it may well have the effect of increasing progression, by transferring funds from rich taxpayers to those in more moderate circumstances. Our information about the financial status of those who benefit from charitable contributions is meager, but it supports the tentative hypothesis that gifts by low-income taxpayers go primarily to the churches of which they are themselves members, thus effecting little redistribution, but that rich taxpayers contribute heavily to private colleges and universities (both directly, and through private foundations), whose student bodies, though not poor, are likely to be drawn—increasingly, these days—from families with far less income than their benefactors. Though the amounts donated by upper-bracket taxpayers are smaller, gifts to community chests, the Red Cross, hospitals, and similar social welfare agencies probably generate an even greater degree of redistribution. I would add museums, art galleries, symphony orchestras, and other cultural institutions to this list; I am familiar with—but do not accept—the assertion that, since the public has not seen fit to support them with governmental funds, they must be dismissed as mere playthings of the rich.

I might summarize my comments on the barrage of recent criticism of the deduction for charitable contributions as follows:

1. The assertion that a deduction for charitable contributions is inconsistent or incompatible with a proper measure of taxable income is devoid of merit.

2. We know too little, other than by intuition, about the incentive effect of the deduction to justify its repeal or major overhaul on grounds of inefficiency.

3. As to "vertical equity," there is no necessary inconsistency between the deduction and a progressive rate structure, and if there were, this criterion might conflict with the criterion of "efficiency."

4. A system of matching grants would be a poor substitute for the deduction, but the proposal independently faces such serious constitutional and political obstacles that it can in any event be regarded as a dead end.

Case for Charitable Deduction

I have discussed the criticisms of the deduction for charitable contributions at some length because they represent the considered judgment of eminent authorities, which have not previously, to my knowledge, been subjected to detailed examination. As a result, however, I have little time to make an affirmative case for the deduction, and will move very rapidly. In doing so, I will avoid repeating or paraphrasing the conventional arguments in support of the deduction, but will offer for consideration several other arguments that, in my view, have not received the attention they deserve.[20]

First, charitable contributions can often be properly viewed as business expenses, akin to advertising and public relations, which should be deducted from gross income if the taxpayer's net income is to be properly measured. This is certainly true of much, if not most, corporate philanthropy; quite aside from such familiar donees as the local community chest, business corporations are being pressed to support a wide range of charitable institutions, and they disregard this pressure at their peril. A business nexus is also often present in the case of contributions by partnerships and proprietorships and even by employees. For example, contributions to the community chest by employees who are solicited at work by fellow employees and supervisors, often released from their regular business activity for the purpose, are sometimes not very different from union dues and subscriptions to trade publications.

The fact that charitable contributions may serve a business purpose is acknowledged, albeit backhandedly, by the history of section 162 (b), enacted in 1938 and enlarged in its coverage in 1954, which forbids charitable contributions to be deducted as business expenses. Until 1936, corporations could deduct gifts to charities *only* if they qualified as business expenses, and there is a small but interesting body of law on the requisites of satisfying this condi-

---

[20] The remainder of this article is a slightly revised version of comments that I made at a 1966 conference at Airlie House, the proceedings of which were published in American Alumni Council, *Taxation and Education*, Washington, 1966. An unpublished manuscript by my colleague, Professor John Simon, includes a sympathetic but critical examination of these suggestions, together with his own penetrating analysis of the entire range of public policy issues posed by public aid to private philanthropy.

tion. In 1936, corporations were relieved of this condition by an amendment to what is now section 170, allowing contributions to be deducted up to 5 percent of corporate taxable income. Since section 170 was not explicitly designated as the sole route to a corporate deduction, however, the possibility remained that contributions in excess of the 5 percent limit could continue to be deducted as business expenses, if they could meet the pre-1936 requirement of a close nexus with the corporation's business activities. To close off this possibility, Congress enacted section 162 (b) in 1938, forbidding corporations to deduct "any [charitable] contribution or gift" as a business expense. In 1954, to put individuals and corporations on a plane of equality, section 162 (b) was expanded to cover all taxpayers.

In short, the very existence of section 162 (b) is a reminder of the business context in which some charitable contributions— by individuals and partnerships, as well as corporations—are made. Even today, a business expense deduction is allowable if the transfer to a charitable organization can avoid being characterized as a "contribution or gift" or if the recipient does not qualify under section 170 (e.g., a foreign charity).[21]

The outside boundaries of the concept of "corporate social responsibility" are still unclear,[22] but it is obvious that we have moved a long way since the thirties, when the propriety of corporate charitable contributions of a type and scale that are now routine was the subject of intense debate. It is equally clear, at least to me, that if Congress had not intervened in 1936 and 1938 to restrict the deductibility of corporate contributions under section 162, the judge-made law in this area would have kept pace with changing conceptions of the stake of business in a healthy social environment, with the result that corporate charitable contributions (and, through a "trickle-down" or fallout process, some contributions by individuals and partnerships as well) would be

---

[21] See Treas. Reg. §1.162-15; Marquis v. Commissioner, 49 T.C. 695 (1968) (payments to charitable organizations with which taxpayer, a travel agent, did business); B. Manischewitz Co. v. Commissioner, 10 T.C. 1139 (1948) (foreign religious seminary); Mertens, *Law of Federal Income Taxation*, §§25.114-25.119.

[22] For a comprehensive review, see Phillip I. Blumberg, "Corporate Responsibility and the Social Crisis," *Boston University Law Review*, 50 (Spring, 1970), 157-210.

routinely recognized as legitimate business expenses. Indeed, businessmen regularly deduct (with no likelihood, in my opinion, of successful challenge by the Internal Revenue Service) the expense of special minority training programs, uncompensated services to community organizations, and the like—even if their potential contribution to business profits is speculative and distant, and the motivation is identical with that underlying charitable contributions. It is even possible that section 162 (b), by denying a tax deduction for contributions serving the same business and social functions, has the effect of pushing businesses down more costly and less efficient routes to these objectives.

Secondly, there is another nonvoluntary aspect of charitable giving in our society, stemming from a conviction that charitable functions have a claim of very high priority on one's resources. The weight of this claim varies from person to person, and also with the kind of organization that is soliciting the gift. In the extreme case of a member of a religious order, bound by a vow of poverty, it is clear to me that the income he receives from a trust and must pay over to a religious organization under his vow of poverty is properly excluded in calculating his taxable base. In our secular society, few are bound by oaths of poverty, and even the Biblical tithe is more than we contribute on average. Nevertheless, charitable contributions represent a claim of such a high priority that, in my view, a case can be made for excluding them in determining the amount of income at the voluntary disposal of the taxpayer in question. I would offer two analogies. To the economist, the amount that one pays in alimony is a belated payment for pleasure enjoyed long ago, so that it is just a consumption expenditure. Despite this, the husband is allowed to deduct alimony payments. To be sure, the amounts deducted by the husband are taxed to the ex-wife, but the theory of the deduction (which is granted whether the ex-wife's tax rate is higher or lower, and even if she has offsetting losses or is a nontaxable nonresident alien, etc.) is the husband's inability to use the funds as he chooses. Similarly, section 73 of the Code permits parents to exclude their children's earnings from their gross income, even if the parents are entitled to the earnings under state law. In effect, section 73 subordinates legal rights to the moral obligation that many parents feel to earmark their children's earnings rather than use them as part of the family's general resources.[23]

A third buttress to the deductibility of charitable contributions can be built on the fact that some charities rely very heavily upon the unpaid services of donors (e.g., the Boy Scouts and the Red Cross). Side by side with taxpayers who can satisfy their charitable impulses by making a contribution of their time (from which they report no imputed income), are others who feel the same charitable impulse, but must discharge their moral obligation by contributing cash or property. This raises a question of equity as between these two classes of taxpayers, and a similar question of equity between charitable purposes that can be advanced by the unpaid services of their members and those that depend upon gifts of money and property. The problem of nontaxable imputed income may not be susceptible to a generalized solution, but the deduction for charitable contributions provides an equitable solution in this limited area. A related point is that of two charitably minded persons, one may be able to satisfy his impulse by a transfer of inherited or accumulated property; once he has made his gift, whether in trust or outright, the income from that property is thereafter devoted to the charitable purpose and never again shows up in his tax return. The second person must rely upon contributions out of current earnings to discharge his moral obligation. The deduction helps to equalize their circumstances; its repeal would, in my opinion, create an inequitable disparity between them.

Next, I should like to offer a defense of the deduction even if it turns out to be "inefficient," failing to operate effectively as an incentive to private philanthropy, viz., that something can be said for rewarding activities that in a certain sense are selfless, even if the reward serves no incentive function. I am quite aware of the fact that a contribution to charity may serve some deep-seated need or drive in the donor, just as much as an expenditure on wine, women, and song; and I know that the economist does

---

[23] The announced reason for section 73 was the divergence and complexity of state law, previously controlling in determining whether the child or the parent was required to report the income. S. Rept. No. 885, 78th Cong., 2d Sess. (1944), reprinted in 1944 C.B. 858, at 876-77. But geographical uniformity could have been achieved as readily by requiring the parent to report the income as by imposing this responsibility on the child; either way, some state laws had to be disregarded.

not like to distinguish among the various things on which people choose to spend their money. As previously noted, however, a system of matching grants would be no more "neutral" vis-à-vis the taxpayer's expenditures than the tax deduction of existing law. And, if we were to ask whether Nobel Prizes elicit contributions to nuclear physics or to literature, no doubt the answer would be that they have no significant "incentive" effect. But I do not think life would be enriched by eliminating them and parceling out a few dollars to every educational institution in the world. What has been quite notable about the Peace Corps is the almost unanimous feeling that it provides a model and holds up an ideal of public service. Does not this alone justify the expenditure? What I am suggesting, to return to the deduction for charitable contributions, is that it need not stand or fall on its efficiency. Moreover, since its incentive effect is still veiled in uncertainty, the alleged "waste" is at worst speculative, and there are favorable offsetting externalities.

Finally, I would argue that the deduction can be viewed as a mechanism for permitting the taxpayer to direct, within modest limits, the social functions to be supported by his tax payments. We have heard much in recent years of alienation, discontent with bureaucracy, and of the citizen's inability to exert influence over governmental activity. It has often been asserted—with good reason, in my opinion—that voluntary nonprofit agencies under private control provide an antidote to the citizen's feeling that he is ineffectual and powerless, at the mercy of big business and big government. It has, therefore, been customary to defend tax exemption for these organizations and deductions for their benefactors as enhancing their ability to function as independent, decentralized centers of power. Of at least equal importance, in my view, is the fact that the deduction gives the taxpayer a chance to divert funds that would otherwise be spent as Washington determines, and to allocate them to other socially approved functions. One need not be an anarchist to applaud the modest opportunity that this gives the citizen to control the use of funds that will in any event be taken from him.[24]

---

[24] Another instance is President Kennedy's 1963 proposal for a credit for political contributions to national campaigns (up to $10 per taxpayer, $20 on a joint return) or a deduction (up to $500), an idea that is embodied in a more restricted form in the current tax bill.

What I am suggesting is that the psychological gap between the student who refuses to pay the tax on long distance telephone calls because it was levied to finance the Viet Nam war, and his parents who feel that they have been deprived of control over their destinies, may not be as broad as we sometimes think. William James sought for a "moral equivalent of war" that could tap the martial virtues of discipline, vigor, and self-sacrifice without violence. Perhaps the deduction for charitable contributions serves as a similar escape hatch—as the older generation's substitute for civil disobedience, or, pursuing the military analogy, for alternative civilian public service by conscientous objectors to military training. In a less provocative vein, I remind you that Mr. Justice Holmes liked—or at least said that he liked—to pay taxes, because he bought civilization with them. For those who live in another day, and do not want quite as much of today's civilization as is offered, perhaps the deductibility of charitable contributions provides a constructive alternative.

RECOMMENDATIONS

Against this background, I offer the following recommendations for legislative change in the deduction for charitable contributions.

First, repeal of the percentage limits on the deduction. I believe in having as much of a good thing as possible, and really do not understand—save as a compromise between those who believe in a deduction and those who would repeal it—these limits. If a taxpayer contributes 100 percent of his income to charities, it is preposterous to suggest that his character will suffer if he does not pay "some" amount in taxes.[25] For those who fear that we will be unable to carry on as a nation if everyone adopts the practice of giving all of his income to charities. I suggest that there are greater dangers on the fiscal horizon to which they could turn their attention with profit.

---

[25] In my view, the unlimited charitable deduction of section 170 (b) (1) (C), now being phased out by section 170 (g), was unjustly criticized. Though this is not the place for a funeral oration, it is at least appropriate to note that it should have received high marks for "efficiency," since in effect the taxpayer had to take a big leap to get over the otherwise nondeductible area that extended from 30 percent of adjusted gross income to 90 percent.

Second, repeal of section 162 (b), which now prevents taxpayers from deducting charitable contributions as business expenses. Given the pressures on business taxpayers to contribute to community chests, local hospitals, educational and cultural institutions, and other nonprofit agencies, I see no reason why they should arbitrarily be deprived of the right to establish that their gifts have a business motivation, comparable to advertising and public relations expenses. Rather than prefer conventional advertising over charitable benefactions by allowing only the former to be deducted, my policy preference would be just the reverse; but I am willing to compromise on "neutrality" in applying section 162. This measure would of course be unnecessary if my first recommendation (removal of section 170's percentage limits) were adopted. If there is an administrative problem in separating business-motivated contributions from nonbusiness ones, that can be dealt with when it proves to be more than a figment of the imagination, by statutory guidelines, administrative rules of thumb, percentage limitations, specification, and so on.

Third, enactment of a modest floor, permitting the taxpayer to deduct contributions only if they exceed this amount. I am prepared to believe that a modest amount of charitable contributions would be forthcoming regardless of the deduction, so that a "floor" related to the taxpayer's income (on the model of the deduction for medical expenses) would contribute to administrative simplicity without significantly impairing the incentive effect of the deduction. (I would exempt contributions that can qualify as business expenses from the floor if section 162 (b) is repealed.) Moreover, the reasons leading to my approval of the deduction are more applicable to the taxpayer who goes an extra mile than to the one who stops at the end of the first lap. I would not insist on an above-average contribution, however, but would instead fix the floor so as to exclude, say, the least generous 10 or 20 percent of currently itemizing taxpayers. Setting this floor at 3 percent, a figure that has been supported by others in the past, is plausible, though the level probably ought to be reconsidered in the light of the revised limits on the standard deduction.

Fourth, re-examination of the deductibility of the fair market value of appreciated capital assets, without recognizing the gain, only in the context of general realization of appreciation by gift and at death. Commenting on the taxpayer's right to deduct the fair market value of appreciated capital assets, without recognizing the gain, critics usually compare the taxpayer who sells his capital assets with the one who contributes them to a charity. Aside from the fact that this comparison does not in any event lead irresistibly to the usual conclusion that this state of affairs is intolerable, it is deficient in disregarding the taxpayer's third alternative, viz., an intrafamily transfer of the property by gift or at death without recognizing the gain. While this possibility remains, I see no burning need for a change in the rules governing charitable contributions of such property. Even then, I would give more weight to the practical consequences of a change, than to its contribution to "tax purity," "tax logic," or definitional elegance.

CHAPTER XVII

AN ALTERNATIVE TO
THE FEDERAL INCOME TAX DEDUCTION
IN SUPPORT OF PRIVATE PHILANTHROPY

PAUL R. McDANIEL
Assistant Professor of Law, Boston College Law School

Should we permit a segment of our society to set up a government of its own to render philanthropic services? The others have no such choice, but must go along with the main stream, and not only carry its own burden, but a little bit more. Our tax laws have given one group a chance to escape that basic burden, to let them make their own determination as to what is in the public good, and to decide how to spend that money.

—Congressman John W. Byrnes*

. . . I just continue to plead for the private enterprise factor, the private initiative factor, in our society, and to me today that requires money. . . .

. . . There must be some incentive to get people to accomplish results that are important to our society. . . . I would say that to me this is a form of incentive, this privilege that you are discussing, to encourage people of means to use their funds in venturesome ways that will be meaningful to our society.

—John D. Rockefeller, 3rd**

INTRODUCTION

THE MOST recent public consideration of the effects and efficiency of the federal income tax deduction for charitable contributions was occasioned by the Tax Reform Act of 1969. The above quotations are from a colloquy during the 1969 House Ways and Means Committee hearings on tax reform. They formed part

---

* *Tax Reform, 1969,* Hearings Before the House Committee on Ways and Means, 91st Congress, 1st Session, Washington: Government Printing Office, 1969, Part 4, p. 1573 (hereafter cited as W & M Hearings).
** W & M Hearings, p. 1574.

of an exchange between the ranking Republican member of the committee and one of America's leading philanthropists. The exchange illustrated the context in which the debate over proposed changes in the rules governing the charitable contributions deduction took place. At one pole: tax inequity, favoritism for the wealthy; at the other: incentive for private involvement, pluralism, the vital contribution of charity to American life.

The polar positions seemingly presented by tax reform and philanthropy were never effectively joined in the debate over the Tax Reform Act of 1969. Predictably, what emerged was a compromise that satisfied neither side. The changes in the charitable contribution deduction merely nibbled at tax reform, and the reforms achieved exacted a very high price in terms of complexity. Charitable organizations and their supporters, on the other hand, appeared to emerge from the process with the strong suspicion that tax reformers neither understood nor appreciated the problems that organized charity faced in dealing with the social issues that confront the nation.

As one participated in the tax reform efforts in 1969, it became apparent that what was needed was an alternative to the charitable contributions deduction—an alternative that would satisfy both the legitimate demand for tax reform and the very real and justified insistence of private philanthropy that its efforts be given financial support and encouragement. That alternative was not available in 1969. The proposal advanced herein is an attempt to begin to fill that vacuum.[1]

Briefly, it is proposed that we should substitute for the charitable contributions deduction a system of direct federal assistance

---

[1] Alternatives to the present deduction system usually take the form of proposals for a tax credit in lieu of the deduction, or placing a floor under allowable deductions. These alternatives alleviate, but do not eliminate, tax inequity. They have been analyzed elsewhere and will not be discussed herein. See, e.g., Richard Goode, *The Individual Income Tax*, Washington: The Brookings Institution, 1964, pp. 172-73; Lawrence M. Stone, "Federal Tax Support of Charities and Other Exempt Organizations: The Need for a National Policy," in University of Southern California Law Center, *Major Tax Planning for 1968*, New York: Matthew Bender & Company, Inc., 1968, pp. 45-47; *Tax Reform Studies and Proposals, U.S. Treasury Department*, Joint Publication, House Committee on Ways and Means and Senate Committee on Finance, 91st Congress, 1st Session, Washington: Government Printing Office, 1969, p. 194; Royal Commission on Taxation (Canada), *Report*, Ottawa, 1966, Volume III, p. 222; C. Harry Kahn, *Personal Deductions in the Federal Income Tax*, National Bureau of Economic Research Fiscal Studies No. 6, Princeton: Princeton University Press, 1960, pp. 87-91.

for private charitable organizations through a matching grant mechanism. Each donor's gift would be matched by a predetermined amount from the government, the federal share to be transmitted directly to the charitable institution of the donor's choice.

Before examining the proposal itself, it is helpful first to look at the arguments advanced for the existing deduction system to determine their implications for an alternative.

SOME ARGUMENTS ADVANCED FOR THE CHARITABLE DEDUCTION— AND THEIR IMPLICATIONS FOR AN ALTERNATIVE

I do not propose in this paper to deal at any length with the inequities in the income tax system that result from granting a deduction for contributions to charity; the purpose of this paper is not to detail the case *against* the charitable contributions deduction. Rather the task is to elicit from the arguments *for* the deduction the functions and purposes that the present tax rule is seen to fulfill by its proponents. It is then possible to evaluate the deduction as to the effectiveness and efficiency with which it achieves these purposes. In short, the arguments in favor of the charitable deduction are here analyzed not for the purpose of refuting them, but to determine whether an alternative system can be proposed to satisfy the demands of philanthropy and tax reform alike.

Repeal of the Charitable Contribution Deduction
Will Reduce Private Giving to Charity

This argument was repeatedly advanced during the 1969 tax reform debate by representatives of charitable institutions.[2] Unfortunately the proposition cast in this form misstates the real problem that concerns charity. The concern of charity is not that *private* giving will be reduced if the deduction is repealed, it is that the *federal government* will reduce the financial support to charity that is currently made available through the deduction. Indeed, it is difficult to see how elimination of the charitable con-

---

[2] See, e.g., Statement of C. Douglas Dillon, in *Tax Reform Act of 1969*, Hearings Before the Senate Committee on Finance, 91st Congress, 1st Session, Washington: Government Printing Office, 1969, Part 4, p. 3342 (hereafter cited as SFC Hearings).

tributions deduction would have an adverse impact on private giving to charity.

The matter can be put this way: The deduction for charitable contributions is simply a mechanism whereby the federal government matches private donations to charity. For example, if a 70 percent bracket taxpayer wishes to give $100 to charity, the deduction system matches a $30 gift by the taxpayer with $70 of federal funds. The taxpayer is denominated the paying agent for the government's share and is given the right to designate where that share will go. The taxpayer writes out only one check to charity; but this does not change the fact that it is in reality two checks—one representing his own private gift of $30, and the other the government's matching contribution of $70. The government settles up with the taxpayer for its share on April 15 of each year.[3] As the following analysis indicates, private giving, as so defined, will not be adversely affected by repeal of the charitable contributions deduction.

Viewing the charitable deduction as a matching grant system using individual taxpayers as paying agents for the government's share enables one to make a clearer evaluation of philanthropy's position with respect to the deduction. For, if the deduction were repealed, the individual donor in the above example would presumably continue to write out his $30 check to charity. This is the amount of private giving that is represented in the transaction; the balance is public support for private charity. Repeal of the charitable deduction should not affect the private portion of the gift at all. Indeed to the extent the donor would write a check in excess of $30, *private* giving would be increased by repeal of the deduction.

This view of the impact of the repeal of the deduction on private giving is entirely consistent with testimony that was presented by philanthropy during consideration of the Tax Reform Act of 1969. For example, the Peterson Commission reported the results of a survey among 85 donors who had each given over

---

[3] The settlement may be made on a more current basis if the taxpayer takes charitable contributions into account in computing his quarterly estimated tax liability. Even for those subject to withholding, section 3402 (m) of the Internal Revenue Code allows some taxpayers to reduce withholding by virtue of the presence of itemized deductions.

$375,000 per year to charity in each of the five years preceding the survey. These donors were asked to state the effect repeal of the deduction would have on their giving to charity. The responses indicated a median reduction in charitable contributions of 75 percent.[4]

This response is within the range that is indicated by the analysis above. Assuming that each of the responding donors in the Peterson survey was potentially in the 70 percent marginal bracket, the survey simply shows that, if the deduction were eliminated, the donors would still be writing out their checks to charity for their own private gifts in approximately the same amount, i.e., the net cost of the gift to them under the present system; they would no longer be serving as paying agents for the government's share. But, as will be seen below, the assumption that high-bracket donors will reduce their donations by 100 percent of the increased tax cost resulting from repeal of the deduction is an extreme one, not justified by verifiable data.

In arguing for retention of the charitable deduction, then, it should be clearly recognized that charitable institutions are not concerned with maintenance of the level of out-of-pocket private giving, but with insuring that federal funds will continue to be available at a level provided through the deduction mechanism. Another example will illustrate this basic point. If charitable organizations were really concerned about the level of private giving, i.e., the amount of after-tax contribution that a donor makes, they might have been expected to be concerned about the imposition of the 10 percent surcharge in 1968. For that act could have caused an actual reduction in private giving. In our example, if the 70 percent donor in 1969 continued to write out his combined private-federal $100 check to charity, he really reduced his private giving from $30 to $23. But charities were unconcerned by this result because the government had increased its share to $77 (note: higher tax rates under the deduction mechanism might induce increased contributions from the high-bracket taxpayer).

The argument for "private giving" is thus really an argument

---

[4] SFC Hearings, p. 6137.

to maintain the government's financial support to charity at a level that will insure that the combined checks going to charity continue to total $100 (in our example). It obscures consideration of the issue to assume that the $100 check written by our hypothetical donor constitutes private giving in its entirety. It is private giving only to the extent it represents his own funds, which the deduction system automatically defines as the net after-tax cost of the gift.

The aspect of the argument that must be accepted by tax reform advocates, however, is that charitable institutions cannot accept a reduction in the combined federal-private check. In 1968, the total amount of contributions to charity by living individuals was some $12.6 billion.[5] Of this amount some $2.4 billion represented federal matching funds through the deduction mechanism as described above.[6] It was part of this latter figure that charities were fearful of losing as a result of reforms proposed in 1969. And they were properly concerned since there was no provision in the tax reform bill that would insure that the government would continue its prior financial support through some alternative mechanism. In short, the proposed changes in the charitable deduction represented a net loss in public funds for charitable institutions.

The first requirement of an alternative system for delivering federal matching funds to charity, then, is that it insure a commitment of federal funds to private charity at least as great as is made available through the present charitable deduction.

On the other hand, charitable institutions must recognize the

---

5 American Association of Fund-Raising Counsel, Inc., *Giving USA*, New York, 1971, p. 14. Giving by living individuals was estimated to be $13.6 billion in 1969 and $14.3 billion in 1970. *Ibid.*, pp. 14, 8. This source allocates only $1.44 billion of giving to those who use the standard deduction. This figure seems low. Kahn, *op. cit.*, p. 59, assumed 17 percent of the standard deduction should be attributed to charitable contributions. This would indicate some $3.7 billion in contributions from persons filing standard deduction returns in 1968. See United States Internal Revenue Service, *Statistics of Income—1968: Individual Income Tax Returns*, Washington: Government Printing Office, 1970, p. 55 (hereafter cited as 1968 SOI).

This paper deals only with donations by living individuals, who account for 77 percent of all charitable contributions. Contributions by corporations, foundations, and bequests account for the remaining 23 percent.

6 Statement of Assistant Secretary of the Treasury Murray L. Weidenbaum in *Changing National Priorities*, Hearings Before the Subcommittee on Economy in Government of the Joint Economic Committee, 91st Congress, 2d Session, Washington: Government Printing Office, 1970, p. 57. The revenue loss from the deduction for fiscal year 1971 is estimated to be $3.75 billion. See Table in Statement of Senator Jacob K. Javits, *Congressional Record* S18764 (daily ed. November 16, 1971).

irrationality of the present deduction as a means of providing the federal matching funds. If charities were unconcerned about the 10 percent surcharge in 1968, it is safe to say that no member of Congress gave a thought to the fact that by imposing this surcharge Congress was increasing its proportionate share of the matching fund system (effected through the charitable deduction) for support of private charity. Conversely, the increase in the standard deduction in 1972 will automatically decrease the federal share for millions of gifts; but again there was no discussion of this fact in congressional consideration of the Revenue Act of 1971. Combined total giving to charity may be unaffected by these actions, but it seems difficult to defend so unknowing an approach to federal spending for the support of charity. Conscious and open congressional action which would insure continued federal financial assistance to charity would appear to be the goal.

Charitable Deduction Is Incentive to Private Giving

The incentive effect of the present deduction as analyzed above is twofold: (1) the government has a standing offer to match the gifts of the donor (the matching percentage to be determined by the donor's tax bracket); (2) the donor can designate the recipient of the federal funds and can control the uses to which those funds will be put if he so desires. In its purely matching aspect, the incentive system involved in the deduction is not dissimilar from the incentive system used by the Ford Foundation in encouraging decentralized theater groups in the United States.

Two questions are raised by the incentive argument: To the extent that there is an incentive effect, what does the deduction look like as an incentive system? What is the extent, efficiency, and effectiveness of the incentive?

Assuming that the deduction operates as an incentive for charitable giving, it is appropriate to analyze its dimensions as an incentive program. So viewed, the first feature that is apparent is that the deduction incentive program is structured so that it can operate as such for at most 30 percent of the taxpayers. This is just another way of saying that the deduction has no incentive effect for the 70 percent of taxpayers who in 1972 will be claiming

177

the standard deduction rather than itemizing deductions,[7] nor for those who file nontaxable returns. If the matching grant provided by the deduction is an incentive to give for the $12,000 wage earner who itemizes his deductions, then it would seem that a similar incentive can and should be provided for the $12,000 per year nonitemizer who gives the same amount to charity.

Further, the incentive effect seems to be triggered for most taxpayers by factors totally unrelated to charitable giving. Based on 1968 data, it appears that over 95 percent of those who will claim charitable deductions in 1972 will do so in amounts constituting less than the allowable standard deduction, i.e., 15 percent of adjusted gross income and $2,000.[8] If the charitable deduction were the only itemized deduction, then, there would be no incentive for these taxpayers to give to charity. Thus, the incentive is conditioned for this overwhelming majority of taxpayers not on the act of charitable giving, but by the taxpayer's status in life as a homeowner, installment purchaser, consumer of durable goods on which local sales taxes are levied, owner of a car, etc. Viewed from the standpoint of charity, it is at least an odd incentive system that says if you own a house, we will give you an incentive to make a charitable contribution; but if you are an average apartment dweller, the incentive is probably not operative.

Finally, the incentive is upside down. Operating as a function of tax brackets, the deduction appears to provide the greatest financial incentive to those who have the least financial need for an incentive. It is presumably less burdensome for a person with $200,000 to give 10 percent of his income to charity than it is for a $12,000 per year wage earner to give the corresponding 10 percent. Yet the incentive through the deduction requires the government to expend $14,000 to obtain $6,000 from the high-bracket taxpayer; but the government is required to expend only $324 to obtain $876 from the wage earner. Or, to put the matter another way, for some reason it is felt that a larger incentive is required to induce the high-income taxpayer to give the same percentage of his income to charity as his lower-income counterpart.

---

[7] United States Congress, Joint Committee on Internal Revenue Taxation, Staff, *General Explanation of the Tax Reform Act of 1969,* Washington: Government Printing Office, 1970, p. 218.
[8] Derived from 1968 SOI, p. 75.

However unusual the contours, proponents of the deduction insist that the federal matching grant is an incentive to private giving.[9] Accepting that proposition, it would then appear that an alternative system could provide an incentive effect through a direct matching system. It would also appear that the erratic nature of the present incentive could be smoothed out by limiting the incentive effect to the act of charitable giving unaffected by other economic activities of the individual taxpayer. And finally, an alternative should provide the same incentive to those who donate similar percentages of their income.

But the critical question for the policy maker at this stage is whether the present matching grant system in fact operates as an incentive to private charitable giving. If it does not, then there is little point in structuring an alternative system to reflect the deduction.

Unfortunately the policy maker does not have a ready answer to the incentive question. Certainly fund raisers for charitable organizations hold to few articles of faith more firmly than that the deduction is a significant incentive to charitable giving.[10] One observer, T. Willard Hunter, relying primarily on survey data, concluded that the charitable deduction did not affect the *fact* of charitable giving, but it did have an impact on the *amount* and *timing* of charitable giving.[11]

Economists who have looked at the problem, however, have generally concluded that the deduction has little, if any, incentive effect. And to the extent there is an incentive effect, the deduction is an inefficient means of achieving the desired result.[12]

How is the policy maker to make a decision when confronted

---

[9] Dillon, *op. cit.*

[10] See, e.g., Statement of John J. Schwartz, Executive Vice President, American Association of Fund-Raising Counsel, Inc., in W & M Hearings, p. 1446.

[11] T. Willard Hunter, *The Tax Climate for Philanthropy*, Washington: American College Public Relations Association, 1968, p. 130.

[12] The most detailed study is set forth in Michael K. Taussig, "Economic Aspects of the Personal Income Tax Treatment of Charitable Contributions," *National Tax Journal*, 20 (March, 1967), 1-19. See an earlier study reaching similar conclusions in Kahn, *op. cit.*, Chapter 4. Similar views were expressed by Professors William S. Vickrey and Melvin I. White in American Alumni Council, *Taxation and Education*, Washington, 1966.

with opposing views from two camps of experts, each with its own expertise? Perhaps we can make a start toward resolving the policy maker's dilemma if we can narrow the area of dispute between the fund raisers and the economists.

The economists' view that there is little incentive effect in the deduction for individuals at the lower end of the income scale seems now to be implicitly accepted by fund raisers as well. If tax considerations played a part in charitable giving by lower-income persons, the institution of the standard deduction in 1942, and the reduction in tax rates and introduction of a minimum standard deduction in 1964, should have produced an adverse impact on charitable giving by such individuals. No such impact can be discerned.[13] In a review of the testimony in 1969 by representatives of charitable organizations, it was the rare fund raiser who still would assert that an increase in the standard deduction would have an adverse impact on charitable giving.[14]

In 1968, some 56 percent of United States taxpayers were thus offered no incentive for charitable giving through the federal tax system. Standard deduction taxpayers generally fell in adjusted gross income (AGI) brackets under $15,000[15] and hence rate brackets below 22 percent. It seems also fair to assume, from the data above, that their counterparts in the same brackets who itemize charitable contributions generally would not reduce charitable giving if the deduction were repealed. If so, the data indicate that no incentive effect is operative for 25.5 million of the 30.1 million returns itemizing the contribution deduction in 1968. Taking the standard deduction into account, the existence of the charitable deduction then had no ascertainable incentive effect on some 67 million out of the 73 million returns filed in 1968.[16] Assuming that standard deduction returns accounted for

13 Taussig, *op. cit.*, p. 6; Kahn, *op. cit.*, p. 71.
14 See, e.g., W & M Hearings, p. 1666. Congressman Byrnes was openly incredulous that a charitable institution would take such a stand: "You would prefer to see most Americans, for whom we are trying to simplify the tax process, continue to tear out their hair keeping their records, still burn the midnight oil making sure they have taken all the deductions to which they are entitled, just because you believe that tax-exempt contributions would be decreased?" W & M Hearings, p. 1668.
15 1968 SOI, p. 55.
16 *Ibid.*

$1.4 billion of giving that year,[17] then, at a minimum, $7.7 billion ($1.4 billion plus $6.3 billion from itemizers below $15,000 AGI) out of the $12.6 billion given to charity by individuals in that year was uninfluenced by the existence of the deduction. Assuming an average 16 percent marginal rate for the lower bracket taxpayers who did itemize, then some $1 billion of the federal charitable "incentive" in 1968 went to taxpayers who needed no incentive to give.

At the other end of the income scale we also seem to find general agreement. Fund raisers and economists alike believe that the tax incentive has its most potent effect on high-bracket taxpayers, although they may differ on the degree of the incentive effect. Taussig's study found an incentive effect only for taxpayers with above $100,000 AGI.[18] This would indicate no incentive effect for taxpayers in brackets below 58-60 percent. Under Taussig's analysis, at 1968 levels, the federal subsidy of $2.4 billion was operative as an inducement for less than 1 percent of all United States taxpayers, who gave about $1.2 billion (or 10 percent) of the total donations by individuals.

To test the efficiency of the incentive even at levels where it is operative, it is essential to know what the donors would have given without the deduction. Taussig's data here indicate a maximum reduction in charitable giving of 40 percent of the increase in taxes resulting from repeal of the deduction.[19] Assuming an average marginal rate of 60 percent for those above $100,000 AGI, some $720 million of the federal incentive in 1968 went to these individuals to obtain at most $288 million (.40 × .60 × $1.2 billion) in contributions in excess of those that would have been given in any event.[20]

We may compare Taussig's conclusions with what the high-bracket donors surveyed by the Peterson Commission say they would do if the deduction were eliminated. It will be recalled

---

[17] American Association of Fund-Raising Counsel, Inc., *op. cit.*, p. 14.

[18] Taussig, *op. cit.*, p. 6, Table I.

[19] *Ibid.* The range is estimated from 24-40 percent.

[20] This is a very conservative conclusion from Taussig's study. In American Alumni Council, *op. cit.*, he indicated that the "efficiency ratio" was about 20:1, i.e., for every $1 spent by the federal government via the deduction, charities received only $.05 in incremental donations. American Alumni Council, *op. cit.*, p. 26.

that the donors expressed their anticipated reduction in terms of the amount of the check that they would expect to write to charity in the absence of the deduction. The median reduction asserted was 75 percent. These donors then were claiming that they would reduce their giving by 100 percent (or more) of the increased taxes resulting from elimination of the deduction. This response is undoubtedly unduly pessimistic.[21] In 1964 the top marginal tax bracket for these donors was reduced from 91 percent to 70 percent. For some high-bracket taxpayers this step tripled the net cost of seeing that $100 goes to charity. But there is no indication of a reduction in giving at anything like the levels indicated by the Peterson Commission survey.[22] Yet for the 70 percent taxpayer removal of the charitable deduction would have about the same percentage effect: it would triple his net cost of insuring $100 for charity, assuming no federal matching funds at all.

While the policy maker may not feel constrained to accept the range of maximum adverse impact observed by Taussig (a reduction only by over-$100,000 AGI individuals of 24-40 percent of their increased taxes resulting from repeal of the deduction), the observable responses (as opposed to survey responses) of donors to tax changes that had impacts similar to repeal of the deduction lead one to reject also the claim that their checks to charity will be reduced on a dollar-for-dollar basis with increased taxes.

Thus far, the rough computations above have accounted for some $9 billion out of the $12.6 billion donated in 1968 ($7.7 billion by taxpayers below $15,000 AGI and $1.2 billion by taxpayers above $100,000 AGI). We have also accounted for approximately $1.75 billion out of the $2.4 billion in revenue expended through the incentive. That $1.75 billion appears to have pro-

---

[21] The discussion here does not consider the effects where gifts of appreciated property are involved. That problem is considered separately under "Problem Areas in the Proposed Alternative."

[22] Individual giving as a percentage of personal income was 1.79 percent in 1969 and 1.79 percent in 1970. As a percentage of disposable personal income, the comparable figures are 2.04 percent in 1964, and 2.09 percent in 1970. Total giving to charity doubled between 1960 and 1970. American Association of Fund-Raising Counsel, Inc., *op. cit.*, p. 30; *U.S. News & World Report*, "Giving in U.S.A.: Now Double 1960," 70 (June 28, 1971), 44. From 1955 to 1968, charitable giving increased by 155 percent compared to an increase in gross national product of 118 percent over the same period. Commission on Foundations and Private Philanthropy, *Foundations, Private Giving and Public Policy*, Chicago: University of Chicago Press, 1970, Appendix V, p. 257.

duced at most $288 million in donations (a generous figure under Taussig's analysis; $720 million under Peterson Commission survey) that would not have otherwise been made.

Turning now to the middle-income group, primarily the 25-50 percent bracket taxpayers, there are also data to indicate that the deduction as an incentive to charitable giving is a distinctly inefficient mechanism. The Treasury Department *Tax Reform Studies and Proposals,* submitted to Congress in early 1969, contained a variety of proposals dealing with the charitable contributions deduction. The most important of these was a recommendation to allow the charitable deduction outside the standard deduction, but subject to a 3 percent floor.[23] This proposal was designed to eliminate the wasteful effects of the deduction for relatively small gifts. But, coupled with an increase in the limit on the deduction to 50 percent of AGI, it was also designed to provide an incentive for giving significant amounts. Of interest here is the Treasury conclusion that the package of proposed changes, while picking up a net $1 billion per year in revenues, would reduce charitable giving by only $100-$300 million per year at most. In other words, for the taxpayers affected, the government was spending $1 billion to obtain at most an extra $300 million in private funds for charity.[24]

Important here is the Treasury assumption with respect to the price effect of eliminating the deduction for some taxpayers and reducing it for others. Treasury economists assumed an "unrealistically high" price effect of 50 percent, i.e., that taxpayers affected by the proposal would reduce charitable giving by one-half of the additional cost.[25] This price effect was significantly higher than any observed by Taussig for high-income taxpayers. But with the application of the effect to middle- and lower-bracket taxpayers, for whom Taussig found no price effect at all, Treasury data still showed a markedly inefficient system of delivering federal dollars to charity.

The following implications for an alternative to the charitable

---

23 *Tax Reform Studies and Proposals, loc. cit.*
24 *Ibid.,* p. 200.
25 *Ibid.,* p. 199.

deduction appear to be warranted by this analysis of the "incentive" argument:

1. There is almost certainly no incentive effect from the deduction at lower income levels; for taxpayers in this group, the deduction is purely a windfall form of sharing by the government. Removal of the deduction will probably leave the level of private contributions from these donors unchanged.

2. In the middle brackets, it is uncertain whether there is an incentive effect, but to the extent there is, the inefficiency of the deduction as an incentive is high.

3. There probably is some incentive effect from the federal matching funds at the highest income levels. However, the incentive is almost certainly an inefficient one. If the goal is to get $100 to charity from a 50 percent bracket taxpayer, the government can reduce its share at least from $50 to $25 and still be assured that the charity will receive $100 (i.e., the donor will reduce his gift by one-half of his increased taxes from repeal of the deduction) in the aggregate. Or, in the alternative, if the government share is held at $50, charity ought to be able to expect a total of $125 from the donor's contribution.

The government in 1968 was willing to commit $2.4 billion to charity ($3.75 billion in 1970). Charitable institutions see this expenditure as an incentive that induces private charitable contributions, at least when coupled with the corollary right of individual donors to name the recipient of the federal funds. For purposes of this analysis, we can accept the argument that a program of federal matching grants will operate as an inducement to greater private giving. But it is submitted that the incentive can be offered in a more efficient and equitable fashion than is possible through the deduction mechanism.

Charitable Deduction Avoids Red Tape Involved in System of Direct Government Expenditures

What is presumably meant by the argument is that there would have been bureaucratic wastage of the $2.4 billion spent in 1968 if, instead of the deduction, additional taxes had been collected by the Internal Revenue Service and then disbursed to charitable institutions. But the argument must be sharpened. For the deduction system *is* a collecting and disbursement system via the filing of federal income tax returns. There are expenses of collection (processing the returns) and of disbursement (auditing the returns to see that the contributions were in fact made in the amounts claimed). The costs of collection and disbursement through the Internal Revenue Service run about $\frac{1}{2}$ of 1 percent.[26] This compares to a range of 2-14 percent for most charities.[27] Therefore, the question is whether a shift to a direct grant system would add more than say $2\frac{1}{2}$ percent to the Internal Revenue Service costs. As long as the grant system is modeled mechanically along the lines of the present deduction system, it would appear that the federal system of support to charity could stay well within the charities' own ratio—which is, I assume, efficient by definition! Indeed a direct grant system would surely reduce the wastage involved in the suspected overreporting of charitable donations at present.[28] Efficiency will thus be enhanced, to the benefit of charitable institutions.

One suspects that this "efficiency argument" is a disguised way of expressing the fear that federal controls will be imposed on funds paid out directly by Treasury checks. We will address this concern below.

Charitable Giving Provides Funds for Activities That Otherwise Would Have To Be Paid for by Increased Taxes

The argument may well be correct, but it does not follow that we should grant a deduction for charitable contributions. Because of the deduction, some American taxpayers paid $2.4 billion in increased taxes in 1968 to provide federal funds to charities. Maintenance of federal support at that level coupled with repeal of the deduction does not mean any increased taxes from the aggregate of United States taxpayers; it merely redistributes the incidence of the $2.4 billion in taxes for charities differently among the taxpaying population. Higher-income taxpayers will bear a larger

---

[26] Statement of Commissioner of Internal Revenue Sheldon S. Cohen, *Hearings on Department of Treasury and Post Office and Executive Office of the President Appropriations for 1968 Before Subcommittee of House Committee on Appropriations*, 90th Congress, 1st Session, Washington: Government Printing Office, 1967, p. 493.

[27] W & M Hearings, p. 1453.

[28] See Taussig in American Alumni Council, *op. cit.*, p. 26, where he estimates that one-fifth of the purported contributions itemized on income tax returns are fictitious.

share of the cost of federal support to charity than they now do. Only if federal support of charity is increased over that provided by the deduction will a higher aggregate tax cost be involved. But so long as the federal share remains at levels presently provided by the deduction, this "substitution" argument can be satisfied: charities will get at least the same amount of total funds; no higher taxes are paid in the aggregate; but there is some redistribution of the tax cost of supporting charity from the less affluent to the more affluent (i.e., the regressive effect of the deduction is eliminated).

Charitable Deduction Promotes Pluralism and Effects Dispersion of Power

Pluralism under the present deduction system is achieved by giving to certain individuals the right to designate how the federal funds for charity will be spent. The choices of these individuals control the uses to which the federal funds will be put, free of governmental directive or control. But the present system confines this kind of pluralism to 30 percent of the taxpaying population. If the present degree of pluralism is good, would our society not be greatly enhanced if the pluralism could be extended to 100 percent of charitable contributors? Or, if it is good to disperse government power over $2.4 billion, why do only 30 percent of the taxpayers get to control the dispersion of funds contributed by all taxpayers?

Proponents of the pluralistic argument seldom face the fact that the charitable deduction mechanism achieves relatively little pluralism. And that pluralism is operative in the most part only for the upper-income individuals in the country. If private control of federal funds provided to charity is good, then is the pluralistic ideal not achieved just as well when a $5,000-a-year wage earner is the designating agent as well as the $250,000-per-year Wall Street lawyer or investment banker?

At this point, some charitable institutions begin losing their enthusiasm for the pluralism argument. For the data show that high-income individuals and low-income individuals do not give to the same charities. Thus, a system that shifted some of the designation power over federal funds from higher-income to lower-income individuals could have an adverse impact on the charities currently favored by the wealthy. Representatives of institutions of higher education, for example, worry about this problem. While 17 percent of all charitable giving in 1970 went to education at all levels,[29] the Peterson Commission survey showed that wealthy donors directed 45 percent of their contributions to higher education.[30] The concern of colleges and universities is that a shift of the power to designate federal funds from the wealthy to the lower-income groups would produce a corresponding shift of funds from higher education to the charities more favored by lower-income individuals, notably religion.[31]

But the argument for pluralism only for upper-income individuals has a decidedly elitist caste to it. And higher education need not necessarily suffer from a shift in paying agents. If lower-income individuals had the right to control the allocation of federal funds for charity, higher education might well receive increased donations from these individuals.

The argument for pluralism has merit, however, and is one that must be taken seriously by any advocate of an alternative system. The argument represents a viewpoint shared by many Americans. We sense intuitively that multiple approaches to problems are desirable; that individuals and organizations outside government can provide programs and ideas that might have difficulty surfacing in the government; and that giving the individual the power to designate the objects of his charitable interests is conducive to achieving these ends.

The proposal set forth below accepts the case for individual control over the federal funds for support of charity. It does not, however, accept the limitations inherent in the deduction mechanism: all, regardless of income, who give to charity will be entitled to designate a predetermined portion of the federal share for the charitable purpose of their choice. Thus the values of pluralism will be preserved, with a decided democratization of the present system.

---

29 American Association of Fund-Raising Counsel, Inc., *op. cit.*, p. 2.
30 SFC Hearings, p. 6136. See also Kahn in American Alumni Council, *op. cit.*, p. 17.
31 Religion received almost 45 percent of all charitable giving in 1970. American Association of Fund-Raising Counsel, Inc., *op. cit.*, p. 2.

Charitable Deduction Insures That Charitable Institutions Will Receive Funds Free of Government Controls Over Their Use

Two concerns are expressed in this argument for the present deduction. The first is a judgment that the federal government will be unwilling to grant directly appropriated funds to charitable institutions with no strings attached. The deduction, however imperfect it might be in other respects, is seen to achieve this end.

To discern the implications of the "government control" argument for an alternative, it is helpful to understand what the argument is not about. It is not by and large an argument for restricted versus unrestricted funds. For example, colleges and universities frequently advance the government control argument, with overtones of academic freedom lurking in the background. But in fact 70 percent of the funds received by higher education from living individuals are restricted as to use.[32]

If this be the case, the "control" argument is not one over the *fact* of control, but over *who* will exercise the control over the federal share. Apparently colleges and universities are more comfortable with control imposed by wealthy donors than by Congress or the Department of Health, Education, and Welfare. It should be noted, however, that the Higher Education Act of 1971 as passed by the House[33] indicates a considerable willingness by Congress to provide general purpose funds to institutions of higher education.

The other aspect of the control argument is a quantitative one. Charitable institutions are fearful of having the federal funds represented by the deduction subjected to the annual appropriations process. The concern here is that, in the battle for allocation of limited funds, charitable institutions will not have the political power to hold these funds for this purpose (the results of the lobbying effort by charities in the Tax Reform Act of 1969 indicate that charities are unduly modest on this point).

---

[32] Council for Financial Aid to Education, *Voluntary Support of Education 1969-1970*, New York, 1971, p. 12; Melvin I. White, "Proper Income Tax Treatment of Deductions for Personal Expenses," in *Tax Revision Compendium*, Compendium of Papers on Broadening the Tax Base Submitted to the House Committee on Ways and Means, Washington: Government Printing Office, 1959, p. 371.

[33] See Title VIII of H.R. 7428, 92d Congress, 1st Session (1971).

But the appropriations process aspect of the argument does not stand up under scrutiny. After all, Congress has examined the charitable deduction with varying degrees of intensity 4 times in the last 17 years.[34] Thus tax appropriations for charity are examined periodically by Congress and adjustments are made in the federal funds that go to charity. The question is whether that examination could go on in a more rational context under a direct expenditure system, even if one decided not to conduct it every year.

The government control argument does, however, teach two lessons for an alternative system. First, donors, rather than the government, must be free to control the objects and uses of funds. Second, fear of adverse effects from the appropriation process must be alleviated perhaps by a permanent appropriation to provide the matching funds (modeled after the appropriation for interest on the national debt). I suspect that budget experts would think that a permanent appropriation probably goes too far; however, an appropriation for a 10-year period would seem to satisfy the dual requirements of periodic budget review and the need for financial certainty by charitable recipients.

Charitable Deduction Is Reward for Those Who Give Up Part of Their Disposable Funds for Purposes That Benefit the Public

Assuming for the moment that the argument is true, the charitable deduction viewed as a reward system for contributions in the public interest has all the peculiarities noted when we examined the deduction as an incentive device. The events that trigger the reward and determine the size appear to have little to do with reward systems as we generally understand them.

The reward theory is presumably based on the assumption that the donor has sacrificed some part of his disposable income for the public good. But if so, why condition the reward not on sacrifice, but on the extent of the donor's other income and deduction-producing activities? Why is John Smith, the apartment dweller earning $10,000 per year, who gives 5 percent of his income to charity

---

[34] Internal Revenue Code of 1954; *Tax Revision Compendium*, Compendium of Papers on Broadening the Tax Base Submitted to the House Committee on Ways and Means, Washington: Government Printing Office, 1959, Volume 1, pp. 365-472; Revenue Act of 1964; Tax Reform Act of 1969.

not entitled to a reward; but a reward is granted to his neighbor Ed Jones, also a $10,000-a-year wage earner but a homeowner (with resulting interest and tax deductions), who may donate only 2 percent of his income to charity? For some reason the $100,000-per-year executive who gives 5 percent of his income to charity is entitled to a reward whereas our friend, Smith, who made at least the same relative sacrifice for the public, is passed by in the rewards ceremony each April 15.

Examples of the oddities of the charitable deduction as a reward system can be endlessly multiplied. But the point here is that if there is to be a reward for charitable giving, the incidence and amount of the reward should bear some rational relationship to the act of charitable giving. The reward should be the same for persons who make a similar sacrifice, however measured. This appears to call for a system that increases the reward as the individual sacrifices a greater proportion of his income to charity.[35]

A Brief Note on Tax Theory and the Charitable Deduction

As noted above, it is not the function of this paper to deal in detail with the issues of tax theory raised by the deduction for charitable contributions. The arguments against the deduction on tax equity grounds are well known and have been detailed elsewhere.[36] A brief summary of the tax equity argument will suffice: expenditures for contributions to charity do not help define net income in economic terms; they constitute consumption expenditures of that income.[37] Granting a deduction for such expenditures therefore permits tax liabilities between persons of identical incomes to vary because of factors unrelated to the production of income. And in a progressive rate system, the benefits of the deduction are distributed regressively up the income scale, thereby

---

[35] I fully realize that the reward-sacrifice problem is more complex than indicated in the text. While the percentage of total income that a person gives to charity is not the only possible measure of "sacrifice" it is more justifiable than the indicia presently utilized in the deduction system.

[36] See, e.g., White, "Proper Income Tax Treatment of Deductions for Personal Expenses," *op. cit.*, p. 370.

[37] Henry C. Simons, *Personal Income Taxation*, Chicago: The University of Chicago Press, 1938, pp. 57-58.

negating in whole or in part the fundamental assumption of a progressive tax system. Internal structural rules produce further inequities in the disparate treatment accorded contributions of cash and appreciated property. From the standpoint of tax reform *alone*, therefore, the solution to the tax equity problems is abolition of the deduction for charitable contributions.

But brief mention of two arguments sometimes advanced in favor of the deduction on theoretical grounds is in order at this point since they bear on the desirability of removing federal support for charity from the tax system.

Charitable Contributions Are to Some Extent Involuntary and Deduction Is Therefore Appropriate[38]

Presumably the involuntary argument is based on an analogy to the deduction for losses suffered by a taxpayer, or to payments of alimony. If so the deduction appears difficult to defend on these grounds. The act of contributing to charity, even under social pressure, seems to have little in common with the financial loss involved in having one's home destroyed by fire. Professor Simons dealt with charitable contributions on the consumption side of his equation, not as an aspect of determining the increase or decrease in net worth. If the charitable contribution is a consumption item, then its involuntary nature is a good deal less clear than expenses for food and clothing, which are nondeductible. The alimony deduction is defended on assignment of income principles in situations where the assignee is generally taxed on the income. Where the assignee is tax exempt, the analogy to the alimony deduction begins to lose force.

The characterization of charitable contributions as voluntary or involuntary seems to be of little assistance in evaluating the deduction as a form of federal financial support for charity. If the federal government is to carry on such a program, the funds should be provided on a neutral basis, i.e., for all private gifts, whether voluntary or involuntary.

---

[38] Boris I. Bittker in American Alumni Council, *op. cit.*, p. 29.

*Charitable Deduction Equalizes Tax Results Between Those Who
Give Money or Property to Charity and Those
Who Donate Services*[39]

This argument is based on the following analysis: Adams, a profit-seeking individual who takes off time from work to give services to charity, should theoretically be treated as having derived income from that activity under the Simons definition of income. He is not, however, perhaps for reasons of administrative convenience. On the other hand, his friend Wilson who keeps working, but donates cash to the same charity, must pay tax on the income he earned. Deductibility of the contribution therefore puts Wilson on the same after-tax position as Adams.

The problem with the above argument is that there are all kinds of nondeductible expenditures for personal services, the performance of which by the individual himself could theoretically give rise to income. For example, shaving myself in the morning could be seen as an income-producing activity, but we do not give my neighbor a deduction for the cost of a shave at the barbershop because of the failure to tax the imputed income involved in my shaving myself. On theoretical grounds what makes the expenditure for charity any different? Nothing that I can see, except a desire to encourage charitable activities more than barbering. And we are then brought back to the question we have been considering of whether the deduction is the best way to achieve the desired goal.

Resort to the donated services situation by proponents of the deduction thus seems less than decisive of the tax equity issue. But in terms of encouraging donation of services to charity the matching grant proposal seems much superior to the tax system. If we desire to encourage volunteer work, then a program of direct federal assistance could match contributions in services just as it could contributions in cash.

A Proposal for a Direct Federal Matching Grant Program for Contributions to Charity

Many commentators have noted the similarity between the charitable contributions deduction and a system of direct federal

---

[39] *Ibid.*

matching grants.[40] Reference is sometimes made to the English matching grant system.[41] But so far as I have been able to discover, there has been little effort in the United States to formulate a model of a direct system of federal support to charity to replace the tax deduction.

The following proposal is set forth not because it represents a definitive statement of what a substitute for the deduction ought necessarily to look like. Rather, it is offered as an illustration of the dimensions of a direct matching grant system that consciously seeks to satisfy the criteria enumerated by charitable institutions and philanthropists as they have argued for retention of the deduction system. Accepting their value judgments—pluralism, incentive to provide giving, no diminution in total funds going to charity, reward for personal sacrifice, and the like—it is submitted that a direct matching grant system can accomplish the goals of private philanthropy better than the present tax deduction.

It is proposed that all gifts to charity by living individuals be matched by a direct federal grant on the following basis:

PERCENTAGE OF "TOTAL INCOME" DONATED	MATCHING FEDERAL GRANT AS PERCENTAGE OF DONATION
Under 2%[42]	5%
2-3	10
3-4	15
4-5	20
5-6	25
6-7	30
7-8	35
8-9	40
9-10	45
Over 10	50

---

[40] See White, "Proper Income Tax Treatment of Deductions for Personal Expenses," op. cit., p. 370; Paul R. McDaniel, "Alternatives to Utilization of the Federal Income Tax System to Meet Social Problems," Boston College Industrial and Commercial Law Review, 11 (June, 1970), 875-77; Stanley S. Surrey, "Federal Income Tax Reform: The Varied Approaches Necessary to Replace Tax Expenditures With Direct Governmental Assistance," Harvard Law Review, 84 (December, 1970), 381-94; Stone, op. cit., pp. 47-48; Gwyneth McGregor, "Charitable Contributions," Canadian Tax Journal, 9 (November-December, 1961), 444.

[41] See Royal Commission on the Taxation of Profits and Income (United Kingdom), Final Report, Cmd. 9474, London, 1955, Chapter 7. The English system is analyzed in Kahn, Personal Deductions in the Federal Income Tax, op. cit., p. 87; McGregor, op. cit., pp. 445-47.

[42] Throughout this paper I have assumed for ease of analysis that all contributions, regardless of size, will be matched. Very small gifts, by their sheer numerical volume, might create an unacceptable administrative burden. If this were found to

The donation base—"total income"—should be federal adjusted gross income increased by the items of tax preference that constitute economic income but are presently excluded from AGI.[43] The percentage of his total income that an individual gives appears to be the proper measure for determining the amount of the federal matching grant. It is consistent both with the "incentive" and the "reward" arguments analyzed above. Adjusted gross income is not an adequate measure because of its erosion by tax preferences. While use of AGI at lower income levels would not present any significant problems (except perhaps for the exclusion of social security benefits), higher-income individuals would be unduly favored by such a base. Data presently available show that higher-income individuals give larger percentages of AGI to charity than do lower-income taxpayers.[44] But these data are surely misleading.[45] Utilization of tax preferences predominates in the high brackets and thus use of AGI as the donation base would produce a higher matching grant for a smaller relative gift by high-bracket taxpayers.

The individual contributor will be allowed to designate the charity or charities that he wishes to receive the matching federal funds. Administratively the system can be effected through the filing of the income tax return form. On a separate schedule, the individual can list his charitable contributions, as he does now. He would compute his "donation base" by adding back to AGI the specified items of tax preferences. The federal matching percentage could then be computed. The individual would designate the charities to receive the federal funds triggered by his gifts, making such allocation between charities as he wished.[46] The amounts for the various charities could be accumulated in ac-

---

be the case, it could be provided that an individual's gifts would be required to exceed a specified minimum to a particular charitable organization in a given year before the matching grant would be triggered.

[43] The Tax Expenditure Budget listing of items would be an appropriate starting point for determining the includible items of tax preference. See Surrey, *op. cit.*, p. 356.

[44] 1968 SOI, p. 75.

[45] Vickrey in American Alumni Council, *op. cit.*, pp. 32-33.

[46] An administrative problem that must be considered further is that the proposal would require filing of returns by some individuals who are not now required to do so for tax purposes, and in addition, some taxpayers claiming the standard deduction will be required to itemize their charitable contributions, if they are to generate the matching grant.

counts for the various tax-exempt organizations by the Internal Revenue Service (which already has an employer identification number for each charity). Periodically the Treasury could issue checks to these organizations for the balance in their respective accounts. As a control, the Internal Revenue Service would be authorized to require verification from a charitable institution that it had in fact received the donations claimed by individual donors.

The organzations qualifying as recipients of the federal matching grants could be the same as those presently qualifying for deductible contributions under section 170 of the Internal Revenue Code. No distinctions in the grant formula should be made based on the nature of the organization. But obviously, Congress may want to look more closely at the present definitions of qualifying organizations—a long overdue action even under the present deduction.[47]

The percentage specified for the federal matching share is set at levels that would have been sufficient to generate approximately the $2.4 billion in revenues spent through the tax deduction system in 1968. As contributions rise, the federal share will automatically increase, as it does under the present system. Appropriations for the matching fund could be made on a 10-year basis. This would appear to be a reasonable balance between the needs of charitable institutions for financial certainty and the interests of the public in periodically reexamining its priorities.

As to present tax rules, the charitable contribution deduction would, of course, be repealed.[48]

EVALUATION OF ALTERNATIVE PROPOSAL IN LIGHT OF ARGUMENTS FOR THE TAX DEDUCTION

Impact on Amounts Received by Charity

The alternative proposed should provide larger amounts of dol-

---

[47] One does wonder whether Congress would put funds directly into private foundations to be perpetually under the control of the creator of the foundation and his own selected trustees. The direct grant model emphasizes the importance of the Treasury proposals to require diversification of foundation management. See *Tax Reform Studies and Proposals, op. cit.,* p. 305.

[48] Contributions by businesses might be deductible under section 162, Internal Revenue Code, subject to the limitations imposed under that section, for example, the limitation as to capital expenditures. See Bittker in American Alumni Council, *op. cit.,* p. 29.

lars than charities have been receiving via the deduction matching grant system. Table 1 is intended to indicate the amounts that could have been expected to have been received by charity in 1968 had the proposed matching grant system been in effect at that time.[49]

The direct matching formula provides approximately $2.5 billion to charity in direct federal matching funds. This compares with $2.4 billion in federal funds provided in the same year by the deduction.

The assumption in Table 1 is that all itemizing donors will reduce the size of the checks they have been writing to charity by 50 percent of the amount of the increased taxes resulting from repeal of the charitable deduction. Based on available data, this seems to be a conservative assumption. Even at AGI levels above $100,000 it substantially exceeds any effect observed by Taussig. It is consistent with the assumption of the 1968 Treasury proposals. And it is rendered more conservative by applying the reduction factor at all AGI levels although it is probable that little if any reduction in private giving will occur at the lower income levels.[50]

From the standpoint of charitable institutions, the formula insures that the federal government share will continue at levels that would be derived from the present deduction. Private giving, defined as the net cost of the donation to the contributor, will increase under the assumptions made in Table 1. For example, on an individual basis, a 60 percent bracket taxpayer who now incurs $40 of the cost of a $100 contribution can be expected to write out a check for $70 under the new system. Private giving from this donor has thus almost doubled. The result is not far from what some wealthy donors themselves have reported they would do fol-

---

[49] The computations in Table 1 are derived from data in 1968 SOI, p. 75. The figures shown are not the result of a computer run and are therefore illustrative only of the effects that might be expected from the proposed system. More sophisticated analysis is required to determine exact effects.

[50] There are actually two simultaneous price effects involved in repealing the deduction and introducing the proposed direct matching grant system. The first effect is the adverse one to charitable giving which is reflected in Table 1. The other effect which should be built in is the positive one resulting from introduction of the matching grant. This latter price effect would offset the adverse price effect from repeal of the deduction to some extent. Omission of the favorable price effect from the computations in Table 1 results in an understatement of the amounts that could be expected from private contributions.

PROJECTION OF CHARITABLE CONTRIBUTIONS IN 1968 UNDER PROPOSED FEDERAL MATCHING GRANT (FMG) SYSTEM

(thousands of dollars)

Adjusted Gross Income Class	Donations under 2%	5% FMG	Donations 2-3%	10% FMG	Donations 3-4%	15% FMG
Under $5,000	$ 43,044	$ 2,152	$ 55,869	$ 5,587	$ 58,171	$ 8,725
$5,000 under $10,000	366,654	18,332	369,687	36,969	338,158	50,724
$10,000 under $15,000	495,402	24,770	462,179	46,218	396,462	59,469
$15,000 under $20,000	256,480	12,824	232,600	23,260	166,360	24,954
$20,000 under $25,000	108,714	5,436	101,043	10,104	78,738	11,811
$25,000 under $30,000	61,063	3,053	51,005	5,100	42,775	6,416
$30,000 under $50,000	111,218	5,561	86,663	8,666	67,169	10,075
$50,000 under $100,000	73,011	3,650	51,310	5,131	44,348	6,652
$100,000 under $200,000	23,746	1,187	13,979	1,398	13,868	2,080
$200,000 under $500,000	8,967	448	5,561	556	4,639	696
$500,000 under $1,000,000	2,608	130	1,621	162	1,721	258
Over $1 million	3,353	168	1,925	192	2,026	304
Total under Proposal	$1,554,260	$77,711	$1,433,442	$143,343	$1,214,435	$182,164
1968 Itemized Donations	$1,651,971 $1,797,817		$1,576,785 $1,645,881		$1,396,599 $1,343,331	

Adjusted Gross Income Class	Donations 4-5%	20% FMG	Donations 5-6%	25% FMG	Donations 6-7%	30% FMG
Under $5,000	$ 62,117	$ 12,423	$ 57,500	$ 14,375	$ 50,812	$ 15,243
$5,000 under $10,000	250,695	50,139	177,279	44,320	138,700	41,610
$10,000 under $15,000	231,600	46,320	161,836	40,459	114,767	34,430
$15,000 under $20,000	113,759	22,752	72,995	18,249	59,641	17,892
$20,000 under $25,000	52,013	10,403	35,907	8,977	25,346	7,664
$25,000 under $30,000	25,676	5,135	20,979	5,245	12,310	3,693
$30,000 under $50,000	53,139	10,628	37,533	9,383	38,199	11,460
$50,000 under $100,000	34,322	6,864	27,998	6,999	22,637	6,791
$100,000 under $200,000	12,066	2,413	10,817	2,704	8,900	2,670
$200,000 under $500,000	5,300	1,060	4,922	1,230	4,682	1,405
$500,000 under $1,000,000	1,716	343	1,488	372	2,072	622
Over $1 million	1,553	311	1,434	358	1,855	556
Total under Proposal	$843,956	$168,791	$610,688	$152,671	$479,921	$149,976
1968 Itemized Donations	$1,012,747 $ 969,952		$763,359 $703,269		$623,897 $554,544	

197

TABLE 1 (continued)

PROJECTION OF CHARITABLE CONTRIBUTIONS IN 1968 UNDER PROPOSED FEDERAL MATCHING GRANT (FMG) SYSTEM

(thousands of dollars)

Adjusted Gross Income Class	Donations 7-8%	35% FMG	Donations 8-9%	40% FMG	Donations 9-10%	45% FMG
Under $5,000	$ 41,435	$ 14,502	$ 40,905	$ 16,362	$ 35,363	$ 15,913
$5,000 under $10,000	105,732	37,006	100,669	40,268	85,574	38,508
$10,000 under $15,000	87,313	30,559	87,639	35,056	74,538	33,542
$15,000 under $20,000	46,004	16,101	37,479	14,992	33,292	14,981
$20,000 under $25,000	20,100	7,035	17,307	6,923	18,959	8,531
$25,000 under $30,000	12,484	4,369	9,438	3,775	6,982	3,142
$30,000 under $50,000	23,501	8,225	16,814	6,726	15,756	7,090
$50,000 under $100,000	19,752	6,913	15,578	6,231	14,019	6,308
$100,000 under $200,000	10,294	3,603	7,577	3,031	7,691	3,461
$200,000 under $500,000	4,456	1,560	4,670	1,868	4,990	2,245
$500,000 under $1,000,000	2,176	762	2,016	806	1,596	718
Over $1 million	2,195	768	1,602	641	1,228	553
Total under Proposal	$375,442	$131,403	$341,694	$136,679	$299,988	$134,992
1968 Itemized Donations	$506,845		$478,373		$434,980	
	$437,404		$394,223		$347,010	

Adjusted Gross Income Class	Donations over 10%	50% FMG	Total under Proposal	Total Itemized Donations (1968)
Under $5,000	$ 323,752	$161,876	$ 1,036,126	$ 831,249
$5,000 under $10,000	513,165	256,582	3,060,771	2,704,678
$10,000 under $15,000	300,051	150,025	2,912,635	2,661,821
$15,000 under $20,000	155,072	77,536	1,417,223	1,339,443
$20,000 under $25,000	71,139	35,569	641,659	617,391
$25,000 under $30,000	45,416	22,708	350,764	341,610
$30,000 under $50,000	134,991	67,495	730,292	739,560
$50,000 under $100,000	184,207	92,103	634,824	665,903
$100,000 under $200,000	176,863	88,431	396,779	414,202
$200,000 under $500,000	171,678	85,839	316,772	333,309
$500,000 under $1,000,000	98,279	49,139	168,605	177,372
Over $1 million	185,883	92,941	299,846	312,389
Total under Proposal	$2,360,496	$1,180,244	$11,966,296	
1968 Itemized Donations	$3,540,740			

lowing repeal of the deduction. According to Hunter's survey, the donors responding indicated a 42 percent decline in giving if the deduction were repealed.[51] These donors, however, were thinking of the contribution in terms of the $100 check now being written to charity. The $58 check the wealthy donors would intuitively expect to write is not too far from the somewhat larger check that Table 1 would indicate.

The aggregate results illustrated in Table 1 bear out this analysis. Private giving, as so defined, would have increased by some $850 million in 1968 under the proposed direct matching formula. Given the demonstrated inefficiency of the deduction system, this figure reflects the anticipated result from the expenditure of the same amount of federal funds in a more efficient fashion.

The important point, however, is that the total amount going to charity can be kept constant even assuming a reduction in charitable giving equal to 100 percent of the increased taxes. As long as the formula is structured to insure a federal matching contribution equal to the revenue gained from repealing the deduction, charitable institutions in the aggregate will receive at least as much as they are receiving under the present deduction system. No data exist to indicate that this extreme response would occur. Therefore it seems reasonable to conclude that the direct matching formula will actually assure funds to charities in amounts in excess of that they now derive from the deduction system.

While the aggregate funds flowing to charity can be expected to increase under the proposals, there may well be a shift in the relative amounts that particular types of recipients receive through private sources. The dollars donated by individuals up to the $20,000 AGI level will generate a substantially greater federal response than under the present deduction system. Therefore, charitable activities favored by these contributors, notably religion and general civic campaigns such as united fund appeals, could well expect an increase in total available funds. Table 1 indicates, for example, that total amounts going to charity from taxpayers in the under-$5,000 AGI class would have increased from $831 million to $1 billion; in the $5,000-$10,000 AGI class, from $2.7

---

51 Hunter, *op. cit.*, p. 117.

billion to $3 billion. Similar increases are reflected in AGI classes up to $25,000.

On the other hand, total contributions to charity from higher-income donors may decrease somewhat under the proposed system. Total giving by over-$100,000 AGI donors in 1968 was $1.24 billion.[52] Table 1 indicates combined contributions from this group under the proposed system of $1.19 billion, a total decrease of only $50 million. This decrease is probably somewhat under-stated, however, as the matching formula is based on "total income," as defined above, rather than on AGI. Nonetheless, the feared decrease from higher bracket individuals from repeal of the deduction seems entirely within manageable proportions even for those charities that rely primarily on contributions from this group.

The reason for this result is to be found in the greater incentive provided for gifts that represent a significant portion of the donor's income. Table 1 shows, as would be expected, that smaller contributions than at present will go to charity from those who make gifts of less than 4 percent of AGI. For gifts amounting to 5 percent or more of AGI, however, Table 1 shows a significant increase in the total giving compared to present contributions. Since the wealthy give a larger percentage of AGI to charity than do lower bracket taxpayers, the progressive incentive effect of the matching grant almost offsets the repeal of the deduction for those high-bracket donors. For example, assume a 70 percent taxpayer has been giving more than 10 percent of his income to charity. Under the assumptions in Table 1 he will reduce his $100 gift to $65 ($30 plus one-half of the $70 tax increase from repeal of the deduction). But with a 50 percent matching grant, his total gift will still amount to $97.50.

As noted earlier, higher education is a charity favored by the wealthy. But as the above analysis indicates, amounts going to higher education even from high-bracket donors would not be substantially reduced. If higher education absorbed one-half of the projected $50 million decrease in cash giving from over-$100,000 AGI donors, the reduction would constitute less than

---

[52] 1968 SOI, p. 75.

2 percent of total gifts to higher education.[53] And, it seems reasonable to expect that the increase in gifts to higher education resulting from the matching of gifts by lower-income donors would substantially offset, or entirely eliminate, this small decrease. On balance, therefore, it would seem that higher education would not experience a significant adverse effect in aggregate cash giving as a result of the proposed change, although its share of total combined private-federal donations might decline relative to other charitable recipients.

In sum, it appears that a direct matching grant system structured along the lines indicated can insure charity that its total combined private-federal funds will not be diminished. Private giving should be increased with the removal of the inefficiency built into the deduction system. If this anticipated reaction occurs, charitable institutions will experience a net increase in combined federal-private support.

The Incentive Effect

As we have seen, the incentive in the present deduction in part consists of the right to designate where the government's matching share will go. The incentive is greater for the high-bracket individual because the deduction system gives him the right to command a greater percentage of federal funds for the object of his charitable interest.

The proposal accepts the assumption that this right to control federal funds does in fact constitute an incentive to give. It extends that incentive to the 70 percent of the taxpayers claiming the standard deduction, who, under the present deduction system, are given none, and to those individuals who incur no tax liability.

The matching grant system also removes the inefficiency inherent in the deduction as an incentive. First, the direct matching grant is triggered by the act of charitable giving itself and by no other factor; hence the wastage involved where taxpayers claim

---

[53] The estimate here disregards the impact on gifts of appreciated property. (See section on "Problem Areas in the Proposed Alternative.")

To keep the matter in perspective, it should be noted that contributions by living individuals accounted for some 46 percent of the total funds donated to higher education in 1969-70. Council for Financial Aid to Education, *op. cit.*, p. 5.

the contributions deduction only because they have other deductions is eliminated. Second, the windfall element is eliminated; only the amount of incentive presumably necessary to elicit the donation is provided.

Further, the proposal is structured to tie increases in the incentive to increased giving. The present deduction system increases the incentive as a function of income, not as a function of increased giving.

The federal government in 1968 spent $2.4 billion in support of private charitable institutions through the deduction. It could have spent this same sum for charity in a manner that would have insured that charity would have received more than the $12.6 billion it derived through individual giving. To put this conclusion another way, the real loser from using the charitable deduction as an incentive device in 1968 was charity, if we assume that the government was prepared to honor its committment to private charity to the full extent of the $2.4 billion. Charity paid for the inefficiency in terms of lower amounts of funds than it otherwise could have had with the same expenditure of federal funds. And I share with charity at this point the view that all society was thus the poorer.

In proposing the alternative outlined above, I assume that the federal government is willing to continue paying to private charitable activities the same amount that it is presently expending through the deduction system. If this assumption is valid—and since Congress has now been shown the effects of the deduction as an expenditure mechanism for 1968-71, I think it is—then charity has only to gain from an alternative that will improve the efficiency of the present incentive device. For improvement in efficiency is just another way of stating that more private dollars will be induced by the same amount of federal funds.

The proposed matching grant, viewed as an incentive, also represents a distinct improvement in equity over the deduction system. As noted above the incentive is extended to all individuals who make contributions to charity. But more, the incentive is equalized as between those who presently get the benefits of the deduction. Use of the matching grant formula outlined above insures that each individual's contribution will be matched on the same basis regardless of his income tax bracket or his deduction-generating economic activities. A person in the 70 percent bracket who contributes 5 percent of his income to charity will trigger the same percentage matching federal grant as does a 14 percent bracket taxpayer who contributes 5 percent of his income to charity.

Pluralism Under the Proposal

The benefits in terms of pluralism are obvious. The direct grant system would expand the potential paying agents for the federal system from 30 percent of the taxpaying population to 100 percent of the population, whether taxpaying or not. Simultaneously, overtones of elitism in the pluralism argument when directed to retention of the charitable deduction are eliminated.

The control aspect of the pluralism argument is also satisfied. Each donor will be entitled to direct the matching federal grant triggered by his contribution to the charity of his choice. Thus, the fund-raising activities of the charities will still be directed to the individual donor, not to the government.

Government Controls

Under the proposal, no greater power is vested in the federal government to control the uses to which the federal funds are put than currently exists under the deduction system.

The long-term appropriation contemplated assures charities that they can plan financially on predictable levels of federal support through the matching grants. Congress has recently begun to place some limitations on certain tax provisions intended as incentives for specific economic actions:[54] a 10-year appropriation, open-ended as to amount in any particular year, would correspond to these limits.

Conclusions as to Overall Effects

The direct matching grant system proposed above appears to satisfy the values that organized philanthropy discerns in the charitable deduction. And in some instances the proposed system

---

[54] Five-year limitations were imposed on the provisions for rapid amortization of pollution control facilities (I.R.C. § 169 (k)), railroad rolling stock (I.R.C. § 184), and coal mine safety equipment (I.R.C. § 187); and low income housing rehabilitation projects (I.R.C. § 167 (k)).

seems to do a much better job of meeting the needs of charities than does the present system. As we enter a decade in which the need of charities for increased funds is even greater, the proposal almost certainly assures increased giving through the private contributor. Accompanying benefits are a numerical increase in the number of contributors who will have an incentive to give and a resulting direct involvement in charitable activities by more people. Efficiency in use of the federal dollar is enhanced and the inequities involved in the present deduction system are substantially eliminated. An area of uncertainty does exist for those charities that rely heavily on giving by high-income individuals who may reduce ther combined private-federal checks to charity, but it does not appear significant in the aggregate.

Problem Areas in the Proposed Alternative
Gifts of Appreciated Property

The foregoing analysis has focused on the charitable contribution made in the form of a cash donation. This approach, in addition to simplifying analysis, appears justified since cash contributions account for some 92 percent of the total charitable contributions.[55]

Nonetheless, some account must be taken of the fact that some donors utilize appreciated property to a significant extent[56] in making their charitable gifts, and some types of charitable institutions rely heavily on such gifts. Of the $1.2 billion in charitable giving by over-$100,000 AGI donors, as much as one-half may have been in the form of noncash donations, some undetermined portion of which represented accrued gain.[57] Higher education, museums, and libraries[58] have a particular interest in this form of charitable giving since, as we have noted, they are the favored charities of the wealthy.

Under present tax rules, generally, the donor who gives appreciated property received both a deduction for the contribution

---

[55] 1966 SOI, p. 50.
[56] SFC Hearings, p. 6136.
[57] See 1966 SOI, p. 50.
[58] SFC Hearings, pp. 2168, 2140, and 6037.

and an exemption from tax on the accrued gain.[59] This latter effect makes the present deduction system even more inefficient when appreciated property is given to charity. The Tax Reform Act of 1969 took steps to deal with the problem where the gain would constitute ordinary income upon sale.[60] But ironically, "reforms" in the capital gains area just made the charitable deduction problem worse where capital assets are transferred. Prior to the 1969 act, the contribution of a capital asset with $100 of appreciation cost the Treasury $95 ($70 from the deduction, $25 in forgiven capital gains tax). But with the repeal of the alternative tax for gains above $50,000, the cost of a gift of the same asset to charity went to $105. When the potential impact of the minimum tax and maximum tax is added in, the cost to the Treasury can now rise to $115.50 to get the same $100 gift that cost only $95 before "tax reform."[61]

How should the proposed matching grant system interact with tax rules on charitable contributions of appreciated property? The simplest solution would appear to be to treat contributions of appreciated property as having a value equal to cost basis for purposes of determining the matching percentage. This solution would correspond to present tax rules with respect to donations of ordinary income property. It would leave the broader issue of whether transfers to charity should constitute realization events to be resolved in the context of proposals that deal with donative transfers of appreciated property generally.[62]

Data are not available to indicate precisely how much of the noncash gifts to charity in 1968 constituted appreciation. If one assumed that one-half of the estimated $600 million in noncash gifts in 1968 by high-bracket donors represented accrued gain, then the federal matching share for those donors might be cor-

---

[59] See generally, Harry J. Rudick and John A. Gray, "Bounty Twice Blessed: Tax Consequences of Gifts of Property to or in Trust for Charity," *Tax Law Review*, 16 (March, 1961), 273-313.

[60] Internal Revenue Code section 170 (e) limits the deduction to the donor's cost basis in such cases. Some limits are also placed on donations of capital gain property to certain kinds of recipients.

[61] See Surrey, *op. cit.*, p. 386, n. 61.

[62] See *Tax Reform Studies and Proposals, op. cit.*, p. 331.

respondingly reduced. (The private share assumed in Table 1 would not be affected since the tax increase would result solely from repeal of the deduction; there would be no change in the tax rules with respect to the appreciation itself.)

On this very rough assumption, the federal matching share for the over-$100,000 AGI group might be reduced from an estimated $300 million to approximately $150 million. If we assume that higher education would bear three-fourths of this amount,[63] it might face a loss of some $120 million from present levels. Taking into account some overlap with the loss in cash giving by the wealthy to higher education predicated above, there might be a net reduction from present gifts to higher education by living high-bracket donors; but the net reduction would still appear to be well under 10 percent of total contributions to higher education.[64] These are rough estimates and probably overstate the impact on higher education. Again, it must be emphasized that the gain in contributions from middle- and lower-income donors could be expected to reduce substantially, or entirely eliminate, this shortfall.

Church-State Relations

The channeling of direct matching grant funds to churches raises the constitutional question: Can Congress provide aid to religion through the tax system but not through a direct grant system modeled on the tax structure?

The Supreme Court has never had occasion to answer the question with respect to the federal tax system. However, it did consider a similar issue in a case involving local property tax exemptions for religious institutions. In *Walz v. Tax Commission of the City of New York*,[65] the Court held that the exemption did not constitute an abridgement of First Amendment rights. But the Court's analysis of tax subsidy versus direct subsidy rivals some of the early New Deal decisions for a display of economic naiveté:

---

[63] SFC Hearings, pp. 2168, 2140, and 6037.
[64] See note 53 *supra*.
[65] 397 U.S. 664 (1970).

Granting tax exemptions to churches necessarily operates to afford an indirect economic benefit and also gives rise to some, but yet a lesser, involvement than taxing them. In analyzing either alternative the questions are whether the involvement is excessive, and whether it is a continuing one calling for official and continuing surveillance leading to an impermissible degree of entanglement. Obviously a direct money subsidy would be a relationship pregnant with involvement and, as with most governmental grant programs, could encompass sustained and detailed administrative relationships for enforcement of statutory or administrative standards, but that is not this case. The hazards of churches supporting government are hardly less in their potential than the hazards of government supporting churches; each relationship carries some involvement rather than the desired insulation and separation. We cannot ignore the instances in history when church support of government led to the kind of involvement we seek to avoid.

The grant of a tax exemption is not sponsorship since the government does not transfer part of its revenue to churches but simply abstains from demanding that the church support the state.

If the justices think that tax preferences involve only "minimal and remote involvement" in the affairs of the beneficiaries of those preferences, they might do well to peruse the pages of the Code dealing with private foundations.

If the consitutional test is really one of the degree of permissible entanglement between religion and the government, and if the present charitable deduction satisfies that test, then a direct grant system can be drafted to satisfy it also.[66] The Supreme Court's assertion that a direct subsidy is more "pregnant with involvement" than a tax subsidy will just not stand up to analysis, even if one resorts to history rather than logic.

---

[66] Although reaching the same result as the majority in *Walz,* Judge Oppenheimer displayed a higher degree of economic sophistication: "Indubitably, religious organizations benefit from the exemption. Economically, they are in the same position as though they paid taxes to the city and state and then received back the amounts paid in the form of direct grants. Moreover, members of the general public pay higher taxes than they would if the exemptions were not in effect; the same amount of revenue must be raised and, by reason of the exemption, the rate paid by non-exempt taxpayers is higher." Murray v. Comptroller of the Treasury, 241 Md. 383, 216 A.2d 897, 906 (1966).

It must be confessed that one who is not a constitutional lawyer is bemused at the Court's concern over payments for such things as bus transportation for parochial school children, when 20 percent of the *total* cost of parochial elementary and secondary education is paid for by the general public through the federal income tax deduction for charitable contributions. See Ernest Bartell, *Costs and Benefits of Catholic Elementary and Secondary Schools,* Notre Dame: University of Notre Dame Press, 1969; John M. Swomley, Jr., "Parochaid and Taxes," *The Christian Century,* 88 (September 1, 1971), 1024-25. On the constitutional issue generally, see Herbert J. Korbel, "Do the Federal Income Tax Laws Involve an 'Establishment of Religion'?" *American Bar Association Journal,* 53 (November, 1967), 1018-24; Harold D. Hammett, "The Homogenized Wall," *American Bar Association Journal,* 53 (October, 1967), 929-36.

Income Effects

It may be suggested that the proposed matching grant system does not fully satisfy equity or distribution of wealth principles. That is to say a wealthy donor can still control a larger *amount* of federal dollars than a lower-income contributor, even if the matching percentage is the same for each.[67] Since the wealthy individual has greater resources from which to make the same percentage gift, the question arises as to whether the federal matching grant should be reduced as income increases by a factor that would reflect this fact, say by the inverse of the taxpayer's marginal rate.

The proposed system does not take this income effect into account. In the first place those who have studied the present tax system have concluded that the income effect has little impact on charitable contributions.[68] I have accepted this conclusion and have accordingly not built it into a direct federal incentive plan. Secondly, if one wants to achieve the desired income effect, it should be done by means other than a system of federal aid to charity, e.g., rate reductions confined to lower-income individuals.

Transition Problems

To enable donors and charities alike to adjust to the new system gradually, it could be phased in over a five-year period of time.[69] The allowable deduction could be decreased by 20 percent each year. Correspondingly, the revenue saved could be allocated to be distributed under the matching grant system. It would also appear appropriate during the transition period to match all gifts in excess of a specified dollar amount, say $10,000, with the top 30 percent grant even though the donor might not

---

[67] Surrey, *op. cit.*, p. 393.
[68] Taussig, *op. cit.*, p. 3; *Tax Reform Studies and Proposals, op. cit.*, p. 198.
[69] The timing of delivery of the federal checks to charities might create an additional first-year transitional problem. The federal check could be paid only after April 15 of year two of the new system because the federal matching share is correlated to personal income reported on the federal income tax returns. Many charities might have expected to have received substantial funds by December 31 of the preceding year (year one of the new system), because of the habit of many donors of making gifts in December under the present deduction system. This problem, if it is one, appears solvable and could be handled, for example, by estimated prepayments of the federal share.

otherwise qualify for that percentage under the regular formula. This special rule would allow time for those charitable institutions that rely on large individual gifts to adjust to the new system without experiencing sharp drops in total donations. The special rule could be justified only as a transition measure, however, and could not equitably be made a part of the permanent matching system.

Conclusion

The matching grant system for federal support of private charitable activities outlined here had its origins in an interest in achieving tax reform. But federal tax reform involving provisions that are directed to nontax objectives can be achieved only by evaluating the demands of the sector of our economic or social life that is being aided by the tax rules, and taking those concerns into account where justified. Alternative direct means of financial assistance may then be conceived which retain the advantages perceived to inhere in the tax mechanism. The system proposed herein tries to achieve that goal in the area of charitable contributions.

CHAPTER XVIII

FEDERAL ENCOURAGEMENT OF PRIVATE GIVING

HENRY AARON
Senior Fellow, The Brookings Institution;
Associate Professor of Economics,
University of Maryland

THE discussion of charitable contributions frequently is overly complicated. I would like to try to reduce it to four basic questions.

PRINCIPLE OF FEDERAL ENCOURAGEMENT

First, should the government allow its revenues to be reduced at the discretion of individual taxpayers? The charitable contribution is clearly an instance in which we do that. A checkoff for political contributions would be another.

I see no objection to this procedure as a matter of principle or in the particular instance of the charitable contribution or any other device for encouraging private giving.

SPECIFICS OF FEDERAL ENCOURAGEMENT

The second question concerns whether the government should spend public resources or allow federal revenues to be reduced to support the purposes covered by this contribution deduction, not as a matter of principle but as a matter of specifics. One consideration in answering this question should be whether some need is now being fulfilled that the government would have to step in and fulfill if private giving were curtailed. One implication of this consideration, however, is that the deduction should be disallowed for purely sectarian religious giving.

Generally speaking, most people wish to see the purposes now covered by the charitable contribution continue to be served in some way and preferably through some kind of individual acts. I differ with respect to the religious contribution, but I recognize that I am part of a minuscule minority view and I would not press it.

I am puzzled, however, that it is possible to seriously defend the constitutionality of the charitable deduction and yet to maintain that a matching grant or a credit perhaps would be judged unconstitutional. There is no logical distinction whatsoever between credits, deductions, and matching grants.

If you name me a deduction, I can give you a matching grant or a credit; it will not take any fancy computer to calculate an equivalent formula or a genius to understand it. In some cases deductions may be simpler, in others, credits or matching grants, but you name the distribution you want and I can give it to you through any one of the three devices. For this reason, it really surpasses my understanding as an economist how the lawyers and courts in general can sustain distinctions among these various tax devices, calling some constitutional and others unconstitutional.

Is the Deduction Effective?

The third question is: Does the charitable contribution deduction encourage giving to eligible recipients and does it provide as much encouragement as other possible devices?

As is quite clear, the evidence on this particular topic is quite scant, but the numbers of charitable contributions suggest that it is inconceivable that the effect could be very large in the aggregate. I tabulated some numbers from the Brookings Institution tax file which indicate that nearly two-thirds of all charitable contributions are made by people with adjusted gross incomes of under $15,000 in 1966 (based on 1971 tax law). The maximum marginal tax rate in that range cannot possibly be a major incentive to charitable giving. There may be some effects in higher brackets. Even if one acknowledges that every dollar given by people with incomes over $50,000 a year would not be given at all, in the aggregate that comes to 11 percent of total charitable contributions. It is difficult to imagine that one could not conceive of some device, perhaps along the lines suggested by Mr. McDaniel, perhaps along the lines of a tax credit, to increase charitable giving by other groups if the deductibility provisions were entirely removed.

IS THE DEDUCTION FAIR?

The final question seems to me the most important: Is the implicit matching grant in the contribution—that pattern of deductibility and its effect on taxes—fair?

Fairness is a matter of judgment. I would just like to reiterate a couple of the observations Mr. McDaniel made and make one or two more. First: Why should the implicit matching rate—which the deductibility provision in effect is—differ for people at different income levels?

It would appear to me that the burden of proof should rest upon anybody who would advocate different effective matching grant rates for people at different income levels. The present tax provisions represent a 14-cent matching grant for somebody in the 14 percent bracket who gives 86 cents; a 70-cent matching grant for somebody in the 70 percent bracket who gives 30 cents.

I would argue that the burden of proof should rest on those who contend there should be any difference in the implicit federal matching grant between those in different income classes. I can see no clear reason why there should be.

The burden should also rest on those who would argue that the implicit federal matching grants should differ between those who itemize and those who do not. I confess that I cannot perceive any persuasive reason why the rates should differ. If the question of the relative responsiveness of various groups to the implicit matching grant contained in the tax system arises, then I think those who advocate differences should produce evidence that the responsiveness is different, and thus far I have not seen any.

We do know—we have very strong evidence from Taussig's study—that if people face a 70-cent matching grant for every 30 cents they give, they will give more than they will if they face a 14-cent matching grant for every 86 cents they give. That should not surprise any of us. But nobody has produced any evidence that if everybody received, let us say, a 25-cent matching grant for every dollar given total giving would be reduced or increased. I can see reasons why it might rise or fall, but I can see no argument in equity for the present system. It would seem to me that the argument that a system to encourage private giving should do so equally should have the presumption in its favor, and that the burden of proof should rest on those who wish to deviate from that norm.

CHAPTER XIX

IT DEPENDS UPON HOW YOU LOOK AT IT

Thomas B. Curtis
Vice President and General Counsel,
Encyclopaedia Britannica, Inc.

I WELCOME this opportunity to participate in a discussion which covers all three major sectors of our society and their basic relationships, namely, the governmental sector, the profit private sector, and the nonprofit private sector. All too often the discussion in the parlor, in a symposium, or in a governmental forum, covers the governmental and the profit private sector and only as an afterthought includes the great nonprofit private sector which has played such an important part in the history and development of the American society.

Decline of Nonprofit Private Sector

I find that in the struggle in recent decades between the governmental sector and the private sector only the nonprofit private sector has been diminished; both government and the profit private sector have flourished.

The nonprofit private sector historically has been concerned with the fields of welfare, education, health, culture, and research, and has been, until recent decades, relatively well organized, operating under the egis of the religious institutions of the society. It is significant that in the Middle Ages and even in the Renaissance in Europe the Church tended to dominate these fields of social endeavor, but the transplant of European society on the eastern shores of the relatively unpopulated American continent occurred at the same time the Catholic Church was being pushed back and splintered in its power and jurisdictions internally and also by the outside growing power of political governments.

Furthermore, organized church and state did not keep pace with the primitive social structure of the frontier and perforce independent cooperative and nonprofit enterprises sprung up to fill the vacuum.

A third important development occurred at the same time, the industrial revolution, the embodiment of the growing and proliferating profit private sector.

The decline of the nonprofit private sector in our society may merely reflect the continuing decline of the Church, splintered and anemic as it is. Though the Christian Church was not powerful and unified in eighteenth and nineteenth century America as it had been in the Middle Ages in Europe, it was not confronted with strong governments and it continued to service the areas of health, education, and welfare, although it had abandoned the fields of culture and research. Indeed, with the increased emphasis on good works in both Catholic and Protestant churches resulting from the Reformation, most schools, hospitals, orphanages, and old folk asylums were developed in America under their egis.

The decline of the nonprofit sector may also be reflecting the increase of the profit private sector which has demonstrated an interest and ability to service these areas. Certainly cost accounting, which government forced upon the profit private sector through the development of the federal income tax on profit corporations and individuals, has rationalized an economic discipline, that of not going broke, which both the nonprofit private sector and the governmental sector lack.

The decline may also be reflecting the movement of government into these areas because of an ineptness on the part of the nonprofit private sector to properly meet the social needs in the areas of its historical jurisdiction and/or an increasing ambition on the part of those in the governmental sector to increase its powers and jurisdiction.

Certainly in the field of taxation we run into the basic relationships of these three sectors, and we can alter these relationships through the tax structure we establish. The tithe of the church, once a powerful tax, like the gorilla is almost extinct, so we are discussing the tax structure imposed by political government.

215

PRINCIPLE OF ECONOMIC NEUTRALITY

I had the pleasure to serve almost all of my 18 years in the United States Congress on the House Ways and Means Committee and on the Joint Economic Committee. After a few years of study and deliberation in the areas of these committees' wide and complementary jurisdictions I began to evolve a basic theory of taxation and economics which I then began to preach albeit with few converts. I remain a zealot, however. This theory has direct bearing on the subject of this symposium and of this panel.

Let me state it. The powers of government to create money and to tax should aim toward economic neutrality. The power of government to spend should be deliberately and openly affirmative.

It is a great temptation to use monetary power to achieve immediate economic goals. Certainly demonstrable results can be achieved. There are many advocates of the theory that monetary power should be used affirmatively and this theory seems to be in practice internationally and in the United States today.

It is probably a greater temptation to use the power to tax affirmatively, because it is more subtle and yet more effective. The advocates of government using tax power affirmatively are in the ascendance in the macroeconomic field and in the descendance in the microeconomic field. Indeed the macroeconomists are in the forefront of striking down such microeconomic use of the tax power and so take on a camouflage which permits them at times to consort with tax neutralists.

We start out with a paradox. As government taxes it has an economic impact usually deleterious to the endeavor taxed. However, the decision of government to spend is the affirmative decision which requires that it tax. If it taxes an endeavor for which it has decided to spend, the total effort toward the endeavor, public and private, might be diminished.

There are several important axioms in tax laws to be considered. Revenue equals tax rate times tax base times a factor of collectibility. As the tax rate rises the tax base and the factor of collectibility tend to decline. There is a point of diminishing returns where the tax base and the factor of collectibility decline to the extent that the increased tax rate is neutralized.

One of the most effective ways to use tax policy to produce

deliberate economic results is to increase the tax rate so that the tax base disappears and no revenue is obtained. This is the theory of the protective tariff. Another effective use of tax policy is to impose a tax on one economic endeavor and not upon another. The endeavor taxed will tend to wane and the endeavor untaxed will tend to flourish.

In both of these examples, and they are only two of many, the economic purpose is achieved at the sacrifice of revenue.

If we approach the writing of a tax law with the neutralist theory, the objective is to obtain revenues as efficiently as possible—which implies with a minimum amount of deleterious economic impact on that which is taxed. If the tax writer knows that one of the governmental expenditure programs is to build hospitals because hospitals are needed, would it be counterproductive to tax moneys going into building hospitals? Would it not be better to complement the affirmative governmental expenditure policy by forgoing that source of revenue?

The exemption of charitable donations provided in the federal income tax laws followed this philosophy albeit the rates in the federal income tax system were initially so low that clearly the only purpose in the mind of its authors was to raise revenues sufficient to cover the then relatively low expenditures.

The exemption of revenues from local and state bonds followed this philosophy, although there was the added problem of whether the federal government could consitutionally tax the financing methods of state and local governments. Certainly it could be a wise exercise of tax selectivity not to diminish the amount of money going into building local governmental facilities by taking away some of it by federal taxation. Furthermore, it seems a much more practical way for the federal government to share tax income with the states and local governments than the proposals presently being considered in the Congress.

Looking at not taxing certain economic endeavors which have become the subject of direct federal spending this way, instead of exemptions, is somewhat difficult because of the efficacy of the federal income tax and its evolution toward comprehensive coverage. To remove exemptions written into the federal income tax law at its inception seems, at first blush, to be a movement toward tax neutrality. However, it takes on a different hue when one considers some of the arguments for it. A tax exemption is alleged to be a way of getting around the authorization-appropriation process of the Congress—the way to avoid taking up directly an expenditure program. This argument would be meritorious if a tax exemption were granted for an endeavor for which Congress had not made an expenditure policy decision. However, once the governmental policy has been made to see that more hospitals are built, the choice becomes one of whether hospitals are built more efficiently and to best meet the needs in kind and by geography through governmental or through private and local action. Certainly it seems appropriate for the tax writers to take this governmental expenditure decision into account and to say we will not seek to get taxes to support this program from moneys being spent privately for this same purpose. The tax writers might well not wish to make such fine distinctions in the tax laws for reasons of efficiencies in collecting the general taxes imposed, or because a governmental expenditure program and policy might be temporary, or because they must be concerned with getting revenues for the broad list of expenditure programs, not just a specific one.

However, when the fields of expenditures are broad, such as welfare, education, health, culture, and research, and religion itself, the tax writers certainly can and I believe should take cognizance of the fact that money spent for these purposes in the nonprofit sector, derived from nontaxed gifts and moneys deducted from the taxable income base of the profit private sector, means that government will not have to finance its programs for these same purposes so heavily. Furthermore, the tax writers might conclude that money spent by the private sector is spent more efficiently and with a better regard for other human values than money spent by government.

In recent years another philosophy of government and taxation has been expressed which I find new and strange and fundamentally out of step with our history and our philosophy and with reason.

This theory seems to say that all assets and endeavors belong to the political government and what the government does not take in taxation from the private sector is a subsidy to it. Exemption for dependents, for example, is a subsidy to the private citizen who has children. The nontaxation of imputed income for rent to the homeowner is a subsidy to homeowners. The exemption of moneys given to nonprofit institutions is a subsidy to philanthropy.

The topic for this panel discussion, "Support of Private Philanthropy Through Federal Tax Laws" is worded with overtones of this inverted philosophy. The title should be rephrased to read "Should Money Given to Philanthropy Be Federally Taxed?" Is this a good additional source of federal revenues?

The political government is only one mechanism available to society to meet its goals; the nongovernmental sector contains many more. I believe that it is a fundamental and dangerous error to equate the political government with the total society and that we should not set up our tax structure on such a theory.

CHAPTER XX

DISCUSSION OF SUPPORT OF PRIVATE
PHILANTHROPY THROUGH FEDERAL
INCOME TAX LAWS

Moderator Herbert L. Chabot, Assistant Legislation Counsel, Joint Committee on Internal Revenue Taxation: We want to give the panelists an opportunity to discuss the comments that have been made thus far, and also to give the audience an opportunity to have an input in the question and answer session. At this point, then, I shall suggest a number of possible items that I hope the panelists, or some of them, will comment on, after which we shall have discussion from the floor.

One of the points that has been mentioned by Professor Bittker is the difficulty of instituting a matching grant system with regard to churches—constitutional difficulties, perhaps practical political difficulties. I would hope that one of the panelists would take up this matter.

In connection with the *Tilton v. Richardson* case, I suppose to some extent the *Walz* decision of the Supreme Court about a year ago might be relevant in this area.

One of the points that was made by Professor McDaniel was that perhaps pluralism ought to be more broadly available, that is, the idea of an incentive for people to make independent private choices. I hope that one of the panelists will discuss this item.

One of the matters that has been suggested but not taken up thus far in the discussion is the idea of substituting for the present deduction system a system of credits, or perhaps working it together with the present deduction system. The Congress in the Revenue Act of 1971 has decided to try a combined credit-deduction system for political contributions. Perhaps one or more of the panelists could comment as to whether a credit approach would be more apt to meet some of his objectives without running into some of his objections.

I shall ask Congressman Curtis to lead the panel discussion.

I. DISCUSSION BY THE PANEL

Mr. Thomas B. Curtis, Encyclopaedia Britannica: What I find missing in the presentations and in a great deal of the tax dialogue that goes on today is a discussion of taxation from the standpoint of raising revenues. I have been in the business for a number of years trying to use the tax structure to this purpose and also trying to maintain an attitude of neutrality because we find that we are going to have an economic impact whatever we do in the way of raising revenues. It's an entirely different approach from the approach taken here, where you are deliberately using the tax structure to produce these results.

I think we have to do some thinking back on the point of the tax system as a revenue raiser because our present level of income tax is certainly not raising the revenues needed to meet the expenditures. We've got a $28 billion deficit for this fiscal year and from various projections it may be as much as $40 billion next year. And when one relates this, as I think one has to, to the devaluation of the dollar and a great many other monetary matters, we have to see how these systems discussed in the papers might affect the income tax as a revenue producer. We must start thinking in terms of how we strengthen it.

We have three other major methods of raising taxes—excises, payroll, and property—in our society, and we can perhaps gain some insight from looking at these other systems. For instance, there are selective excises at the federal level and sales taxes at the state level. There is no equity involved in taxing the telephone industry, if we do, over taxing others. It is, though, a darn good revenue producer. We must look to see whether we kill the sheep from which we take the wool. This is a more traditional way of looking at taxes.

I would argue that our present federal income tax rates are beyond diminishing returns now, and if we reduce rates we shall increase revenues. I think I could establish this point had I the time here, but it's worthy of thought. In fact, I think we could embark upon a program for the next 20 years of gradually reducing federal income tax rates and probably increase the revenues. But it relates to this problem.

The excise was used at one time for revenue purposes in the field of imports. But note the history of what happened when it became used for other purposes, for protective tariff, a neat and easy little way of manipulating the economy. That's the danger of using the tax structure for other than collecting revenues. The rates gradually moved up to become what were protective tariffs. And it was relatively easy for government to shift from a protective tariff to a subsidy, the direct subsidy, which is exactly what we have gone into, on the assumption that government should have this control over imports. But we ended up with little or no revenue.

Another one of our big taxes that is not meeting its responsibilities is the payroll tax, which in most people's vocabulary is the social security tax. Question: Are we really now going to have to move over and use general revenues for social security?

Also, there is the property tax which the federal officials know very little about because it has never been used as a federal tax.

But again these tax systems fall, I think, into certain basic patterns. They enable us to study taxes from the standpoint of raising revenues, which reveals, among other things, that it's almost impossible to get a good tax system of raising revenues unless there is some sort of tie-in with expenditures. That's where our subject matter today needs examination.

My concept of tax neutrality is to extract the revenue with a minimum of economic impact. So one doesn't tax an endeavor that is anemic. You tax an endeavor that can stand it. If it happens to be telephones, fine; it can stand it. If it happens to be income, as it usually is, it can stand it up to a point. And you don't tax endeavors in a way that would render them anemic. So I say, following the neutralist theory, that we should not tax social endeavors in the private sector that will require government to perform those services if they are diminished. This is where tax policy ties in with expenditure policy, which in the government sector should be affirmative, not neutral.

The nonprofit private sector, which in the beginning was largely identified with the church, went way beyond the church in the fields of health, education, welfare, culture, and research and development. Initially there was little federal expenditure in these areas. Query: What does happen if the federal government taxes the money that is spent for these purposes? Isn't it perfectly proper tax policy for those who are trying to raise revenues, to consider whether the Congress would have to spend more money affirmatively to meet these essential needs in our society if the private funds are diminished?

That's why I suggested that the topic, support of private philanthropy through the federal income tax law, begs the question, because it almost presumes that what the federal government doesn't take is a subsidy. I would reverse it and simply say that the title should be: Should money given to philanthropy be federally taxed?

Professor Paul R. McDaniel, Boston College Law School: I would like to ask Professor Bittker a question about the church-state issue: If the only deduction in the federal tax system were one for contributions to churches, would that be held unconstitutional?

Professor Boris I. Bittker, Yale Law School: I think there is a possibility that it would be. It would involve singling churches out from other nonprofit institutions, and it would be much easier to say that that was an aid to religion than to say that general aid to all types of nonprofit institutions is an aid to religion. When all nonprofit institutions are treated the same, however, it is arguable that a tax on income simply doesn't make sense for such groups.

Professor McDaniel: It seems to me, then, that the case is pretty clear that the matching grant system I have proposed meets that test; it gives the same benefits to all types of charities just as the present deduction system does. I agree with your response, but I would conclude from it that the proposed matching grant system does not lead to a constitutional problem; or at least not any that is not present in the existing tax system.

Professor Bittker: I don't know that we can solve the question of the status of grants to religion, although I realize I may be responsible for having introduced it. But the fact is that the last Supreme Court decision we have on the subject was one in which grants to church-related colleges did have to encounter certain very serious obstacles that, in the Court's view, were not encountered by grants to non-church-related colleges. I must say that after studying that decision, as well as other cases in this area, I don't have any confidence at all that the Court will agree with Henry Aaron or Stan Surrey, logical as their point may seem to be, that there is no difference between tax deductions and direct expenditures.

A second point is that in Professor McDaniel's presentation, I found a lack of clarity in his approach to a question that I touched on in my presentation: Is the matching grant system to take as its objective the precise duplication of what we now have in terms of ultimate receipts by charities in the proportions in which they now get them—or not? If the objective is to get just what we now have, then my reaction, as I said before, is why force change on us? I, therefore, cannot help but believe that the enormously powerful intellectual apparatus that has been brought to bear on the tax deduction, must have coupled with it some notion that if matching grants are to be established, they will produce a different result from existing law.

What I don't understand from Professor McDaniel's presentation is this: The revenue that is now lost through the charitable contributions deduction is said to be $2.4 billion for a recent year. I'll accept his estimate of $3.75 billion for the current year and next year. Does he propose that this amount of revenue loss should be preserved, but somehow redistributed among the charitable organizations? Why would that be a step forward? Or are we, rather, to take his plea, for which something can clearly be said, that persons claiming the standard deduction don't participate in the existing system; and conclude that what he would like to see is matching grants that would go beyond $3.75 billion by giving an appropriate amount to those who do not itemize, so that it's $5, $6, or $7 billion that we're talking about.

Or, looking to McDaniel's comments on efficiency—and even more the comments on efficiency made by others—are we to assume that the virtue of the matching grant system is that it will disregard those charities whose private gifts would hold up in the absence of charitable contribution deductions? This approach would focus on those areas where private giving would fall off and limit the matching grant system to the amounts that would be lost to private charities when the charitable deduction is repealed. This amount is estimated in Taussig's study as only $57 million. Is the matching grant's contribution to efficiency to be estimated by subtracting this amount, which would be replaced, from the revenue loss of $2.4 or $3.75 billion attributed to the charitable contribution deduction?

Professor Henry Aaron, University of Maryland: Professor Bittker cited two studies of the impact of charitable contributions, one by Mike Taussig and another done at New York University. I think I could characterize his presentation of Professor Taussig's points in the following way. I believe he said that it violated his intuition and therefore he presented various quotations from Taussig acknowledging that there were qualifications to his work. At no time did he present any evidence that the conclusions were incorrect. The methodology was never explicitly criticized or challenged. Indeed, many of Taussig's qualifications were made to indicate that his results were probably unduly conservative in the sense that they overstated the impact of taxation on charitable giving.

Professor Bittker: In response to Professor Aaron's comment, I have read the Taussig study fairly carefully and was puzzled by the fact that his recommendation for the total abolition of the deduction on the ground that it merely benefits charities to the extent of $57 million, which appeared in the dissertation, is totally absent from the article. Whether this suggests a change in view on his part I don't know.

At any rate, my point is, are we talking about giving charities just what they now get by a combination of private donations and matching grants, or of something more efficient which would focus only on the $57 million that Taussig talks about or twice that amount, if one wants to be more conservative and cautious? And are the grants to go to the charities that now benefit from the deduction, i.e., higher education and private foundations; or are we to accept a footnote in Stan Surrey's article implying that one could hardly defend direct government grants to private foundations, and eliminate them as recipients of grants?

I am not so much puzzled by Professor McDaniel's ultimate proposal as I am by why he argues that his or any other matching grant system is better than the tax deduction before identifying what it is to accomplish. Is it to do the same as the existing deduction for everybody at the standard deduction level and for non-taxpayers—many of whom may contribute, for example, to their churches? Or is it to get the efficiency that would be achieved by cutting down the total cost of governmental aid to $57 million? Or is it to redistribute the benefits so that the amounts received by private foundations and higher education are drastically cut down and the amount going to religion is drastically increased?

Any one of those proposals, I think, could be defended by the arguments that Professor McDaniel advances, but I am not sure which of them is the model that we are to focus on in discussing a system of matching grants.

Moderator Chabot: I am sure that a panel composed of three professors and one encyclopaedist would not be in favor of a proposal to drastically reduce aid to higher education. But although the discussion is interesting and something that could continue, I think in view of the small amount of time left, we ought to yield at this point to the audience. Does somebody have a question?

II. Discussion by the Audience

Professor William Vickrey, Columbia University: I just wanted to associate myself with Aaron's comments on the elasticity question. I do think that there is no question but what the actual figures overstate the elasticity.

As to the problem of the legality of direct grants to religious institutions: On the one hand, I am inclined to agree with people who might regard the pew rents in a fashionable church as not too different from the membership fees in a club across the street or, for that matter, the fees paid to a psychiatrist or a mortician as not too different from the contributions made to the support of the pastor of a local church. Nevertheless, obviously, I don't think there are very many who would agree, and I think that the political implications of withdrawing the benefits to churches would be serious.

I wonder if Mr. McDaniel has in mind that one might allow the individual to list all contributions on his return. One might take a tax credit rather than a matching grant, which of course would not take care of the nontaxpayer. It might, on the other hand, be open to the individual to list all his contributions, including contributions to church. On the basis of this total a matching grant would be computed, and then the taxpayer could list only those nonreligious organizations among which he wanted to have this matching grant distributed. This would at least avoid the picture of a check going directly from the Treasury to the church, which seems to worry the lawyers.

I must say that although I agree with Aaron that the logic of this is that in fact there is no difference, the tax laws are riddled with situations in which for no logical reason arbitrary distinctions are drawn.

Moderator Chabot: Paul, would you want to respond, or would any of the panelists?

Professor McDaniel: As Professor Aaron said, if one thinks that there is a greater cosmetic effect in providing the credit for religious institutions on constitutional grounds, one can do so. As I say, speaking strictly as a non-constitutional lawyer, the constitutional distinction between direct matching grants and tax credits eludes me. But it would be possible to do what Professor Vickrey suggests.

Mr. Gabriel G. Rudney, U.S. Treasury Department: I'd like to comment on Professor Bittker's statement. He comments about the supporters of the comprehensive tax base approach. It's rather unfortunate that he lumped all comprehensive tax base proponents into one group committed philosophically and through implementation to the Haig-Simons approach without reservation. There are many who support a form of comprehensive base with simplification and low rates and retain the revenues that Congressman Curtis talked about, but who would also continue a deduction for charitable contributions. These people are presumably in Professor Bittker's corner, at least on the subject that he's discussing today. But they are not in his corner when he opposes the comprehensive tax base. They believe that a low-rate, gross-income system may have great advantages or incentives for investment and effort in the economy.

Professor Bittker: I would accept that qualification. I did say, or meant to say, that I detected among the comprehensive tax base people, some persons who seem now to be opposing deductions in the interest of progression, who formerly seemed to oppose them in order to reduce progression. But I agree with you, there are a lot of people on the side you describe.

Mr. Robert B. Bangs, U.S. Department of Commerce: In the discussion of vertical equity, which I found very interesting, I also found one thing missing, namely that the 14 percent tax bracket income consists basically of wages and salaries, whereas the 70 percent bracket income consists of capital gains, dividends, and interest, including tax-exempt interest. Large and small incomes consist of quite different things which are taxed in the first instance at different rates. Would any of the panelists care to comment on this?

Professor Bittker: I didn't hinge my argument at all on any support for differential rates at the 70 percent bracket. I agree with you that capital gains make up a larger proportion of income at high levels so that marginal rates may be 70 percent, but the effective rate is less than that. I would still take the position, however, that even if that were corrected, it would not necessarily be true that vertical equity would be violated by the charitable contribution deduction. This is partly for the reason I suggested earlier: that any amount lost through the charitable deduction could be recouped from persons with the same adjusted gross income, if that's the definition you want, or total economic income, if you prefer that definition, by increasing the rates in that area. I might add one other point that I might have made with respect to the progression argument. It is puzzling that those who argue that the rich man misses 70 cents no more than the poor man misses 14 cents, in order to justify progression, also seem to think that the restoration of 70 cents to the rich man gives him a great deal more pleasure than the restoration of 14 cents to the poor man. I would think that what's sauce for the goose is sauce for the gander. If there is a declining marginal utility in money, one should feel it equally when he kisses 70 cents good-bye and when it is returned to him.

Moderator Chabot: Professor Aaron, I wonder if you would comment on the implication that there might be differences in composition of income at different levels.

Professor Aaron: Not really, no. I don't have any comments to make.

Professor C. Lowell Harriss, Columbia University: I have biases on this issue, admitted but not catalogued (to your boredom). Several points trouble me. First, I have sympathy with the objectives of the people who use the term "tax expenditure" or something similar. Yet this usage, coupled with the talk of federal "spending" of money which has not been collected, seems to imply that since the federal government *could* take everything in taxes, the fact that it does not do so is an act of grace. This unstated assumption is disturbing. Government does *not* "properly" "own" what it does not actually take in taxes.

A second point. The American people, it seems to me, are not at their best when they are acting through the political process of elections and what follows. The congressional procedures are not necessarily those that show us at our best. We can devise schemes of bringing congressional decisions more into the selection process of which agencies will get how much of the funds which qualify for tax deductions. But would the results be better? Really? How does Congress actually make decisions?

Another point results from wide differences in tax rates, 14 to 70 percent under the income tax or 3 to 77 percent under the estate tax. Anomalies are inevitable. I do not see how we can expect any kind of a reasonably consistent or rational system when rates under the same tax vary so greatly.

There is a final point, one on which I would not insist. But may there not be a presumption that the people who are subject to the 70 percent income tax rate—or near it—or the estate tax at the 77 percent rate, may be better able to use funds in the general interest, constructively, than people who make the political decisions?

Professor Aaron: I'd like to speak to the first point. The first thing is that I believe nobody used the phrase tax expenditures today unless it was Professor Bittker. Second, the term tax expenditures presumes nothing regarding the right of the government to claim each and every dollar. The tax expenditure approach asks a simpler question. Suppose you curtail some deduction or credit or exemption the tax code now provides; that would change federal revenue. The federal government could then use those revenues if it so desired to cut tax rates, to increase other tax deductions, or to increase expenditures.

Given the objectives which the deduction or the credit or the exemption is designed to achieve, is it better at achieving that objective than any of the other devices around?

Asking such a question is an essential to good government planning. To ask it makes no presumption regarding government's right to anything. To ask it simply expresses recognition that the tax provision is probably there for some reason. Congress had a reason for enacting it, and it asks whether Congress, if it considered a wider variety of means to a given objective, could accomplish that objective more efficiently. It is not an assault on private property to question whether the particular means Congress has chosen to accomplish some objective is the most efficient.

Mr. Curtis: I would simply say, put it in different semantics, to ask, if you tax that area, will you get more revenue? In this context, we could have a good dialogue. It has been put in a different context, and I think Professor Harriss is absolutely right. If you follow through the logic, an exemption might be called a subsidy —and I've heard it expressed just that baldly—it can mean just that. But taxes are not being discussed with the object in mind of trying to figure out how best to get revenues. Rather the discussion is in which way can we more efficiently manipulate or affect the society to achieve social goals we are interested in. To raise revenues most efficiently is not the design. The dialogue isn't around that point. It must be around that point, I believe, or the tax system will be destroyed.

Professor Aaron: As long as we adhere to that principle, we should tax salt and other essentials. Since there's no chance really of escaping such taxes you'll raise a lot of revenue. That is a prescription for taxing essentials. Whether that is regressive or progressive apparently is of no concern to Mr. Curtis. Whether it promotes economic efficiency or not is apparently of no concern.

Mr. Curtis: No, now wait a second. It is of concern, and this is notable, the way you try to turn this around.

Professor Aaron: I was simply drawing out the implications of what you said.

Mr. Curtis: No, you turned it around to say that those of us who are tax neutralists have no concern about the society. Part of the neutralist thesis is that federal spending, government spending, should be affirmative. We should discuss and know what we are doing when we are spending tax money. I have always considered the use of a salt tax as an example of a society that has really gone down the drain, because that's the only damn thing it can get money from. It isn't a very good way of getting money. We are talking about getting money, but we are also talking about getting money in order to pay for what the government's affirmative expenditure policies are.

Professor Bittker: I would just like to add this. I would take no exception at all to Professor Aaron's statement of what is meant by the phrase "tax expenditure." I think that's a legitimate way of looking at the problem, indeed a highly appropriate one. But I must say that the phrase is also used for rhetorical purposes, as in statements such as "the charitable contribution deduction is just like a check written by the Secretary of the Treasury to a stated charitable organization or to the donor," depending on who is supposed to be getting the subsidy in question. And I do think that at some point, this kind of rhetorical use, whether deliberate or not, is open to the objection that Professor Harriss offered to it.

Let me offer a further example. When the tax rate on earned income is reduced from 70 percent to 50 percent, we do not hear it repeatedly asserted that the people who benefit from that tax reduction and who spend money on summer vacations or yachts are acting just as though the Treasury Department were sending checks to pay for those summer vacations. What is objectionable about the shorthand use of the term "tax expenditures" is that, wittingly or not, there is conveyed again and again the suggestion that there is no difference between a Treasury expenditure and a tax deduction. The result is that all the rest of the comparisons between tax deductions or subsidies—based on efficiency and other criteria—somehow either get relegated to a footnote, or else are put in the way in which Professor Aaron seemed to put them— that is, the burden of proof is on somebody else. The rhetorical

231

signal conveys the message that this is presumptively government money, and therefore it's up to you to prove that it should be influenced in any way by private choice.

Moderator Chabot: Mr. Barlow, would you want to join in this discussion?

Mr. Joel Barlow, Covington & Burling, Washington, D.C.: Yes. I'd like to subscribe to the statements made by Lowell Harriss. But what disturbs me among other things in Professor McDaniel's presentation is that there is a kind of palpable fraud—if you'll excuse my using that expression—just in terms of political reality. Even if the government started out by making the matching grant the equivalent of the tax benefit to the taxpayer in the high marginal bracket, that wouldn't last long. That carrot on the stick suggests that you could have a system—and this is Mr. Aaron's point, and I agree with him—with a 14-cent contribution and an 86-cent matching grant. This is just a little ridiculous in terms of political reality.

I have always subscribed to Stanley Surrey's view that we should not have a proliferation of tax credits. After we get the one that we're interested in, of course then we don't want any more proliferation. But it seems to me that it makes no sense to move the tax credit into the area of charitable deductions because then you'll go through the whole spectrum of deductions in the tax structure.

As far as the tax expenditure aspect is concerned—tax expenditure against tax deduction—I think I share the view of Professor Bittker that names are only labels for our ignorance, and you just are not really creating any distinction, either in terms of meaningful tax language or in terms of what happens when the government taxes.

Moderator Chabot: We have time for one more question. Professor Surrey?

Professor Stanley S. Surrey, Harvard Law School: At some point I probably should ask for equal time to answer Professor Bittker.

Professor Bittker: You've had it in your articles!

Professor Surrey: I wonder if Paul McDaniel would want to respond briefly to Mr. Bittker's question, because I think in his question he didn't perceive what Paul McDaniel was talking about.

Professor McDaniel: I have assumed that the federal government has undertaken to spend $2.4 billion—now it's up to $3.75 billion—for support of charity. I assume that is a conscious decision. Under my proposal of federal financial support that level remains the same, and the matching grant system is geared to produce that same federal revenue for charity. Now, spending that same amount of federal money results in charities getting more combined federal-private money, because the inefficiency factor in the deduction has been eliminated. Table 1 in my paper quantifies this result.

You can go at it the other way around. If one only wanted charities to get the same amount of total income or revenues that they derived through the present charitable deduction, then the amount of federal contribution in the matching system could be reduced, but I haven't proposed that. I have assumed that it is a rational decision to spend federal funds in support of charity at levels represented by the present revenue loss through the charitable deduction.

I did try to indicate in the fourth section of the paper what effects one might see among varying types of potential recipient institutions as a result of a change to a matching system. There is going to be some change. I have to say Mr. Harriss articulated what I think is the elitist argument. On the other hand, I am willing to accept the judgment of one hundred percent of our charitable contributors as to which charities the federal money ought to go to. A redistribution of funds among types of charitable recipients does not bother me if it results from the collective judgment of all contributors; and I think it is decidedly more consistent with the democratic processes than is the present system which freezes out lower-income contributors from the judgment process, insofar as allocation of federal funds is concerned.

There is going to be matching for the standard deductors as a matter of equity on the basis of percentage of income donated to charity. There may be some redistribution of federal funds among charities; but if that's the way the public says it ought to be redistributed in terms of support for private charity, then I am willing to live with it.

Moderator Chabot: This discussion has perhaps gotten to its warmest and therefore most fruitful at the very end. Thank you.

Mr. Leonard L. Silverstein, Silverstein and Mullens, Washington, D.C.: In summarizing may I state that our speakers at this symposium have given information and ideas here to stimulate another meeting and certainly to establish the need for more symposiums of this character. The discussions have underscored the obvious point that private philanthropy remains very much alive, giving full effect to the Tax Reform Act of 1969. Problems of complexity persist, both as to individual donors and managers of private foundations. While large private foundations recognize and can cope with the 1969 act's requirement for additional administration, smaller foundations, particularly, may have some initial compliance difficulties, especially with respect to overseeing of expenditure responsibility grants.

On the other hand, those foundations with adequate staff apparently have been able to function administratively much as they did before the 1969 law was passed.

Notwithstanding general agreement that our society should remain pluralistic, doctrinal differences exist respecting the manner in which pluralism may best be maintained—whether through the route of tax allowances, or whether another approach would be more effective.

With that we shall return the symposium to President Baker for conclusion. Thank you.

President R. Palmer Baker, Jr., Lord, Day & Lord, New York: I have a very simple and pleasant job to do. To thank all of our speakers, to thank all of the panelists, to thank the chairmen of the symposium committees and their members, to thank all of you, and Leonard in particular, to thank you. We are adjourned.